HIGH SCHOOL

HIGH SCHOOL

A REPORT ON SECONDARY
EDUCATION IN AMERICA

*THE CARNEGIE FOUNDATION
FOR THE ADVANCEMENT
OF TEACHING*

Ernest L. Boyer

HARPER & ROW, PUBLISHERS, New York
Cambridge, Philadelphia, San Francisco, London
Mexico City, São Paulo, Sydney

1817

FIRST EDITION

Designer: Sidney Feinberg

Library of Congress Cataloging in Publication Data

Boyer, Ernest L.
  High School.

  Includes bibliographical references and index.
  1. High schools—United States. I. Carnegie Foundation for the Advancement of Teaching. II. Title.
LA222.B68   1983   373.2'38   83-47528
ISBN 0-06-015193-5

---

83 84 85 86 87 10 9 8 7 6 5 4 3

CONTENTS

ACKNOWLEDGMENTS

While preparing this report on the American High School I have been reminded almost daily that it would be impossible even to imagine carrying out such a task without the help of many people. Support has come from a host of friends and colleagues. For this I am deeply grateful.

The trustees of The Carnegie Foundation for the Advancement of Teaching were among the first to recognize the significance of this study. The author and the staff assume full responsibility for the accuracy and the conclusions reflected in the text. Still, in formal discussion and informal communication, the trustees have given endless encouragement and wise counsel. The report would not have been possible without them.

I'm similarly indebted to members of our national advisory panel. These distinguished colleagues were profoundly influential. Men and women with different perspectives on the purpose of schooling exchanged information, debated issues, and searched together for ways to enrich our schools. Working with each member of the panel has been, for me, a special joy.

Some colleagues served as consultants, others drafted background papers or steered us to vital information. I feel especially indebted to: Mortimer J. Adler, Ernest L. Boyer, Jr., E. Alden Dunham, Joseph Featherstone, Emily Feistritzer, Chester E. Finn, Jr., John W. Gardner, Gerald Grant, Fred M. Hechinger, Harold

Howe II, Martin Kaplan, Francis Keppel, James A. Perkins, Diane Ravitch, David Tyack, Ralph Tyler and Janice Weinman.

In the Appendix are the names of the educators who spent over 2000 hours in high schools from coast to coast. These scholars observed with care and expressed with great sensitivity their findings and impressions. The performance of these men and women was outstanding. I am especially indebted to Vito Perrone, who was brilliantly effective as leader of this study team, and to Marilyn Cohn, who was always available to us just when her help was needed most.

At one time or another, every single member of the foundation's staff pitched in to help. Whether they engaged in research, prepared working drafts, tracked down references, compiled charts and tables, reviewed manuscripts, or coaxed our word processors into producing daily miracles on incredibly short notice, they all have had a part. I'd like to extend a special word of thanks to Michael O'Keefe, and to Paul L. Houts, the project director, and his colleagues Margery Thompson, Nancy Adelman, and David Haselkorn. Lane Mann and Lisa Cziffra have been tireless and resourceful beyond belief in collecting information and statistics and finding needed information. And warm thanks to Marissa Burch, who cheerfully read and reread every word and miraculously brought us clean copy from the clutter. Robert Hochstein, Warren Bryan Martin, Gertrude Dubrovsky, and Jo Ann Greenfeld were unusually helpful during the final weeks of the preparation of this report. They devoted endless hours to reading and editing the final copy. Our sessions together were not only remarkably productive but professionally satisfying as well. To each I extend deep thanks.

Two other people were critically important. Verne A. Stadtman, my colleague at the foundation, worked tirelessly—far beyond the call of duty—in bringing all of the loose ends together, polishing text, checking citations, and maintaining liaison with the publisher. This project could not have been completed without his remarkably effective work. Sallie Coolidge, Associate Editor at Harper & Row, was extremely helpful, too. From the first, she expressed interest in the value of this report, gave great encouragement and wise counsel throughout and exercised endless patience every step of the way. Working with Ms. Coolidge has been for all of us a special joy.

Two great foundations were partners in this project. The Carnegie Corporation of New York gave us a generous grant. I'm most grateful to Alan Pifer and to E. Alden Dunham, who encouraged us every step along the way. The Atlantic Richfield Foundation also helped fund the study and provided a major grant to prepare a film of the report. In addition, Atlantic Richfield has established a major fund to support grants to schools. Working with Eugene Wilson and Fred Nelson has been satisfying in every way. Above all, W. M. Marcussen has brought to the project a special blend of common sense and inspiration, and I am very grateful.

To the schools participating in our study I extend a special thanks for welcoming us, for sharing with us your experiences, and your counsel. I hope this report accurately reflects your dreams.

Finally, I wish to express my profound respect for the students, teachers, principals and superintendents who work each day to make the nation's schools succeed. I complete this project with renewed confidence in these dedicated people who shape the lives of future generations.

To Kay, words fail.

E.L.B.

FOREWORD

BY ERNEST L. BOYER, *President,*
  The Carnegie Foundation for the Advancement of Teaching

In the spring of 1980, the Board of Trustees of The Carnegie Foundation for the Advancement of Teaching met to consider a proposed study of American secondary education.

The trustees quickly acknowledged that home influences are exceedingly important, that the first years of formal schooling are crucial, that each level of learning depends upon the other, and that if students make a poor beginning, prospects for future academic progress are diminished. Education is a seamless web.

Still, the trustees agreed that the upper years of schooling are strategically important, too. For many students, high school is the last opportunity for formal learning, and it is during late adolescence that critical life decisions frequently are made.

There was also broad agreement that American high schools are severely buffeted by changes in the community, in family life, and in student attitudes. They also have been weakened by reduced support, declining public confidence, and confusion over goals. We could not ignore these signals of distress.

The trustees concluded the time had come to examine the current condition of American secondary education; the time had come for the nation's high schools to serve their students more effectively and regain public confidence and support. The proposed study was approved.

Two key decisions followed. First, while acknowledging the

importance of nonpublic education, we agreed to limit our investigation to *public* high schools, where 91 percent of the nation's secondary school students—more than 13 million young people—study every day.

Second, we agreed to focus on the high school as an *educational* institution, a place where people come to study and to learn. Our specific aim was to look at teachers, at students, at what is being taught, searching for ways to strengthen the academic quality of the public school.

In choosing the theme of quality in education, we were determined to push vigorously for equity as well. Equity and excellence are connected. Expanding access to the nation's schools must be seen as only the first step toward oportunity for all. And it was our conviction that equality be advanced as the *quality* of education is improved for *every* student.

Having defined in broad terms the scope of the study, a national panel of teachers, principals, superintendents, university administrators, parents, school board members, and citizen representatives was asked to help us in our work (see list on page xvii). Over a two-year period, this distinguished advisory group visited schools, reviewed findings, and debated proposals for reform.

The national panel was not asked to endorse either the conclusions or the recommendations we present. Still, its thoughtful insights and careful judgments were essential, and panel members, both individually and collectively, contributed immeasurably to the shaping of the report.

Meanwhile, the foundation's staff reviewed the literature, visited schools, and talked with educators from many sectors. These discussions, along with our literature search, helped define the issues for investigation.

Two studies were particularly helpful. John I. Goodlad, Professor of Education at the University of California, Los Angeles, was just completing "A Study of Schooling,"[1] an eight-year investigation of American education that explored almost every facet of the school. Goodlad gathered data from thirty-eight schools, including twelve senior high schools. Similarly, James Coleman of the University of Chicago conducted a major study, "High School and Beyond."[2] Coleman surveyed more than 50,000 students in 869 public high schools. These two studies were a rich source of information.

We then selected fifteen public high schools in order to carry out field studies of our own (Appendix A). These schools were geographically dispersed. They were large and small; urban, suburban, and rural; comprehensive and specialized; rich and poor; homogeneous and culturally and racially mixed. We were not seeking "good" schools or "bad" schools. Our purpose was to examine a cross-section of American public secondary education.

A team of twenty-five educators was chosen to visit our preselected schools (see Appendix B). Before the visits, the observers received information about the schools to which they were assigned. Planning meetings were held. Key questions were examined: What behavior would cause one to believe that students were deeply involved in learning? How can the role of the principal be assessed? In what ways can the shared purposes of a school be discovered? These and other questions were discussed.

Visits were scheduled for twenty school days at each institution; in some cases observers spent more time at a school. During their visits, team members talked with principals, teachers, students, and parents. They went to classes, attended pep rallies and sports events, sat in on faculty and PTA meetings, observed counselors and principals at work, and conducted extensive interviews. In all, school visit time exceeded two thousand hours.

Although twenty days were not enough for a rigorous ethnographic study, they did allow sufficient time for our team of experienced educators to learn a lot about the schools. In every case, observers came away with powerful and important impressions. School conditions—both good and bad—were candidly assessed, and each observer presented written reports of what he or she saw and heard.

Vito Perrone, Dean of the School of Teaching and Learning at the University of North Dakota, was leader of the school visit project. He helped select those who visited the schools. He also reviewed the fifteen school reports, searched for themes, priorities, and contradictions, and prepared a synthesis of what the reports revealed. The field studies, plus Perrone's excellent interpretive work, form the basis for many of the observations and conclusions in our report.

By mutual consent, we do not identify the schools visited and individuals interviewed. Pseudonyms are used. We do provide, however, a brief description of each institution (Appendix A) to help the reader better understand the kind of schools we visited. In the report we also mention, from time to time, other high schools from which information was received. In most cases the schools are referred to by name.

Drafts of this report were reviewed by our trustees and a wide circle of respected colleagues. The help of these distinguished educators was invaluable. While we drew extensively from their constructive comments, as well as from our field visits and from the research of others, the conclusions and recommendations submitted in this report are those of the senior author and members of the Carnegie Foundation staff.

We recognize that ours is not the only voice in the great debate about the future of American education. In 1982, Mortimer Adler released the widely debated *Paideia Proposal.* A National Commission on Excellence in Education, the Twentieth Century Fund, and the College Entrance Examination Board have also issued reports. Other studies are still in progress. We applaud this wide-ranging effort and the renewed interest in the public schools it represents. There are many ways by which excellence is achieved. Strategies to improve public education will differ from one school to another, and many points of view, constructively presented, can only enrich the quality of the debate and, ultimately, the quality of education.

In this report on the American high school, a long list of recommendations is presented. Some are new; most are drawn from successful programs currently in operation.

There may be those who feel we are asking too much from high schools and from students. In response, we can only observe that today we ask too little. Indeed, our investigation has convinced us that student aspirations can be raised and that the academic quality of the American high school can and must be strengthened.

This report has no single audience. We direct our recommendations to students, teachers, and school administrators, who are immersed in high schools every day; to college professors, who can make a difference in how school issues are resolved; to policy makers on school boards, in state houses, and in Washington, who have inescapable responsibilities for education; and to members of teachers' and other education organizations in positions of influence.

But education of high quality is not just a professional and political concern. It is a citizen concern. We also direct our recommendations to parents, grandparents, and everyone who deeply cares about the quality and prospects for life in America now and in years to come. Thus, we have quite intentionally prepared this report for a large and diverse audience.

Our aim is to offer recommendations, stimulate discussion about secondary education, and, in the end, reaffirm the nation's historic commitment to the public schools. If these purposes are achieved, then our study of the American high school will have served a useful purpose, and the Carnegie Foundation's commitment to excellence in education will have been advanced.

Members of the National High School Panel*

MYRON ATKIN
Dean, School of Education
Stanford University

BEVERLY JOYCE BIMES
St. Louis, Missouri

DEREK BOK
President
Harvard University

ANNE CAMPBELL
Commissioner of Education
Lincoln, Nebraska

JOAN GANZ COONEY
President
Children's Television Workshop

LAWRENCE A. CREMIN
President
Teachers College
Columbia University

ALONZO CRIM
Superintendent of Schools
Atlanta City Schools

WALTER CRONKITE
CBS News

EMERAL A. CROSBY
Principal
Northern High School
Detroit, Michigan

PATRICK L. DALY
Vice President
American Federation of Teachers

NORMAN FRANCIS
President
Xavier University of Louisiana

MARY HATWOOD FUTRELL
Secretary/Treasurer
National Education Association

JAMES R. GADDY
Principal
New Rochelle High School
New Rochelle, New York

PEGGY HANRAHAN
Principal
Mentor High School
Mentor, Ohio

LESLIE KOLTAI
Chancellor
Los Angeles Community College
    District

MARIGOLD LINTON
Professor of Psychology
University of Utah

WILLIAM M. MARCUSSEN
Vice President
Atlantic Richfield Company

RALPH McGEE
Principal
New Trier East Township School
Winnetka, Illinois

JAMES L. OLIVERO
Project Leadership Executive
Professional Development Program
    Association of California

RAYMA C. PAGE
President
National School Boards Association
    and
Chairman, Lee County School
    Board
Fort Myers, Florida

*With titles held as of time of appointment in 1980.

HIGH SCHOOL

PROLOGUE:
THE GLOBE, THE NATION,
AND OUR SCHOOLS

Education is in the headlines once again. After years of shameful neglect, educators and politicians have taken the pulse of the public school and found it faint. Concern for the health of public education, stirred by a spate of new studies, offers fresh hope that in the years ahead we'll be able to adopt a serious, coherent plan for school reform. Getting the public's attention always has been the first step in the march toward progress in our nation.

This Carnegie report on the American high school begins with the conviction that the time for renewing education has arrived. We believe that today America has the best opportunity it will have in this century to improve the schools. There is a growing national consensus that our future depends on public education. There is a spreading awareness that every mind is a precious resource we cannot afford to waste. There is an eagerness to move beyond the alarming headlines; to begin to rebuild, with confidence, the public schools. As in the past, a new and more compelling vision of education is required to meet this challenge. And if we do not seize this special moment, we will fail the coming generation and the nation.

In 1957, the Soviets hurled a 184-pound satellite into space. America was stunned. Our confidence was shaken. Our very survival seemed threatened. This nation was determined to recapture its leadership and pride. And, of all the steps we took, the one most hotly debated and most vigorously pursued, the one most revealing of our national character, was our renewed commitment to public education.

President Dwight Eisenhower, in his call for a national response to *Sputnik,* said that there is a compelling national need for federal action now to help meet emergency needs in American education. In his statesmanlike message to Congress, the president concluded: American education faces new responsibilities in the cause of freedom, and if we are to maintain our leadership, we must see to it that today's young people are prepared to contribute the maximum to our future progress.[1]

If the challenge symbolized by *Sputnik* was enough to alarm Americans and generate a national response, consider the vastly greater challenge represented by conditions in the world today. Since *Sputnik* circled the earth in its solitary orbit, more than 40 astronauts and 50 cosmonauts have logged over 7 years in space.[2] Nearly 5,000 objects are now orbiting the earth; more than 3,400 of them are officially listed as debris.[3] The space shuttle *Columbia* can carry a 65,000-pound payload, 353 times the weight of *Sputnik.*[4]

On the continents below, the number of human beings has dramatically increased. In 1957, there were 2.8 billion people on earth.[5] By 1981, the number had grown to about 4.5 billion, with prospects of doubling again in less than forty years.[6] In the world's most populated nation, China, forty-five babies are born every minute.[7]

Since World War II, political boundaries of the earth have been transformed. Students who entered high school twenty-five years ago found that twenty-eight new independent nations had been created before they were given their diplomas four years later: Algeria, Burundi, Cameroon, the Central African Republic, Chad, the Congo, Cyprus, Dahomey, Gabon, the Ivory Coast, Jamaica, Kuwait, the Malagasy Republic, Mali, Mauritania, Niger, Nigeria, Rwanda, Senegal, Sierra Leone, Somalia, Tanzania,

Togo, Trinidad and Tobago, Uganda, Upper Volta, Western Samoa, and Zaire.

Today, the world's 165 independent nations and 60-odd political units are interlocked.[8] High interest rates in the United States hurt Common Market countries; bad harvests in the Soviet Union help Canadian farmers; a Middle East oil glut means less pressure in Brazil to aid capital-starved Africa; unemployment in Germany sends ripples to Spain and Yugoslavia; a robotics breakthrough in Tokyo makes a difference in Detroit. Pretoria and Peoria are connected.

The world may not yet be a global village, but surely our sense of neighborhood must include more people and cultures than ever before. Refugees flow from one country to another, but too many Americans can neither point to these great migrations on a map nor talk about the famines or wars or poverty that caused them. Philosophers, statesmen, inventors, and artists from around the world enrich our lives, but such individuals and their contributions are largely unknown or unremembered.

What happens in the farthest corner of the world now touches us almost instantly. When *Sputnik* was launched, every fifth house on the block was still without a television set;[9] the arrival of each new bulky box with its glowing little screen caused quite a stir. No young American today, save perhaps a recent immigrant, can recall ever living in a world without television. Ninety-eight percent of American homes have TV—more than have indoor plumbing.[10]

This ubiquitous box has connected us irreversibly to all the world. Through it we watched Neil Armstrong's foot touch the surface of the moon; we followed American soldiers on their tense patrols in distant jungles; we traveled with Jacques Cousteau to the bottom of the sea and attended the coronations and funerals of heads of state in distant lands. Through technology we share a common classroom.

And through technology our world also has become more threatening and unsafe. In the 1950s the *Ed Sullivan Show* ran films of a hydrogen bomb explosion. Parents were warned that children might be too upset to watch. Today, at least four nations stockpile an estimated 17,000 nuclear warheads, the equivalent of 16 billion tons of TNT and more than 5,000 times what was exploded in all of World War II.[11] For the first time in human history, a generation has grown up with headlines that describe destruction on a global scale.

A quarter century ago, it seemed relatively easy to isolate our challenge and respond. Today, with dozens of crises crowding our universe, we see not a single gleaming speck but a dark foreboding cloud. The world has become a more crowded, more interconnected, more volatile and unstable place. If education cannot help students see beyond themselves and better understand the interdependent nature of our world, each new generation will remain ignorant and its capacity to live confidently and responsibly will be dangerously diminished.

Since *Sputnik*, America too has undergone dramatic transformations. Twenty-five years ago, the nation's work force was about equally divided between white-collar and blue-collar jobs, between goods and service industries. There are now more people employed full time in our colleges and universities than in agriculture.[12] In 1981, white-collar jobs outnumbered blue-collar jobs by more than three to two.[13] And the number of people employed by United States Steel is smaller than the number of employees at McDonald's.

In the last decade, American productivity increased by only about 23 percent—less than half the average increase of ten Western European nations and Japan. In 1979, the United States's share of world manufacturing slipped to just over 17 percent. Less than 50 percent of the consumer electronics sold in America were made in the United States.[14] A generation ago, America was riding the wave of the postwar baby boom. Then the boom became a bust. By 1990, the school-age population will have declined 14 percent from its peak in 1970. By the year 2000, only 34 percent of all Americans will be under 25, while about 28 percent will be 50 and over.[15] The comparable percentages in 1981 were about 41 and 26.[16]

While the population as a whole is aging, the youth population among black and Hispanic Americans remains large and is proportionately increasing. In 1980, slightly less than one-third of all white Americans were 19 years of age and under, but 43 percent of all Hispanics and about 40 percent of all blacks fell into this youth category.[17] These changes have profound significance for education.

In 1981, only 52 percent of all white families had school-age children (under 18 years of age). In contrast, 71 percent of all black and 75 percent of all Hispanic households had children in this category.[18] With fewer school-age children, the commitment of white American families to public education may well decline. And while minority parents have a growing stake in education, historically they have had limited power to help the nation's schools.

Of special concern is the fact that black and Hispanic young people are precisely those with whom our schools have been least successful. In 1980, 78 percent of white nineteen-year-olds in the United States were high school graduates. However, that same year, 61 percent of black and 56 percent of Hispanic nineteen-year-olds held high school diplomas.[19] Opportunity remains unequal. And this failure to educate *every* young person to his or her full potential threatens the nation's social and economic health.

Today, the push for excellence in education is linked to economic recovery and to jobs. We're being told that better schools will move the nation forward in the high-tech race. And, echoing the post-*Sputnik* era, we're being told that tougher math-science standards are required to keep the nation strong.

Clearly, education and the security of the nation are interlocked. National interests must be served. But where in all of this are students? Where is the recognition that education is to enrich the living individuals? Where is the love of learning and where is the commitment to achieve equality and opportunity for all?

Our schools have adjusted successfully to a host of new demands. They now serve more students from different racial, cultural, and social backgrounds. They have responded to enrollment declines and budget cuts. Experimental programs, such as magnet schools, have been introduced, and public schools are now educating vast numbers of handicapped students who previously were locked out.

There remains, however, a large, even alarming gap between school achievement and the task to be accomplished. A deep erosion of confidence in our schools, coupled with disturbing evidence that at least some of the skepticism is justified, has made revitalizing the American high school an urgent matter. The world has changed—irrevocably so—and quality education in the 1980s and beyond means preparing all students for the transformed world the coming generation will inherit.

And in the debate about public schools equity must be seen not as a chapter of the past but as the unfinished agenda of the future. To expand access without upgrading schools is simply to perpetuate discrimination in a more subtle form. But to push for excellence in ways that ignore the needs of less privileged students is to undermine the future of the nation. Clearly, equity and excellence cannot be divided.

We do not suggest that schools can be society's cure for every social ill. A report card on public education is a report card on the nation. Schools can rise no higher than the communities that support them. And to blame schools for the "rising tide of mediocrity" is to confuse symptoms with the disease.

Still, without good schools none of our problems can be solved. People who cannot communicate are powerless. People who know nothing of their past are culturally impoverished. People who cannot see beyond the confines of their own lives are ill-equipped to face the future. It is in the public school that this nation has chosen to pursue enlightened ends for all its people. And this is where the battle for the future of America will be won or lost.

How should America proceed?

After completing our visits to the schools, reviewing literature, and talking with colleagues both in and out of education, and considering a variety of alternatives, we conclude the time has come:

To clarify the goals of education.

To stress the centrality of language and link the curriculum to a changing national and global context.

To recognize that all students must be prepared for a lifetime of both work and further education.

To strengthen the profession of teaching in America. This means improvement of conditions in the classroom, better recruitment and preparation, better continuing education, and better teacher recognition and rewards.

To improve instruction and give students more opportunities for service in anticipation of their growing civic and social responsibilities as they become adults.

To take full advantage of the information revolution and link technology more effectively to teaching and learning in the schools.

To smooth the transition from school to adult life through more flexible class scheduling and by making available to students new learning places both on and off the campus.

To reduce bureaucracy in education and give school principals the support they need to lead.

To recognize that excellence in education is possible only when connections are made with higher education and with the corporate world.

Finally, the time has come for public schools to be aggressively supported by parents, school boards, and government as well; and for the nation's historic commitment to public education to be vigorously reaffirmed by all.

These topics—goals, curriculum, teachers, teaching and learning, technology, structure, school leadership, connections beyond the campus, and community support—emerged as critically important issues in our study and they provided a framework for our report. In the chapters that follow, we discuss these major themes and set forth, for national discussion and debate, a series of proposals to promote school revival and reform.

PART I

A TROUBLED
INSTITUTION

1

A DAY AT RIDGEFIELD HIGH

It is eight in the morning. The doors of 16,000 public high schools open.[1] More than 13 million students begin to arrive for the start of another school day.[2]

In a small midwestern town, about 1,000 students go to Ridgefield High. Hundreds are deposited by bus at the front door of the two-story brick building built in the 1930s, now showing its years and lack of care. Ridgefield has cracked sidewalks, a shabby lawn, and peeling paint on every window sash. Some students walk to school; others park their cars on a gravel lot just beyond the macadam-covered spaces reserved for teachers.

The front foyer of the building leads off in three directions. To the right there is a large cafeteria with long rows of narrow tables and chairs. Straight ahead is a large hallway lined with bright-colored lockers. To the left is the main corridor.

The office also is to the left, with a front wall of glass. On the brick wall opposite the office is the weekly activity board, announcing sporting events, assemblies, and the message "Happy Birthday, Linda Gutowski."

Very little decorates the walls—a few posters here and there. One handwritten announcement of Teenage Christian Fellowship meetings. No graffiti. Fairly clean.

Inside the building there is much milling about. The halls are crowded. Students meet with friends. They noisily stuff possessions into lockers. Boyfriends and girlfriends have already met. The bell rings. The public address system warns the students not to be late for "first-hour" class.

Students at Ridgefield High are predominantly white, the families working class. For boys, normal dress consists of running shoes, jeans (without designer labels), and T-shirts (football and rock group). Some girls wear feminine versions of this "uniform." Others wear either conservative dresses or imitations of the latest fashions, too much makeup or none at all, long straight hair or bouffant curls.

The office has a pleasant atmosphere: popular music plays on the radio; lunch tickets are sold; students and teachers wander in and out. A student comes in to pick up a form from the attendance secretary and regales her with a story about seventeen busboys being fired from a nearby country club restaurant for "getting into the beer."

The office walls contain posters of teachers' assignments, a schedule of events, and a Nike shoe poster of marathon runners after the race.

The principal, Tom Moss, is accessible to students. Almost immediately, several sophomore girls walk in and ask to see him. These four cheerleaders are upset about a conflict between their sponsor, Ms. Johnson, and the volleyball coach, Ms. Plummer. Janice, the fifth member of their squad, is both a cheerleader and a volleyball player. Both groups practice at the same time, and Janice was benched the previous night during cheerleading because a schedule conflict caused her to miss a practice session. An apparent compromise solution (splitting the time) had been ignored by Ms. Johnson.

Mr. Moss has already discussed the issue with the superintendent, the cheerleader's stepfather (who is a Ridgefield High School teacher), and Ms. Johnson. Moss now spends forty minutes with the girls, assuring them that he will speak to all the concerned parties once again. The communication has been direct and caring.

By now, the day's activities are in full swing. At the beginning of the second hour, the main office secretary makes announcements over the school-wide public-address system. Her tone is informal as she runs down the schedule for yearbook pictures, and promises that tomorrow's special assembly will be good, "so don't forget your twenty-five-cent admission."

Physical education classes, a favorite of most students, are going on in the gym and out back. Study hall for this hour is in the cafeteria. There, students are quiet—either sleeping or reading.

In the library, a group of students learn how to locate books, others help the librarian; still others study quietly; a few read magazines from the library's large collection (for example, *Outdoor Life*, *Guitar Player*, *Family Circle*, *American History*).

Down the hall, in the cramped teachers' lounge, four or five people are drinking coffee, eating snacks purchased from the vending machine, and chatting.

In English classrooms, students pick out verbs and subjects from worksheets. In history classes, they are listening to lectures on Indians, Vikings, and the religions of China. Trigonometry students work independently, solving problems in the text.

In "functional" math, several "slow" students work individually, but not seriously. They have been given packets that have catchy titles—Prime Time, Wit Kit, Math Path, Skill Drill, and Game Frame—and include equipment such as headphones, tapes, and projectors. The students, however, are not caught up in the materials; they talk and wander around while the teacher works with one student at her desk.

Biology II students listen to a lecture on the coloration of fall leaves, while Biology I students look at exhibits on an overhead projector and then have a lively debate about pollution. In Spanish class, students watch slides of the teacher's stay in Peru. Conversation in Spanish is interspersed. In Home Economics, students do a "seek-and-find" worksheet on sewing terms, and wait while the teacher helps one student with a sewing pattern at her desk.

In Introduction to Business, students listen and follow directions as the teacher gives step-by-step instructions, in a loud and precise voice, related to the use of a new instructional packet:

> First, put your names and *second period* on the outside of the packet, then take out every item in the packet and put your name on each of the items [she waits]. After your names are put on all materials, put all of them back except for the booklet entitled *Instructions*. Now, look at me, please. I will go slowly and you can put what I say into your own words, but these statements are to be written inside of your instructional manual. One: These packets may not leave the classroom. Two: If absent from school, you need to come before school, during study, or after school, to make up for time that you've missed in class. Three: Pay attention. If you don't pay attention, you may get lost and, since we are going to be working on this for three weeks, you'll be lost for all three weeks. . . . Now let's go back to page one of the instruction booklet. Pages one, two, and three are introductions to the packet. On pages four and five is the actual beginning of the packet and page nine is where you actually start working on your packet.[3]

As students move from class to class, the routine is predictable. For the first half of the period, they mostly sit and listen, occasionally taking notes. During the last portion, students discuss material, fill out worksheets and study guides while their teacher circulates to give individualized assistance.

It is lunchtime. Groups of students shuttle in and out of the cafeteria. There is much half-serious complaining about the food and the meager choices on the menu. Students in one small group eat hurriedly and make their way out the back door to the smoking area, where they visit with one another or smoke cigarettes or dope.

A security guard monitors the area during lunch. He does not like what is going on, but his problem is similar to that of other adults who might be upset about the use of drugs. He does not know how to stop it. A student explains: "Teachers don't like it, but what are they going to do about it? When we see them coming, we flip the joint away and that's that." Around school, these kids are called "burnouts"—in contrast to the "jocks" or the group called "socies."

Two boys caught fighting in the washroom are in the principal's office. Their statements are taped by Mr. Moss. All such conferences are recorded so the affected students and parents hear the same story. The two boys spend most of the time arguing about who won the fight; each seems desperately in need of winning.

When the boys are questioned individually, John starts crying because the expected suspension means he will not be able to play football. Athletics are exalted at Ridgefield High; the jocks are the heroes of students, administrators, and parents. The coach is in on the meeting, assuring John that if he takes the punishment "like a man" he may be allowed to regain status and rejoin the team.

Lunch is over. Some Ridgefield High students take a school bus to Burr Community College to participate in a vocational program. A few leave early to work; most return to class. The corridors begin to clear.

It is two in the afternoon, now. The school day is almost over at Ridgefield High. Students who have broken one rule or another are herded into the library for "eighth-hour" detention time. Usually, they are punished for coming late.

Students on athletic teams head for buses. Others take a final class or study hall before the day ends. Some linger after school for a club meeting. Still others drive around or just hang out with friends before going home.

Some students hurry off to work. Many have chores to do at home. A few are heard complaining about too much homework, but they also claim that they can get away without doing it. One student is overheard saying, "Nothing much happens here."

Tomorrow is another day at Ridgefield High; it will probably be a lot like today.

Ridgefield High has much in common with most high schools from coast to coast. It is neither trouble free nor terrible. Classes are at times inspired, occasionally dreadful, and, most often, routine. A few students tackle ideas as if they were in a college seminar. Most graduate without being stretched to their potential. At Ridgefield and elsewhere, there is a kind of unwritten, unspoken contract between the teachers and the students: Keep off my back, and I'll keep off yours.

Ridgefield, along with most other high schools in the nation, falls somewhere in the middle ground of academic quality. Exceptional institutions are at either end. At one extreme are the very bad, trouble-ridden schools that hold few, if any, academic goals for students; at the other are outstanding institutions—supportive and demanding—where students receive a first-class education.

Troubled high schools frequently are in inner cities where problems of population dislocation, poverty, unemployment, and crime take priority over education. They also may be found in decaying suburbs or in rural communities racked by poverty and neglect.

Students in failing urban schools[4] often jam into battered buildings with wire-covered windows and graffiti-covered walls.* Tile and other hard surfaces reflect the glare from naked light bulbs hanging in protective cages of wire.

Changing classes is like the morning rush hour in Manhattan. Students push and shove in crowded stairways, or ride dangerous elevators and escalators often brought to a quick halt by pranksters. Neighboring residents complain of noise, vandalism, and drugs.

Security guards patrol the halls, attempting to keep order. When violence breaks out, teachers often turn away. They're afraid. On a good day in such a school, the attendance is 50 percent.

Once inside the classroom, students pay little attention to the teacher, who, in turn, expects little from the students. In one such school we heard the teacher say, "I'll write on the blackboard what you need to know." In another, "Helium, we won't worry about

*In this study, "urban" schools are institutions located within the central city of a standard metropolitan statistical area (SMSA). "Suburban" schools are located in an SMSA, but outside of the central city. "Rural" schools are located outside of an SMSA.

that." In still another, "Don't worry, we won't have any hard problems on the test."

Many students are two or more years below grade level in reading and math. Few have a sense of real accomplishment. Heroic teachers can be found, but generally the faculty feel discouraged; some have given up. A handful of kids are high achievers. Most are bored, restless, and rebellious. About half drop out. Those who do graduate get odd jobs or are unemployed. Few go on to college.

At the other end of the spectrum are schools with the highest academic standards. The building may be old or new, but the atmosphere is pleasant. Student art and colorful posters decorate the walls. Announcements of scholarships and overseas study programs are prominently displayed. The occasional graffiti are quickly removed. Students move purposefully from class to class. They take five or six subjects each semester, and do two or three hours of homework every night. They are busy publishing the school paper or telling friends of their American Field Service year of study in Japan.

Graduates from good high schools complete four years of English, social studies, and science; three years of math; and two or more years of a foreign language. Many take advanced placement or honors classes that are rigorous and fast-paced. The classroom is a forum for lively debate. Some students drift, but most master the material and can apply the information.

Teachers at the better schools often push for responses to demanding questions. Generally, the teaching style is pungent, the pace brisk, the tone provocative and friendly. Precise answers and supportive reasons frequently are demanded.

At one school, we saw a science teacher handing out detailed breakdowns of the semester's assignments for each student. They were all prepared, we found out later, on his home computer.

An English teacher returned themes that she said were "disappointing," but on each were extensive comments and corrections representing many hours of work.

A music teacher (who says she is at school until 5 P.M. every day) has written a textbook and curriculum guide for her class and directs operas and symphonies at the school.

An advanced calculus teacher is tough and demanding. He drills and pushes the students, putting them on the spot. Their questions challenge him, even as he motivates the students.

Over 90 percent of the students in strongly academic schools graduate and go on to college. Many are headed for the most prestigious institutions. At graduation, coveted science awards and National Merit Scholarships are presented in great numbers. Such high schools are as good as or better than any in the world.

When the nation's 16,000 high school doors close at the end of a busy day, each school has had its own special blend of minor victories and defeats.

2

REPORT CARD:
HOW SCHOOLS ARE DOING

The village of Ridgefield, with 1800 citizens, is on a winding two-lane road, forty miles from a large midwestern city. Most of Ridgefield's workers commute to blue-collar jobs or care for small family farms. There are five policemen in the town, a volunteer fire department, and two banks.

Until the late fifties, Ridgefield was a stable rural community with a farm and dairy population. The school population was homogeneous and small. In 1953, there was a total of 147 students in the high school and 18 in the graduating class. A long-time resident and teacher recalls the "good old days": "We couldn't have had a more supportive community. We never had a bond issue that was voted down. Anything the school wanted we would get."

The sixties brought dramatic changes. Gradually, acres of farmland sprouted new homesites rather than crops; new landowners were mostly blue-collar workers with jobs in automotive plants and factories in the city about forty miles away. Ridgefield became a bedroom community with shallow roots, less cohesion, and less involvement in the schools. Bond issues were voted down.

Ridgefield reflects a pattern nationwide. In 1955, more than two-thirds of Americans responding to a Gallup Poll said they were "willing to pay extra taxes, if the extra money were used to raise the salaries of school teachers." In 1980, only 30 percent declared themselves willing to raise taxes.[1] Tax resistance notwithstanding, in

1982 the nation spent 126.7 billion tax dollars to finance the biggest, oldest, most comprehensive system of public elementary and secondary education on earth.[2] How can that system be described and what about the quality of its performance?

Every high school is unique; still America's high schools have much in common. The vast majority call themselves "comprehensive." They offer under one roof (or several roofs) an academic program for those going on to college, a vocational program for those preparing for jobs, and a general studies program for those still unclear about their goals.

About 4 percent of the public high schools are "specialized," including the so-called "magnet" schools.[3] These institutions concentrate on programs of high interest to the students—the arts, business, or science, for example.

A few public schools describe themselves as "alternative" institutions. Growing out of the education reforms of the 1960s, these experimental schools offer custom-made programs for both able and high-risk students.

About 10 percent of the nation's public schools are in the cities. They enroll about 2.9 million students. Fifty-six percent are in rural areas, with school districts sometimes extending hundreds of miles. These rural schools enroll about 4.1 million students. Thirty-four percent of the nation's high schools are in the suburbs and enroll 6.3 million students.[4]

High schools range in size from those with less than 50 students to those with more than 5,000; about half the high schools in the United States enroll fewer than 600 students.[5]

Slightly more than half of the nation's high schools—almost 8,200—are four-year institutions, offering grades nine through twelve. About 4,400 combine junior and senior high. Another 3,200 are three-year schools, beginning at the tenth grade. The remaining 200 public high schools have other grade spans.[6]

Most of the nation's high schools have fewer than 30 percent minority enrollment.[7] On the other hand, enrollments at many large urban schools are over 50 percent black or Hispanic. The public school system in St. Louis is nearly 80 percent minority.[8] The city of Atlanta has a minority population of 68 percent, but public school enrollment is 92 percent minority.[9] Between 1970 and 1980, the proportion of white students in Milwaukee's public high schools fell from 75 percent to 52 percent, while its black enrollment almost doubled.[10] In spite of such a large minority representation in some districts, only 8 percent of all high schools bus students to achieve racial balance.[11]

The average American high school gets about 50 percent of its budget from the state, 42 percent from the local district, and nearly 8 percent from Washington.[12] State support for public education varies from a high of almost 90 percent in Hawaii to a low of 7 percent in New Hampshire.[13]

Organizationally, the typical high school is staffed by a principal, two assistant principals, 50 to 60 teachers, a guidance counselor or two, a librarian, a remedial specialist, and several student teachers or teaching aides.[14] Nationally, the average secondary school teacher-pupil ratio is about 1 to 16—and going down.[15] Here again, there is great variation from state to state.

The retention rate varies greatly from school to school. Some schools graduate almost every student. At others, a dropout rate of almost 50 percent is anticipated.[16] Most states require students to stay in school until age sixteen. Overall, about three-fourths of all students who enter high school complete the course.[17]

High school principals identify absenteeism, class cutting, and parental disinterest as moderately serious problems. About half of all principals place student drug or alcohol abuse in the same category. Contrary to popular belief, however, principals claim that student fights, thefts, and vandalism are relatively minor problems.[18] Even so, more than 4 percent of the nation's teachers say they have been physically abused or threatened.[19] More than 35 percent say they have felt unsafe in school.[20]

The rhythm of the school day is familiar. Typically, the day is divided into six or seven periods averaging about fifty minutes each. Most high schools require hall passes, forbid student smoking, and have a dress code.

Many students have what can be best described as a love-hate relationship with the school. Most seniors agree that there should be more emphasis on academic subjects and that poor teaching has interfered with their education; but they criticize their own study habits, too.[21] In general, students do not seem to feel intensely negative about school, but neither do they consider their high schools as outstanding places to be.

The public, in turn, offers its own report card on the public schools. In 1974, the Gallup Poll began asking Americans to grade their schools. That year, 18 percent of those polled gave the schools an *A*, while 6 percent gave them a *D*. Eight years later, in 1982, only 8 percent were willing to give the schools an *A*, while those believing the schools deserved a *D* had more than doubled, from 6 to 14 percent.[22]

How accurate is the public evaluation?

One popular yardstick used to judge school performance is the Scholastic Aptitude Test, commonly called the SAT. Approximately one-third of all high school graduates take this test annually.[23] The SAT is divided into two major parts—verbal and mathematical skills. The verbal portion consists of 85 questions that test vocabulary and a student's ability to recognize relationships in pairs of words, to complete sentences, and to interpret and analyze written passages. The mathematics portion includes questions in arithmetic, algebra, and geometry. All answers on both sections are multiple choice.

Scholastic Aptitude Test results make news every year. For years, the headlines have been bad. Between 1952 and 1982 the average score on the verbal section of the SAT fell 50 points, from 476 to 426 (Chart 1). Even after one adjusts for a larger and more diverse group of test takers there remains a jolting point spread

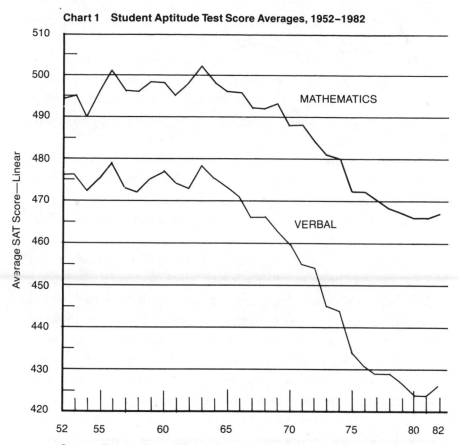

Chart 1   Student Aptitude Test Score Averages, 1952–1982

MATHEMATICS

VERBAL

SOURCE: Data for 1952–1977, College Entrance Examination Board, *On Further Examination: Report of the Advisory Panel on the Scholastic Aptitude Test Score Decline* (New York: College Board, 1977), p. 6. For 1978–1981, National Center for Education Statistics, *Digest of Education Statistics: 1982* (Washington, D.C.: Government Printing Office, 1982), p. 68. For 1982, National Center for Education Statistics, unpublished data.

between scores of today's most academically ambitious young people and those of a generation ago.

In 1975, a panel was convened to investigate possible causes of the downswing of SAT scores. The group identified absenteeism, automatic promotion, reduced homework, lowered textbook standards, decreased emphasis on writing, changes in family structure, television viewing habits, and a host of other factors.[24] The panel concluded with an appropriate caution: "It would be too bad if our concentration on the implications of a decline in the statistical averages on a set of standardized examinations should seem to ignore how incomplete a measure this is of either educational or broader human purpose."[25]

In 1981, the SAT scores leveled off. In 1982, they made a very slight recovery. For the first time in nineteen years the average verbal score for college-bound seniors rose—from 424 to 426. The average math score moved from 466 to 467.[26] However, these increases are too small and the scope of measurement too narrow to allow us to draw conclusions about shifts in school performance.

The SAT is one of two major college admission tests. The other is a test prepared by the American College Testing Program (ACT). About 900,000 students take the ACT each year.[27] This test covers English and mathematics usage, social sciences, and natural science. Students take either or both national tests, depending upon requirements of the colleges to which they apply.

The trend of ACT scores over the past decade (Chart 2) is similar to that of the SAT. In 1970, the combined mean score for English, mathematics, social studies, and science was 19.9. By 1976, the score had dropped to 18.3; by 1982 it reached 18.4.[28] During the same period, the mean mathematics score on the ACT dropped from 20 to 17.2. Scores in science remained at 20.8.[29]

Headlines notwithstanding, neither the ACT nor the SAT was created to measure the quality of schools. For example, when the Scholastic Aptitude Test was first constructed about sixty years ago, the aim was to measure students' underlying "aptitude" for higher

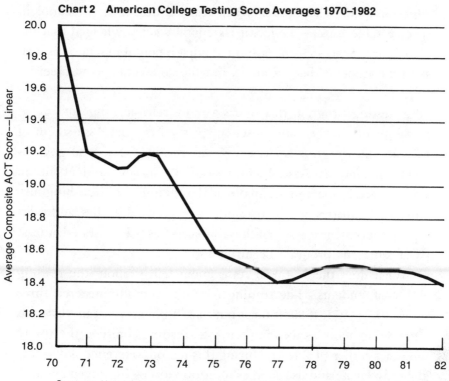

Chart 2   American College Testing Score Averages 1970–1982

SOURCE: Unpublished national data, *The American College Testing Program,* Iowa City,
1982.

education, not what students had learned during high school in specific subject areas. Today, it is generally acknowledged that the SAT scores relate in some fashion to what is taught in school, as well as to the students' backgrounds, but the connection is unclear.

A testing program that offers a more reliable gauge of educational quality in the nation's schools is the National Assessment of Educational Progress (NAEP). Sponsored by the federal government, the National Assessment periodically surveys students in ten subjects: art, career and occupational development, citizenship, literature, mathematics, music, reading, science, social studies, and writing. Achievement in each of these subjects has been assessed at least twice since the program began in 1969.

What does the National Assessment tell us about the reading ability of students? The reading test has been administered three times: 1971, 1975, 1980. It turns out that in 1980 seventeen-year-olds were doing about as well in their total reading ability as they were ten years earlier (Table 1). During this period, reference skills—the ability to locate and use sources of information—improved slightly. However, there was a slight decline in what test makers call "inferential comprehension"—the ability to grasp what a text implies but does not explicitly state. In this skill, the scores of seventeen-year-olds dropped from 64.2 to 62.1 percent. Apparently many students

Table 1 Reading Scores

Changes in mean percentage scores for 17-year-olds
National Assessment of Educational Progress, 1971, 1975, 1980

	1971	1975	1980
Total Reading	68.9	69.0	68.2
Literal comprehension	72.2	72.7	72.0
Inferential comprehension	64.2	63.3	62.1
Reference skills	69.4	70.1	70.2

Source: *Three National Assessments of Reading: Changes in Performance, 1970–1980,* National Assessment of Educational Progress (Denver, Colorado: Education Commission of the States, April 1981).

can decode words but have difficulty understanding whole passages.

The National Assessment also evaluates skills in writing. Students are asked to produce writing samples, which are rated on a scale from 1 (inadequate) to 4 (best). Between 1969 and 1979, there was a slight decline in the overall writing competence of seventeen-year-olds (Table 2). In a storytelling assignment, the number of papers rated "competent" increased by 10.3 percent, a significant improvement; in persuasive writing, there was a drop of 6 percent between 1974 and 1979.[30]

The National Assessment found little change in the students' technical proficiency in writing: 10 to 25 percent of the students had serious difficulty in putting words on paper. The majority of errors were in punctuation, spelling, and sentence structure.[31]

The National Assessment mathematics test measures four categories: knowledge, skills, understanding, and application (Table 3). Between 1973 (when the test was first administered) and 1978, the scores of seventeen-year-olds dropped by 4 percentage points. The most recent assessment, made in 1982, indicates that this decline has been stemmed.[32] There is little reason for rejoicing, however, because most of the improved performance was in routine computation and figure recognition—tasks requiring little of the abstract thinking that gives mathematics its power.

Table 2 Overall Writing Effectiveness

Changes in mean percentage scores for 17-year-olds
National Assessment of Educational Progress, 1969, 1974, 1979

Quality ratings 1 = inadequate 4 = best	1969	1974	1979
1	12.1	14.9	11.9
2	40.3	38.8	46.5
3	31.8	32.6	28.8
4	15.9	13.7	12.8

Source: *Writing Achievement, 1969–1979, Volume I,* National Assessment of Educational Progress (Denver, Colorado: Education Commission of the States, December 1980).

Table 3 Mathematics Scores

Mean percentage scores for 17-year-olds,
National Assessment of Educational Progress, 1978 and 1982

	1978	1982
Total Math	60.4	60.3
Math knowledge	74.7	74.9
Math skills	59.7	60.0
Math understanding	61.8	61.5
Math application	43.5	42.4

Source: *The Third National Mathematics Assessment; Results, Trends and Issues,* National Assessment of Educational Progress (Denver, Colorado: Education Commission of the States, April 1983).

Science assessment includes knowledge of both biology and physical science (Table 4). Measured over a nine-year period, there appear to be modest gains in achievement. Still, an examination of specific questions reveals a disturbing lack of knowledge. When asked what happens when a combustion reaction takes place, only 54 percent of the respondents chose the one answer that contained the word "heat"; 12 percent understood that plastics are petroleum products; 50 percent knew that a star is most like the sun as opposed to a comet, a meteor, the moon, or a planet.[33] A caution: The latest National Assessment report on science is now more than six years old. More recent data are required before we can generalize, with confidence, about the current situation.

The National Assessment also includes a measure of the political

Table 4 Science Scores

Mean percentage scores for 17-year-olds
National Assessment of Educational Progress, 1969, 1973 and 1977

	1969	1973	1977
Total science	45.2	48.4	46.5
Biology	52.3	53.3	52.2
Physical science	42.9	46.8	44.4

Source: *Three Assessments in Science, 1969–1977: Technical Summary,* National Assessment of Educational Progress, p. 15.

knowledge and attitudes of students. Here again, there are no recent data. During the period that is reported, however, the decline in student performance in this area has been most dramatic (Table 5).

Between 1969 and 1976, scores for seventeen-year-olds on knowledge about the government dropped from 64.4 percent to 53.9 percent. In 1976, only 31 percent of thirteen-year-olds and 53 percent of seventeen-year-olds tested knew that each state has two United States senators. Forty-two percent of the thirteen-year-olds knew it was not illegal to start a new political party. One out of every seven seventeen-year-olds thought the President does not always have to obey the law.[34]

In 1972, less than one-half of America's seventeen-year-olds understood how to use a sample ballot. Only one-third of the thirteen-year-olds knew that the United States Supreme Court has the power to declare an act of Congress unconstitutional. And only 17 percent knew that presidential candidates are nominated at national conventions.[35]

In addition to national school measures—the SAT, ACT, and National Assessment scores—many states have assessments of their own.

Iowa, in the nation's heartland, tests students every year in

Table 5 Political Knowledge and Attitude Scores

	Mean average scores for 17-year-olds National Assessment for Educational Progress, 1969 and 1976	
	1969	1976
Respect for others	82.1	79.8
Structure and function of government	64.4	53.9
Political process	65.5	59.0
Average performance		
Political knowledge	73	65
Political attitudes	67	63

Source: Ina Mullis, "Citizenship/Social Achievement Trends Over Time," paper presented at annual meeting of the AERA, 1978.

mathematics and reading achievement. Comparable tests have been given since the mid-1950s. Achievement scores in Iowa began declining in the mid-1960s. Since 1977, however, reading achievement scores for Iowa's elementary school students have been on the rise. Composite scores for grades nine, ten, and eleven also have been going up. Twelfth graders' scores have been improving since 1978 (Chart 3, p. 32).

Iowa is not necessarily typical of the nation; conditions vary from state to state. But positive signs have been noted in other states as well. Philip E. Runkel writes: "In February we reported that scores on reading and math tests given to all Michigan fourth-, seventh-, and tenth-grade students last fall improved at all levels compared to the previous year.

California test scores began declining in 1969. In 1981, its third-, sixth-, and twelfth-grade students had improved, although twelfth graders in California still score below the national norm on most tests.[37]

In all, more than thirty states now require "competency tests." Many seek to measure only "minimum competencies," the ability of young people to function in everyday situations—follow directions, write checks, read a want ad, or fill out a job application. These skills are useful but there is no reason to applaud such a threshold. One state minimum competency test, for example, includes the following questions to test reading comprehension:

EMERGENCY INFORMATION

Fire:	415-2115	Your fire department's number
Police:	555-1155	Your police department's number
Doctor:	515-0734	Your doctor's number
Ambulance:	555-1157	Ambulance number
F.B.I.:		Federal Bureau of Investigation: Dial 481-9110
Coast Guard:		Search and Rescue Emergencies: Call 985-9822

Highway Patrol: To report emergencies, call OPERATOR: Ask for Zenith 1-2000

Secret Service: U.S. Secret Service: Dial 688-4830 or in any emergency, dial the operator

You would dial 555-1155 to reach:
A. the fire department
B. the police
C. an ambulance
D. a doctor

Bonnie has the flu, and her father wants to take her to the doctor for a shot. What number should he call?
A. 515-0734
B. 555-1155
C. 415-2115
D. 555-1157

Here is a sample mathematics problem from another minimum competency test:

Mr. Levi is an hourly employee who receives $5 per hour. He receives time-and-a-half for any time over 8 hours on any given day. The following is his time card for last week.

Monday	Tuesday	Wednesday	Thursday	Friday
8 hours	8 hours	8 hours	9 hours	9 hours

How many hours overtime did he work last week?
A. 1 hour
B. 1.5 hour
C. 2 hours
D. 2.5 hours

Source: Rose Scherini, *High Schools Today: Overview and Implications for the University of California, Berkeley* (Berkeley: Office of Student Research, May 1981), Appendix, pp. 9, 11.

Functional literacy may be a step away from a life of victimization. It is hardly a passport to a life of personal confidence and economic strength.

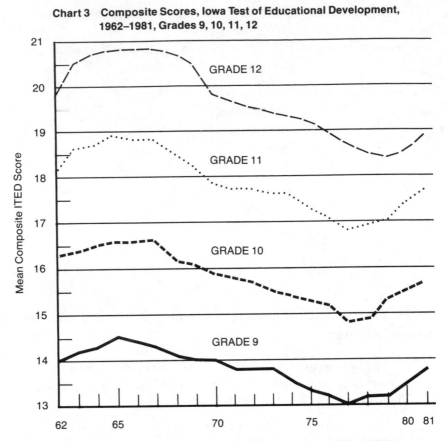

Chart 3 Composite Scores, Iowa Test of Educational Development, 1962–1981, Grades 9, 10, 11, 12

GRADE 12

GRADE 11

GRADE 10

GRADE 9

Mean Composite ITED Score

NOTE: Includes reading, mathematics, social studies, and science achievement scores.
SOURCE: Dr. Leonard S. Feldt, Iowa Testing Program.

How do American schools compare with those of other countries?

In 1967, a twelve-nation study of mathematics performance of thirteen- and eighteen-year-olds was launched under the leadership of Torsten Husén, University of Stockholm, Sweden. Later, from 1973 to 1977, international surveys were conducted in seven subjects: mathematics, science, reading comprehension, literature, English and French as foreign languages, and civic education.[38]

For schools in the United States, the results were not encouraging. The average comprehension score on the reading test, for example, placed United States high school students in the lowest one-third. In mathematics, American students scored lowest among the nations tested, while Israelis, Japanese, German, and French students scored in the top one-third.[39] In civic education, students in Ireland and the United States had the lowest average scores among industrialized countries, while those from New Zealand, Germany, and Sweden had the highest.[40]

Such international comparisons have been challenged because the number of students in the relevant age groups varies greatly from one nation to another. In the United States, for example, about 75 percent of the youth group complete high school. In Sweden, 45–50 percent complete the *gymnasium* (grades 11 and 12) while in the *Oberprimaner* (grade 13) in the Federal Republic of Germany only about 15 percent of the youth group are enrolled.[41]

Husén and his team of researchers sought to overcome the problem by looking, not just at *all* students, but also at the top 9 percent, 7 percent, and 5 percent of the students in each country surveyed. As reported, when the average scores of *all* students are compared, the United States youth performed poorly in most subjects. However, when only *top* students were rated, those in the United States compared more favorably with those in other countries (Charts 4 and 5).

Perhaps the most significant conclusion one can reach (based on

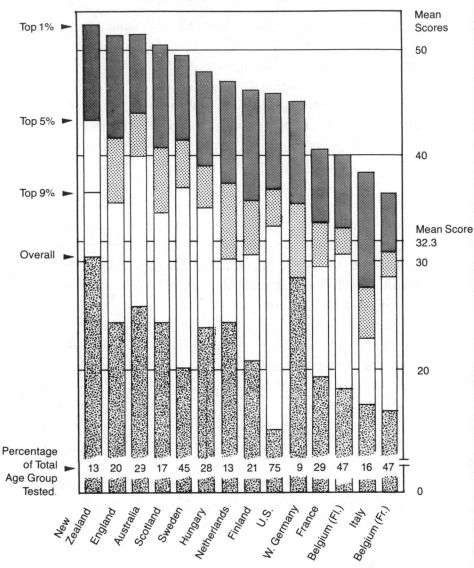

Chart 4   Mean Science Scores of Total Age Group and of Top
1 Percent, Top 5 Percent, and Top 9 Percent

SOURCE: L.C. Comber and John P. Keeves, *Science Education in Nineteen
Countries* (Stockholm and New York: Almquist & Wiksell and
Wiley-Halsted Press, 1973).

**Chart 5   Mean Mathematics Test Scores for Terminal
Mathematics Population in Twelve Nations**

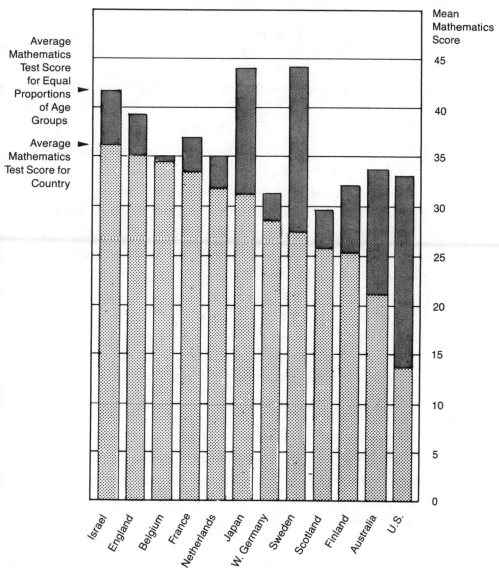

Average
Mathematics
Test Score
for Equal
Proportions
of Age
Groups ►

Average ►
Mathematics
Test Score for
Country

Mean
Mathematics
Score

45

40

35

30

25

20

15

10

5

0

Israel England Belgium France Netherlands Japan W. Germany Sweden Scotland Finland Australia U.S.

SOURCE: Torsten Husén (ed.), *International Study of Achievement in Mathematics: A Comparison Between Twelve Countries* (New York: Wiley, 1967)

limited and dated information) is the one stated in 1983 by Professor Husén:

> The top 5 percent and 10 percent at the end of secondary education (i.e. the elite) tended to perform at nearly the same level in both comprehensive and selective systems of secondary education. Thus the elite among high school seniors did not differ considerably in their performance from their age-mates in France, England or Germany.[42]

Behind the meager international data lie values in the American educational system that explain perhaps both our victories and our defeats. Americans have been less awed than many other countries by "high culture." We have been more reluctant to define what it means to be an educated person. And we are deeply suspicious of central control of education and uniform standards, although we yearn for uniform results.

Further, Americans tend to see schooling as the way for each individual to achieve success and as a way to achieve social equity, too. Viewed separately, none of these beliefs is distinctive.[43] Taken together, they make our education system sharply distinguishable from those of most other countries, and they make international comparisons somewhat risky.

How then should the American high school be assessed?

When viewed in historical perspective, high schools have been, we believe, remarkably successful. These "peoples' colleges"—as they were once called—have educated waves of new Americans, expanded opportunity for historically bypassed minorities, and pro-vided—for millions—a door to work and further education. Perhaps no other institution has reflected more completely the hopes and aspirations of the nation.

Still, with all of its success, public support for public education has gone down. In recent years we have been shocked and disappointed by reports of failing test scores and by the inability of many of our schools to achieve high academic standards. Year after year, school news from a variety of sources has been bad, causing public confidence to plummet.

This decline in the academic performance of our schools accelerated during the 1960s, following a spurt of post-*Sputnik* school reform. During this time when the nation truly was at risk, almost all institutions were battered by the trauma of wars, riots, and assassinations. Willard Wirtz, a perceptive interpreter of social trends, commented on this destructive decade and, in the process, put the decline of test scores in a larger social context:

> We're . . . talking about a period in which . . . test scores were bound to be affected by a decade of distraction, a period in which a war was fought principally by these young people, a divisive war. It was a period of political assassination, particularly of their heroes. It was a period of rioting in the streets. It was a period of corruption of institutional stewardship in this country. It would have been very difficult for young people to place high on their list of personal priorities the goal of getting the highest possible scores on the Scholastic Aptitude Test during that period.[44]

In addition to national problems, the high school has also felt the impact of changing family patterns in recent years. The number of children in America who are affected by divorces has more than doubled since 1960.[45] Nearly one out of five families is maintained by a woman who is either divorced, separated, widowed, or has never married.[46] Two-thirds of these mothers work.[47] About *half* the children now in first grade will have lived in one-parent homes by the time they graduate from high school.[48] This shift in family life has caused schools to take on burdens and responsibilities of the home.

For many teenagers, the high school may be the only place to get support and ease the pain of personal trauma and deep hurt. It frequently becomes a crisis center—helping a pregnant girl, supporting a young student who has had a fight at home, or helping a teenager through the trauma of parental separation or divorce. One student said:

> When my mom and dad separated I thought I'd die. I couldn't study and I felt like I had to cry all day. My English teacher, who I like a lot, stayed after school one day so we could talk. I would have never made it through without her help.[49]

Another student told us:

> One reason I like my school is because I would rather be at school than at home. I even come to school when I have a cold. The reason is because I get bored at home.[50]

High school *is* home for many students. It also is one institution in our culture where it is all right to be young. Here, teenagers meet each other, share hopes and fears, start love affairs, and experiment with growing up. This role will never appear on the report card of the American high school unless perhaps the old-fashioned category "deportment" is added to the list; and unless we grade the school, not just on academic performance, but also on its sensitivity toward students.

In describing these social transitions and upheavals, we do not excuse the schools. Educators have added to the crisis that has swirled around them. Lack of leadership, confusion over goals, a smorgasbord curriculum, a decline of academic standards all have contributed to the weakening of public education. Schools must not just follow, they must lead.

Still, schools reflect both the strengths and the weaknesses of the nation. Caught in the crossfire of competing goals, faced with serious financial problems, and struggling to respond to profound social changes, most secondary schools in the United States are—like the communities that surround them—surviving but not thriving.

For a small percentage of students—10 to 15 percent perhaps—the American high school provides an outstanding education, perhaps the finest in the world. Their schooling combines a solid curriculum with good teaching. Students are not only expected to remember and recite, but also to explore, to think creatively, and to challenge.

A larger percentage of students—perhaps 20 to 30 percent—mark time in school or drop out. For them, the high school experience occasionally may be socially supportive, but academically it's a failure. The majority of students are in the vast middle ground. They attend schools like Ridgefield High, where pockets of excellence can be found but where there is little intellectual challenge.

In short, the academic report card on the nation's schools is mixed. We believe, however, that American public education is beginning to improve. After years of decline, test scores have leveled off and in some states modest gains have been recorded. A core curriculum is beginning to be shaped. College admission standards are being tightened. Most importantly, there is a revival of interest in the nation's schools. Business leaders and governors are promoting education and there are stirrings at the federal level, too. America is turning once again to education.

Still, our celebration should be modest. In the future, citizenship responsibility will be more, not less, demanding; economic pressures will be more, not less, intense. Opportunities for human progress, as well as threats to our quality of life, will increase. The bidding has gone up and the quality of our schools must go up as well. We cannot rest with what we have today.

PART II

A CLEAR AND VITAL
MISSION

3

WE WANT IT ALL

We sat in the teachers' lounge at Ridgefield High. The talk was downbeat; teachers were bone tired. One teacher described why she believed the school was drifting.

> How in the world are you going to know where you're going or if what you are doing is right if you don't have a plan? Things just sort of happen around here. There's no real organization; it's just random happenings.[1]

The Boston Latin Grammar School, founded in 1635, was more than a random happening. The goal was to prepare privileged young men for Harvard, which, in turn, would prepare them to serve both state and church. Historian Lawrence A. Cremin reminds us that, in the early days of the Republic, schooling "was to be only one part of the education of the public, and a relatively minor part at that."[2] In those days, the family and the church were considered powerful educators, too.

As the nation grew, the mission of schooling was extended. In 1751, Benjamin Franklin established a secondary school in Philadelphia to instruct people in more practical skills, such as letter writing and accounting. Franklin's school became the model for "academies" that dominated nineteenth-century secondary education. These schools reflected the new nation's growing commitment to "useful learning."

The academies, although privately controlled, often received community and state support. Their students came from many social classes—from high society to farm families. The curriculum ranged from Latin and Greek, mathematics, English and French, to business and commercial subjects, sewing, and agriculture. Subjects were often grouped to match student aspirations. At Gould's Academy in Bethel, Maine, for example, "different courses of study were arranged for 'those fitting for college, teaching or the counting room.' "[3]

Academies were available only to a paying clientele. Children from poor families had little opportunity for education beyond reading, writing, and arithmetic—the standard subjects taught in the common school. Visionaries, understanding the injustice, argued that if basic education was the right of all, so too was advanced instruction. The popularization of the school had begun.

The first *public* high school in America—the English Classical School—opened in Boston in 1821. An alternative to academies, this school was a free, publicly-supported institution. Other public high schools soon appeared in Portland, Maine, and Worcester, Massachusetts. In 1825, the High School Society in New York City started the first high school outside New England. And in 1826 the city of Boston proposed free secondary education for 130 girls. When applications greatly exceeded that number, the project was abandoned by the city fathers.

The English Classical School—whose name was shortened to English High School—admitted only students twelve years of age or older, boys from the "mercantile and mechanical" classes "well acquainted with reading, writing, English grammar in all its branches, and arithmetic." These young men pursued a three-year course of study in composition, declamation, mathematics, history, civics, logic, surveying, navigation, and moral and political philosophy (see Table 6).

In 1827, the Commonwealth of Massachusetts passed a law requiring every town or village of five hundred or more families to

Table 6 The Curriculum of the Boston English Classical School, 1821

The First Year
- Composition
- Reading from the most approved authors
- Exercises in Criticism; comprising critical analyses of the language, grammar, and style of the best English authors, their errors and beauties
- Declamation
- Geography
- Arithmetic (continued)

The Second Year
- Composition
- Exercises in Criticism
- Reading (continued)
- Declamation
- Algebra
- Ancient and Modern History and Chronology
- Logic
- Geometry
- Plane Trigonometry; and its application to mensuration of Heights and Distances
- Navigation
- Surveying
- Mensuration of Superficies and Solids
- Forensic Discussions

The Third Year
- Composition
- Exercises in Criticism
- Declamation (continued)
- Mathematics
- Logic
- History; particularly that of the United States
- Natural Philosophy, including Astronomy; Moral and Political Philosophy

Source: Elmer E. Brown, *The Making of Our Middle School* (New York: Longmans, Green and Company, 1903), pp. 298–301.

establish a school to teach American history, surveying geometry and bookkeeping, in addition to the common primary subjects. Towns of four thousand also were to offer courses in general history, rhetoric, logic, Latin, and Greek.[4]

Still, for more than fifty years, Massachusetts was the only state that required high schools and, even there, the law was generally ignored.[5] "As late as 1850, when seventy-six towns should have established high school instruction, only forty-seven had actually done so."[6] It was not until 1874, when the Michigan State Supreme Court ruled that taxes could be levied to support public high schools as well as elementary schools, that the American high school began to take firm root.[7]

With urbanization, magnificent high schools were constructed in some of the largest cities in the nation—San Francisco, New York, and St. Louis. These public high schools could compete with the best of the private academies, regardless of their traditions and prestige. Many urban high schools also graduated young women trained in "normal classes" to become teachers.

In Cincinnati, Woodward High School, built in 1856 at a cost of $50,000, had ornate pinnacles and a gothic, wrought-iron fence.[8] It was one of the grandest buildings in the city. The curriculum at Woodward, based upon approved textbooks, was an elaborately developed college preparatory program to appeal to the most academically-minded community leaders (Table 7).

In rural America, it was different. High schools in the nation's villages and farmland offered a more applied curriculum. They often were housed in a single room or two attached to primary schools. In 1896, of the 258 high schools in Illinois, 220 were in elementary school rooms reserved for older children. Historian David B. Tyack observes, "In rural communities, the name *high school* was customarily an honorific label attached to the upper grades, just as the term *college* in the nineteenth century often signified high aspirations but low achievement."[9]

In 1870 there were about 500 public high schools in the nation with about 50,000 students. During this same period, Calvin M. Woodward, a Harvard-trained mathematician, launched a campaign to persuade Americans that high schools were out of touch with the nation's economic and vocational needs. Woodward claimed that high schools were training students to be "gentlemen" rather than preparing them for work. He wanted more "manual training" in the schools, which, he believed, should be an "equal partner" in the broad general curriculum for all students.[10]

Woodward's campaign gained wide support from the ranks of business. The business community felt that getting job training in the schools was particularly attractive, especially as unions began imposing rules on the management of apprenticeships. In the end, vocational education became firmly planted as a central goal of secondary education, but frequently without Woodward's vision of blending the manual and the liberal arts.

With the industrial expansion of America, education increas-

Table 7   Woodward High School Curriculum, Cincinnati, Ohio, 1856

FIRST YEAR	
First Session	Second Session
English Grammar, *Brown or Pinneo,* completed	Latin Lessons, *Weld's,* to Part Second
English History, *Goodrich or Markham,* completed	Physical Geography, *Fitch,* completed
Algebra, *Ray's,* to Section 172	Latin Grammar, *Andrews' and Stoddard's*
Five lessons in each of the above weekly	Algebra, *Ray's,* to Section 305
	Five lessons each week in Latin and Algebra
	Three lessons in Physical Geography, and two in Reading
	Once a week during the year
	Lectures by the Principal on Morals, Manners, &c.
	Aids to Composition, completed
	Composition and Declamation, by Sections, once in three weeks
	Reading and Vocal Music, Penmanship, if needed

SECOND YEAR	
First Session	Second Session
Latin Lessons, *Weld's,* to History	Latin Lessons, *Weld's,* completed
Latin Grammar, *Andrews' and Stoddard's*	Latin Grammar, *Andrews' and Stoddard's*
Geometry, *Davies' Legendre,* to Book V	Geometry, *Davies' Legendre,* to Book IX
Natural Philosophy, *Gray's,* to Pneumatics	Natural Philosophy, *Gray's,* completed
Five lessons per week during the year	*Five lessons a week, in each of the above*
	One exercise per week
	Reading, Elemental Sounds
	Rhetoric and Vocal Music
	Composition and Declamation, by Sections, once in three weeks

Table 7   Woodward High School Curriculum, Cincinnati, Ohio, 1856 *(continued)*

THIRD YEAR

First Session	Second Session
Chemistry, *Silliman's,* to Section 282, five lessons a week	Virgil's Aeneid, *Cooper's three books,* three lessons
Caesar or Sallust, *Andrews',* fifty Sections, three lessons a week	German or French, three lessons
German or French, three lessons a week	Chemistry, *Silliman's,* to Vegetable Chemistry, five lessons
Algebra and Spherics, *Ray's and Davies' Legendre,* completed, five lessons a week	Trigonometry, *Davies',* completed, five lessons
	Once a week
	Constitution of the United States, completed
	Logic, *Hedge's,* completed
	Reading, Rhetoric and Vocal Music
	Composition and Declamation, by Sections, once in three weeks

FOURTH YEAR

First Session	Second Session
Physiology and Hygiene, *Cutter,* completed, five lessons	German or French, three lessons
Cicero, *Folsom's,* three Orations, three lessons	Mental Philosophy, *Wayland's,* completed, five lessons
German or French, three lessons	General History, *Weber's,* completed, five lessons
Astronomy, *McIntire's,* completed, five lessons	Navigation and Surveying, *Davies',* completed
Geology, *Gray's and Adams',* completed, five lessons	Evidences of Christianity, once a week
Moral Philosophy, once a week	*Once a week during the year*
	Critical Readings. Vocal Music
	Compositions, by Sections, once in three weeks
	Original Addresses, once in three weeks

Source: Henry Barnard, "Woodward High School in Cincinnati," *American Journal of Education,* December 1857, p. 521.

ingly was valued in economic terms. Many students saw the new vocationalism as a shortcut to better jobs. They turned away from academic subjects, thus helping to scuttle the intended fusion of intellect and labor. In the end, Woodward himself appeared to cave in. "By multiplying manual training schools," he said, "we solve the problems of training all the mechanics our country needs."[11]

By the turn of the century, the number of high schools had grown to 6,000,[12] with an enrollment of 519,000 students.[13] This represented only about 8.5 percent of the youth group.[14] A still smaller percentage—6.3 percent—actually graduated. During this period, presidents of the nation's most prestigious higher learning institutions were distressed by the uneven quality of high school education, even though a tiny fraction of the nation's youth were going on to college. School people, in turn, were upset by the patchwork of college admissions requirements.

In response, the National Council of Education in 1892 appointed a group of educators, dominated by university professors and chaired by Charles W. Eliot, president of Harvard University, to clarify the goals of secondary education and smooth the transition from school to college.

This nationally prestigious body, known as the Committee of Ten, mapped a core of academic subjects to be studied in the high school. In addition to Latin, Greek, and mathematics, there were the "modern subjects"—English, foreign languages, natural history, physical science, geography, history, civil government, and political economy.

The Committee of Ten stressed "mental discipline." All subjects, the committee said, were to be taught in the same fashion to all students. There was to be no substantial difference between education for college and education for work. Preparation for higher education, the committee argued, was the best preparation for life.[15]

Charles W. Eliot put the matter squarely. While rejecting the notion of universal education, Eliot refused to believe

> . . . that the American public intends to have its children sorted before their teens into clerks, watchmakers, lithographers, telegraph operators, masons, teamsters, farm laborers, and so forth, and treated differently in their schools according to these prophecies of their appropriate life careers. Who are to make these prophecies? Can parents? Can teachers?[16]

Fred and Grace Hechinger have noted the educational and social significance of President Eliot's perspective: "What was remarkable at the time—and important to any understanding of the complex and controversial issues that continued to dominate much of the educational debate of the twentieth century—was this Harvard president's belief that there was no inherent contradiction in the establishment of quality controls and the open democratic society."[17]

With the arrival of waves of new immigrants from Europe, the mission of public education once again expanded. The nation's schools were called upon to "Americanize" the new arrivals, teaching them English, basic lessons in health, sanitation, nutrition, and, most especially, citizenship. One turn-of-the-century writer vividly described how the public school stood as a symbol of hope for the new Americans.

> At the corner of Catharine and Henry Streets in New York is a large white building that overlooks and dominates its neighborhood. Placed in the middle of a region of tawdry flat houses and dirty streets, it stands out preeminent because of its solid cleanliness and unpretentiousness. It is the home of Public School No. I. In it are centred all the hopes of the miserably poor polyglot population of the surrounding district—for its pupils the scene of their greatest interest and endeavor, and for their parents an earnest of the freedom they have come far and worked hard to attain.[18]

In 1913, the National Education Association appointed a blue-ribbon Commission on the Reorganization of Secondary Education. In a report issued five years later entitled *The Cardinal Principles of Secondary Education,* the committee expanded school purposes to include health, citizenship, and worthy home-membership. Almost as an afterthought, "command of fundamental processes" was added to the list. The report said:

> Education in a democracy, both within and without the school, should develop in each individual the knowledge, interests, ideals, habits, and powers whereby he will find his place and use that place to shape both himself and society toward ever nobler ends.[19]

Early in the twentieth century, secondary schools also felt the impact of the seminal works of the philosopher John Dewey.[20] Dewey, father of the progressive movement, was alarmed at the extent to which industrialization and urbanization were eroding the traditional American institutions—the home, the community, and the church.[21] Concerned that workers were becoming "mere appendages to the machine they operate," Dewey argued that schools must educate the whole child, filling in where other institutions failed. He looked to the family as the model. "What the best and wisest parent wants for his own child, that must the community want for all of its children."[22] Ironically, while there was much talk about "social learning," this was also a time of increased differentiation in the schools by social class.

The progressive movement that had begun with the preceptive insights of John Dewey soon lost its way. Much of the misinterpretation of Dewey was made by some of his most enthusiastic supporters, and it eventually led to unsound, careless, and even extreme expressions of educational philosophy. In 1913, for example, a Los Angeles superintendent proclaimed: "The principal business of the child is to play and to grow—not to read, write, spell, and cipher. These are incidental in importance. If they can be made a part of the play, it is well to use them; if not, they should be handled sparingly."[23]

And in 1939 Charles Prosser, underscoring his belief that the very usefulness of a subject determines its disciplinary value to the mind, wrote: "On all these counts, business arithmetic is superior to plane or solid geometry; learning ways of keeping physically fit, to the study of French; learning the techniques of selecting an occupation, to the study of algebra; simple science of everyday life, to geology; simple business English to Elizabethan Classics."[24] As Richard Hofstadter put it, "The silly season in educational writing had now opened."[25]

A backlash was inevitable. Indeed, as early as the late 1920s a movement called "essentialist" education attacked what was viewed as the neglect of traditional fields of study, an overemphasis on social studies, and thoughtless curriculum revision. The Essentialist Committee for the Advancement of American Education presented its platform in 1938.[26] The aim: to return school "to the exact and exciting studies," to support the "mental disciplines," and to save such courses as Latin, algebra and geometry.

William Chandler Bagley, a professor at Teachers College, Columbia University, argued for the enduring values:

> It is true that the world of today is a different world from the world of 1913 and from the world of 1929 . . . but this does not mean that everything has changed. . . . The winds that blow still follow the law of storms: *Huckleberry Finn* and *Treasure Island* still delight youth; and the Sistine Madonna is just as beautiful as of yore.[27]

During the depression years, secondary education enrollments continued to increase. Young people went to school when they could find nothing else to do. In a fascinating description of schooling during the depression, Tyack and Hansot report that despite the economic crisis, school people

> were adept in publicizing the schools and in gaining new money from state legislatures. . . . And despite grouses about unnecessary expenditures the public maintained its historic faith in the value of the common school and in the dedication of teachers.[28]

The depression years were productive in other ways as well. In a significant research effort, Ralph W. Tyler led a study that followed students as they moved through high school and through college (1933 to 1941). This landmark investigation, the so-called "eight-year study," demonstrated, among other things, that course titles did not furnish colleges dependable information about what was being taught and learned in school.[29]

By 1930 a quiet, yet profound social revolution was occurring. Total public high school enrollment had swelled to 4.4 million, or 47 percent of the total age group.[30] By 1950, it had increased to 5.7 million and 67 percent of the age group (Chart 6).

Chart 6 Public High School Enrollment, 1900–1981

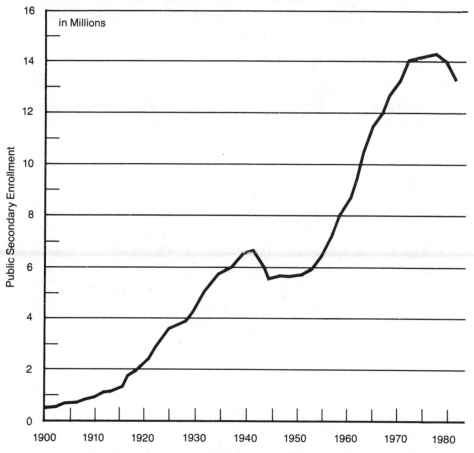

SOURCE: 1900 to 1916: U.S. Department of Commerce, Bureau of the Census, *Historical Statistics of the United States: Colonial Times to 1970.* (Washington: Government Printing Office, 1975), pp. 368-69; 1917 to 1954: Unpublished data, National Center for Education Statistics; 1955 to 1961: National Center for Education Statistics, *Digest of Education Statistics: 1966,* (Washington: Government Printing Office, 1966), p. 24; 1962 to 1973: *Digest of Education Statistics: 1973,* p. 31; 1974 to 1981, *Digest of Education Statistics: 1982,* p. 38.

Soon the majority of America's teenagers were completing high school (Chart 7). And the last to be included were young people from minority populations. Cohen and Neufeld, in a perceptive article, describe the revolution this way:

> Entrance requirements were changed: The admissions exams were dropped in favor of simple elementary school completion. This marked the beginning of the high schools' transition from an elite to a mass institution. . . . And it marked the beginning of a long struggle for a new social goal—universal high school attendance.[31]

The high school had, in fact, become the people's college.

Arthur E. Bestor, a Professor of History at the University of Illinois, charged, in 1953, that schools, in trying to provide "something for everyone," had provided little for anyone. Bestor warned that intellectual training for some people, vocational training and life adjustment for the rest, "is the epitome of a class-structured educational philosophy."[32] Rudolph Flesch, Clifton Fadiman, and Admiral Hyman Rickover soon joined Bestor in the assault.

In a push for excellence to match access, a cadre of university professors began to design and test new curricula for the schools. In 1956, Jerrold Zacharias, Professor of Physics at MIT, developed a new curriculum to update the content of high school physics.[33] A mathematics project was launched at the University of Illinois. National curriculum reform projects in biology and English received federal support.

But it took *Sputnik* to push school improvement to the top of the national agenda. The National Defense Education Act of 1958 provided funds for the improvement of science, mathematics, and foreign-language teaching. It was subsequently broadened to include support for the humanities and social sciences as well. *Rigor* became the catchword of the day.

Symbolic of the time was the now-famous Conant Report. In 1959, James B. Conant, a scientist and former president of Harvard, undertook a study of the American high school. In his best-selling

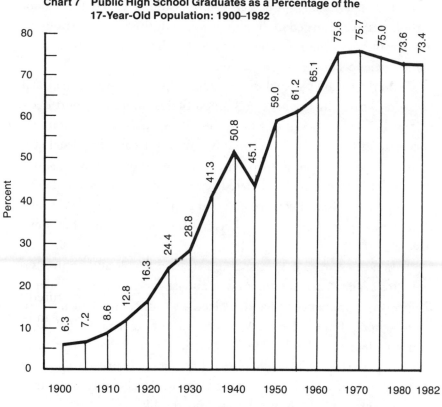

Chart 7 Public High School Graduates as a Percentage of the 17-Year-Old Population: 1900–1982

SOURCE: 1900–1935: U.S. Department Of Commerce, Bureau of the Census, *Historical Statistics of the United States: Colonial Times to 1970* (Washington: U.S. Government Printing Office, 1975), p. 379; 1940–1982: National Center for Education Statistics, *Digest of Education Statistics: 1982* (Washington: U.S. Government Printing Office, 1982), p. 65.

book *The American High School Today,* Conant called for school consolidation and urged high schools to strengthen their curriculum in what were commonly referred to as the "hard" subjects—mathematics, science, and foreign languages.[34]

Soon the nation's schools were caught up in yet another national crusade. Pushed by the historic United States Supreme Court decision in Brown *vs.* Board of Education (1954), public education was called upon to serve more equitably the historically bypassed students—the poor, the underprivileged, and the underachieving. Congress and the courts moved, belatedly, to counter years of scandalous discrimination. Racial balance and compensatory education became urgent new priorities. Schools became the battleground for social justice.

When the Vietnam War sparked student revolt and confrontation, "relevance" became the new mandate for education. Colleges dropped requirements and added electives to meet student interest. High schools followed suit. A new group of reformers, including James Coleman and John Henry Martin, argued that the road to relevance was beyond the school.[35] Educators were urged to provide more "real life" experiences for the young—work-study programs, "action-learning," cities-as-schools, and the like.

Reflecting the spirit of the times, one national panel proposed, in 1973, a cafeteria design for secondary education. High school alternatives, the panel said, might include "minischools, schools-without-walls, open schools, alternative schools, optimal programs, internships, parallel courses, independent study, free schools, and apprentice and action learning."[36] Another commission caught the mood. Options for students, it said, were "limited only by the legitimate needs of adolescents and the vivacity of the imaginations of . . . planners."[37] And so the debate over schools persisted.

In 1953, Arthur Bestor wrote: "The idea that the school must undertake to meet every need that some other agency is failing to meet, regardless of the suitability of the schoolroom to the task, is a preposterous delusion that in the end can wreck the educational system."[38]

Bestor was almost prophetic. Since the English Classical School was founded over 150 years ago, high schools have accumulated purposes like barnacles on a weathered ship. As school population expanded from a tiny urban minority to almost all youth, a coherent purpose was hard to find. The nation piled social policy upon educational policy and all of them on top of the delusion that a single institution can do it all.

Today's high school is called upon to provide the services and transmit the values we used to expect from the community and the home and the church. And if they fail anywhere along the line, they are condemned.

What do Americans want high schools to accomplish? Quite simply, we want it all.

4

FOUR ESSENTIAL GOALS

A high school, to be effective, must have a clear and vital mission. Students, teachers, administrators, and parents at the institution should have a shared vision of what, together, they are trying to accomplish. But is it possible to serve all students and also find a coherent purpose for our schools?

In preparing this report, we looked at the education laws in all fifty states. We discovered a numbing hodgepodge of rules and regulations. In the State of California the education code is four volumes and 3,700 pages long, and in New York it takes five volumes and 4,000 pages to print the education law.

More troublesome are the vague and wide-ranging mandates the states have imposed on public education. Many of these requirements are pushed by special-interest groups. Frequently, they trivialize the mission of public education and, therefore, are rarely taken seriously by schools. Here is a sampling of what state laws say the schools should do.

> *Idaho:* "The school programs shall be organized to meet the needs of all pupils, the community, and to fulfill the stated objectives of the school."[1]

> *Mississippi:* The purpose of education is "to provide appropriate learning experiences to promote the optimum growth and development of youth and adults throughout life."[2]

Oregon: "Each individual will have the opportunity to develop to the best of his or her ability the knowledge, skills, and attitudes necessary to function as an individual . . . a learner . . . a producer . . . a citizen . . . a consumer . . . and a family member."[3]

Maine: The public schools must teach virtue and morality for not less than one-half hour per week. This includes "principles of morality and justice and a sacred regard for truth, love of country, humanity, a universal benevolence, sobriety, industry and frugality, chastity, moderation and temperance, *and all other virtues that ornament human society*" (emphasis added).[4]

California: "Each teacher shall endeavor to impress upon the minds of the pupils the principles of morality, truth, justice, patriotism, and a true comprehension of the rights, duties, and dignity of American citizenship, including kindness toward domestic pets and the humane treatment of living creatures, to teach them to avoid idleness, profanity, and falsehood, and to instruct them in manners and morals and the principles of a free government."[5]

Illinois: All graduates are required by law "to have had adequate instruction in honesty, justice, moral courage, humane education, [and] safety education."[6]

Arizona: A half-unit course is required on the "Essentials and Benefits of the Free Enterprise System."[7]

Rhode Island: Provision must be made for instruction in physiology and hygiene, with special reference to the effects of alcoholic liquors, stimulants, and narcotics on the human system.[8]

Wisconsin: "Every public school shall provide instruction in kindness to and the habits, usefulness, and importance of animals and birds, and the best methods of protecting, preserving and caring for all animal and bird life." And in what can only be described as enthusiastic local boosterism, Wisconsin also requires that every public and private elementary and high school give instruction in "the true and comparative vitamin content and food and health values of dairy products and their importance for human diet."[9]

At the district level we found school leadership frequently preoccupied with administrative procedures. Educational goals appeared to be of only marginal concern. In one district, for example, principals were called together by the superintendent to produce "performance standards" for the year. All schools in the district were expected to accomplish the following objectives:

- Raise the attendance rate
- Reduce teacher absence to 1.5 days per year (which, incidentally, was less than the sick days allowed in the contract)
- Improve parent participation[10]

We also visited schools that were focused on keeping track of the "Carnegie units" earned by students rather than the larger issue of what students should be learning. The Carnegie unit was born about seventy years ago. At that time, there was much confusion about what a high school transcript meant. "Classics" could mean Ancient History twice a week at one high school, or it could mean Latin every day at another.

To rectify the situation, the Carnegie Foundation proposed a standard unit to measure high school work based on time. A total of 120 hours in one subject—meeting 4 or 5 times a week, for 40 to 60 minutes, for 36 to 40 weeks each year—earns for the student one "unit" of high school credit. "The Carnegie unit," became a convenient, mechanical way to measure academic progress throughout the country. And, to this day, this bookkeeping device is the basis on which the school day, and indeed the entire curriculum, is organized. And, at some schools, adding up Carnegie units seems to be the main objective.

Other high schools we visited had written goals. Often they were vaguely stated, offering little guidance as to what schools should teach and students learn. They were generally ignored. At Sands High School, a comprehensive school in the Southeast, we were handed the teachers' manual, which included seven "goals":

- To provide substantial and varied learning experiences that will facilitate life in a multi-cultural changing society.

- To develop programs that are consistent with student interest, ability, and potential.

- To encourage each student to know his worth and to use this sense of worth to productively participate in the school and the larger community.

- To provide a body of learning that will encourage the cohesion of the student body.

- To provide an atmosphere of cooperative interdependence.

- To encourage the student to understand his rights and responsibilities.

- To teach skills that will enable the student to function both effectively and affectively in a changing society.[11]

At Prairie View, a small high school on the western plains, we found this so-called "Statement of Objectives":

The Prairie View Public School is vitally aware that the school of today is the school of the people it serves. The school provides educators who are knowledgeable in their subject matter and who are dedicated to serving all students and their needs.[12]

When we asked teachers, principals, and students about school goals, their response frequently was one of uncertainty, amusement, or surprise. "What do you mean?" "Goals for what?" Some teachers just smiled. Others apologized for not knowing. Some referred us to the teachers' manual. One faculty member told us he thought goals and objectives were something "to be learned in teacher education courses and then forgotten." Another put it more bluntly: "If we had goals, we wouldn't follow them anyway."

When school people did talk to us about objectives, comments differed sharply from group to group. Students said they wanted to "get out," "be with friends," "get into a good college," "pass the competency exam," "get a job." Others were more cynical: "The school is here to keep you off the street and out of trouble until you're old enough to get out there and deal with it."

The principals we talked with spoke of other aims: "develop school spirit," "graduate as many students as possible," "help students pass the state-required exams," "improve relations between different races," "maintain order," "build a sense of community," "improve students' opportunities in life," "successfully mainstream handicapped students."

In one large urban academic school, however, we met a principal who had a special vision of what he was trying to accomplish. In his words:

> I have a dream for the school and for what goes on in the classroom. I'd like every teacher to focus on problem-solving, to make the *process* of learning—not factual recall—the center of instruction. I'd like us to challenge our students to think.[13]

Teachers, on the other hand, spoke frequently about preparing kids to get into a "good" college. Many teachers we talked with shared deeply their students' concerns about "getting good grades" and "getting into an Ivy League institution or to the prestigious state university." These same teachers also expressed nagging doubts about the pressure. As one put it, "All middle-class kids here want to go to college, and it's what their parents want for them, whether or not they have the ability. Many of them frankly don't have it. But if they don't get into college, then we feel we've failed."[14]

Vocational education teachers, on the other hand, said their goal was to "help the kids get jobs." The measure of their success was job placement. The depressed economy seemed to have many teachers worried. As one business education instructor put it: "It's our job to prepare students for jobs. But if there aren't any jobs for them when they graduate, if they wind up on unemployment, then what have we accomplished? What are we doing here?"[15]

A few teachers had distressingly low aspirations for their students. One admitted:

Our goal is to get our students so that they can function adequately in blue collar society. You wouldn't write that down and it would be real embarrassing if someone from the University saw it written, but our goal is to get these kids to be like their parents. We're not really satisfied with their aspirations, but that's our goal.[16]

Still another put it this way:

The goal, I guess, is to keep things quiet and have kids come to school and get their ADA (Average Daily Attendance) . . . have a good team (whatever sport we're doing) . . . and to get through the year.[17]

Not surprisingly, many teachers we met were often confused about new demands confronted by the school. One high school teacher said:

We no longer are expected to just teach a subject. We have to be psychiatrists. We have to take care of the drug problems. Too many demands are being placed on the school by the state.[18]

Another agreed:

We are called upon to act on behalf of many social agencies. We are taking care of human problems every single minute. Just where education fits into that is a very difficult thing.[19]

After visiting schools from coast to coast, we are left with the distinct impression that high schools lack a clear and vital mission. They are unable to find common purposes or establish educational priorities that are widely shared. They seem unable to put it all together. The institution is adrift.

We recommend that every high school have clearly stated goals and purposes that are understood and supported by the students, teachers, administrators, and parents of the institution. But where do we begin? Do we reach back to the Latin Grammar School, to prepare young men—and women—for Harvard and Yale, or for one of three thousand other colleges and universities? Do we recapture the vision of Calvin Woodward, to prepare young people more effectively for the work place? Do we follow the Americanizing impulses of the new immigrations? Or should high schools continue to take over the work of other troubled institutions—the family, the neighborhood, the church?

Garfield High School seems to have found the answer. Garfield is a comprehensive high school in the middle of one of the largest and most distressed cities in the United States. It has a student body of 2,000 students, 80 percent of whom are black or Hispanic. Most students live in a high-rise public housing project.

Just a few blocks north of Garfield, the black and white neighborhoods are not integrated. A few blocks south the neighborhood is all black: middle class, poor, and rich, an integration of class but not race. A half mile west, the community is depressed and dangerous; no place for strangers.

According to its thirteen-year record, Garfield is one of the best high schools in the city. A tradition of success is suggested by high SAT scores and placement of its students into top-flight colleges; daily attendance rates of 96 percent; a student newspaper that wins national awards; and a mathematics team that, in the words of the students, "beats the pants off" the suburban teams.

Garfield's success is reinforced by students who consider the school a special place, by parents who are deeply involved in school affairs, and by a staff who say it is "one of the few schools in the city where teachers work with students and care about learning." One parent caught the spirit we felt at Garfield when she said:

> You know why I like Garfield? It is a no nonsense school. Teachers expect the child to work here, and more than that, they care about your child. My daughter's music teacher, for example, checks up on how she is doing in her other courses. Yesterday, before the first grading period, I decided to call all my daughter's teachers and they were all available. It's not that my daughter is that good in class, always; she has had some trouble in school. But the troubles have always been able to be worked out because the teachers can explain

what they are doing and because they obviously care. As a parent you know something is right when your daughter is getting up early and getting you up early so she can get to school. Before Garfield, I had trouble getting her out of bed, now she gets me up.[20]

Classes are focused and challenging at Garfield High. In a mathematics class, we heard students ask questions like "What does X to the two-thirds power plus Y to the two-thirds power minus one look like?" The teacher in a physics class was heard saying: "You have been told the initial velocity and the rate of acceleration, that it is constant, and the time of the acceleration. Write an equation to tell us how far the object has traveled." In an English class, students were discussing their favorite poets; in a social studies class, a new city law was being skillfully critiqued.

Near the end of a busy day at Garfield High, we chatted briefly with a middle-aged science teacher in the hall. When asked to comment on her own experience, she spoke easily of her feelings:

> You know, I think Garfield is the best an inner city school can be. Not that the staff or the circumstances are perfect; in fact, I'm sure the staff was better eight years ago, when I first came to Garfield. I never saw such professionals, such smart people, in my life as when I arrived here! Of course, many of those have left; a few have stayed and a few new ones have kept Garfield going. When you think about it, this school is resilient. I don't know why exactly, except it must be many things together—the parents, the kids, the teachers, the administration, the tradition. Yes, "resilient" is the best word to describe Garfield today.[21]

Garfield is not trouble-free. One student complained to us about "too much pressure." A mother said, "There is no social program for white students at the school. They are intensely conscious of being in a minority, a new experience." Another mother reported: "One of the greatest problems at Garfield is people's perception of the security problem. Lots of people are antsy because they think it's dangerous." Teachers talk about a shortage of supplies and complicated student scheduling that takes hours of their time.

Still, Garfield is a school that works. There is a shared sense of mission. People know where they are going. What happens there matches well-understood objectives. When we talked to Garfield parents, teachers and students, the following purposes emerged. *First*, develop critical thinking; *second*, prepare students for further education; *third*, increase students' career options; and *fourth*, build a spirit of community and service.

One faculty member spoke movingly, even eloquently, about the need to preserve the value of the common culture, to broaden the horizons of the students to arouse their curiosity, and to teach them to think critically. In his words:

> First, we have to teach students what I'll call survival skills; in other words, the basics. These are absolutes, for any further learning is impossible without them. But beyond those survival skills, there is a cultural and ethical body that binds us all. A culture requires that this body of knowledge be taught, if it's going to survive. Remember, Yeats in one of his poems warned us that a society must not disintegrate into randomness. I think the schools have a critical role to play in seeing that that doesn't happen. We need to put students in touch with knowledge in a coherent way so that they are contributing members of a common culture.[22]

High schools to be effective must have a sense of purpose, with teachers, students, administrators, and parents sharing a vision of what they are trying to accomplish. The vision must be larger than a single class in a single day. It must go beyond keeping students in school and out of trouble, and be more significant than adding up the Carnegie units the student has completed.

We propose four essential goals and the ways these goals can be achieved.

> First, the high school should help all students develop the capacity to think critically and communicate effectively through a mastery of language.

Second, the high school should help all students learn about themselves, the human heritage, and the interdependent world in which they live through a core curriculum based upon consequential human experiences common to all people.

Third, the high school should prepare all students for work and further education through a program of electives that develop individual aptitudes and interests.

Fourth, the high school should help all students fulfill their social and civic obligations through school and community service.

Today, many proposals for school reform are heatedly debated. But, unguided by a larger vision, they amount to little more than tinkering with an elaborate and complex system. What is needed—and what we believe these four goals constitute—is a clear and coherent vision of what the nation's high schools should be seeking to accomplish.

PART III

WHAT EVERY STUDENT SHOULD LEARN

5

SOMETHING FOR EVERYONE

June 1983. The Ridgefield High School gym is overflowing. Families crowd the bleachers. The faculty have assembled. More than 230 seniors, in caps and gowns, are handed their diplomas.

What do those diplomas represent?

About 45 percent of Ridgefield seniors receive what school officials there call a *regular* diploma, with minimum requirements. Another 45 percent are given a *comprehensive* diploma, indicating completion of the minimum course requirements plus a cumulative grade point average of C or better. The remaining 10 percent of Ridgefield's 1983 graduates are handed what is called a *college preparatory* diploma, recognition for meeting minimum requirements plus additional academic courses with an average grade of B. [1]

All Ridgefield students, regardless of diploma, complete a minimum of 21 units—academic credits—for graduation. About half (11½) are required, the rest are elective. Here is the required core:

- Communications (English, literature, speech), 3 units
- Social studies (United States and world history), 2 units
- Mathematics, 1 unit
- Science, 1 unit
- Fine arts, 1 unit
- Physical education, 2 units
- Practical studies (home economics, shop), 1 unit
- Typing, ½ unit

Curriculum requirements at Ridgefield are typical of the pattern nationwide. Most students who graduate from an American high school today complete at least three years of English, two years of social studies, one year of math, one-plus years of science, two years of physical education or health, plus a smattering of local requirements and five or more electives.[2]

At last count, 42 states dictated one or more specific courses for high school graduation (Table 8). Most frequently mandated was a social studies course, usually United States history (42 states); followed by English (39 states). Science (37 states) and mathematics (34 states) came in third and fourth respectively. Significantly, fewer states mandated requirements in core subjects (except for science) in 1980 than in 1972.

Of the eight states not requiring core subjects for graduation, two (Nebraska and Vermont) designated the total number of units to be completed but did not identify specific courses. Six (California, Colorado, Connecticut, Florida, Massachusetts, Wisconsin) had *no* statewide requirements. In these states, all graduation requirements were set at the local level.

While the number of *states* requiring core subjects declined between 1972 and 1980, the number of state-mandated units in core subjects rose slightly (except for social studies) during this same

Table 8   Number of States Requiring Selected Subjects
          for High School Graduation, 1972 and 1980

Core Subjects	Number of states requiring core subjects		
	1972	1980	Change
Social studies	44	42	−2
English	42	39	−3
Science	34	37	+3
Mathematics	36	34	−2
Physical education/health	32	32	±0

Source: *State Graduation Requirements,* National Education Association Research Service, May 1972; *State Mandated Graduation Requirements,* 1980, National Association of Secondary School Principals, 1980.

Table 9 Average Number of Academic Units (Years) Mandated by the States in Selected Subjects 1972–1980 (4-Year High Schools)

	Average number of academic units (years)		
Subjects	1972	1980	Change
English	3.48	3.53	+.05
Social studies	2.14	2.05	−.09
Mathematics	1.22	1.28	+.06
Science	1.22	1.24	+.02
Physical education/Health	1.31	1.38	+.07
Electives/Other	7.34	8.02	+.68

Source: State Graduation Requirements, National Education Association Research Service, May 1972; State Mandated Graduation Requirements, 1980, National Association of Secondary School Principals, 1980.

period (Table 9). State requirements in physical education and health rose more than those in the traditional academic subjects, but the greatest increase was in electives or a category designated "other." In this case, states left specific course decisions up to the local districts.

This trend toward more "nonacademic" enrollments was confirmed in a United States Department of Education study of more than six thousand high school transcripts covering course enrollments from 1964 to 1980. The report concludes: "There seems to have been a systematic devaluation of academic (and some vocational) courses . . . by high school students. While the number of required courses increased in the 1970s, students in 1980 were still spending less time in academic subjects and more time in courses that might be described as "personal service and social development."[3]

During the fifteen-year period covered by this study, the ten courses that demonstrated the most growth were:

> Physical education
> Music performance
> Remedial English
> Driver education

Cooperative education
Health and physical education
Distributive education
General shop
Training for marriage/adulthood
Vocational home economics

What about teacher loads? While enrollments have shifted, the distribution of teachers among school subjects has remained relatively stable over the past 15 years (1966–1981). In 1981, the largest percentages of high school teachers continued to be in English, up from 18 percent to 24 percent; mathematics, up from 13 to 15 percent; science, up from 11 to 12 percent; and social studies, down from 15 to 11 percent (Table 10). While increases are very small, the percentages of teachers in these other fields also have increased: art, industrial arts, special education, and driver education.

Table 10 Subjects Taught by Secondary School Teachers, 1966–1981

Subject	Percentage of teachers in subject			
	1966	1971	1976	1981
Agriculture	1.6	0.6	0.6	1.1
Art	2.0	3.7	2.4	3.1
Business education	7.0	5.9	4.6	6.2
English	18.1	20.4	19.9	23.8
Foreign languages	6.4	4.8	4.2	2.8
Health and physical education	6.9	8.3	7.9	6.5
Home economics	5.9	5.1	2.8	3.6
Industrial arts	5.1	4.1	3.9	5.2
Mathematics	13.1	14.4	18.2	15.3
Science	10.8	10.6	13.1	12.1
Social studies	15.3	14.0	12.4	11.2
Music	4.7	3.8	3.0	3.7
Special education	0.4	1.1	3.0	2.1
Driver education	NA	0.7	0.7	1.3
Vocational education	NA	2.1	3.3	1.3
Other	0.0	0.3	0.0	0.7
Number reporting	1,088	707	670	614

Source: National Education Association, *Status of the American Public School Teacher*, 1980–81 (Washington, D.C.: 1982), p. 39.

During our own field work, we sampled 700 transcripts at six comprehensive high schools to observe more directly how student enrollment patterns changed during the 1970s. We checked enrollments in the four traditional academic subjects (English, social studies, math, and science) at three separate intervals: 1970, 1975, 1981* (Table 11). On average, students in our sample had completed about four years of English, more than three years of social studies, slightly more than two years of science, and about two and one-half years of mathematics.

We also found, however, that the average number of units taken in the four academic fields declined between 1970 and 1981. In English, for example, the number of units completed dropped only slightly, from 4.0 to 3.9. In social studies, the decline was from 3.5 to 3.3. In mathematics, there was a downswing between 1970 and 1975 (2.5 to 2.2), followed by an upswing between 1976 and 1981 (2.2 to 2.4).

The amount of science taken by students went down during the 1970s, dropping from 2.6 units (about two and one-half years) to 2.1 units (about two years). Translated into specific courses, this meant, for most students, a freshman-year general science course plus tenth-grade biology. Our survey of transcripts also revealed that males consistently were taking more science than females.

If we look beyond the traditional subjects, what other courses are mandated either at state or local levels? Certainly driver education. At least two states, Alabama and South Dakota, require all high schools to offer the course. In other states, it is often mandated locally. Mandated or not, the vast majority of schools do provide driver education, and a high proportion of students take it—sometimes for graduation credit, more often for the insurance benefits associated with the resulting certificate.

Consumer education, career development, and practical arts have also made their way into a growing number of graduation

---

*Transcripts were examined in conjunction with descriptive course catalogues provided by the schools.

Table 11   Average Number of Academic Units (Years)
            Completed in Core Subjects

	Average number of academic units (years) completed		
Core Subjects	1970	1975	1981
English	4.0	3.9	3.9
Social studies	3.5	3.8	3.3
Math	2.5	2.2	2.4
Science	2.6	2.6	2.1

Source: Carnegie Foundation analysis of 700 student transcripts at six comprehensive high schools.

requirements. Several states now require a course in the "free enterprise system" as part of a civics course or separately as economics.
State history and/or government is commonly required or strongly
recommended by the states.

A smattering of other topics is also required by state law (see
Chapter 4). They range from "the value of dairy products" (Wisconsin) to "kindness to domestic pets" (California and others). State
requirements such as these are rarely converted into separate
courses; more frequently they are downplayed or ignored.

As reported, thirty-two states in 1980 mandated physical education as a requirement for graduation. Even when physical education
is not required by the state, local districts usually mandate one or
more years of physical activity for all students. Instruction in health,
with particular attention to drug and alcohol abuse, frequently is
included.

Foreign language, a matter we discuss more fully later on, is
currently not required by any state and it appears only occasionally
as a requirement at the local level. Currently, only about 15 percent
of high school students are enrolled in foreign-language study.[4]

State-mandated graduation requirements keep changing. Recently, Rhode Island added a requirement in consumer education.[5]
Beginning with the class entering in the fall of 1980, students in
Georgia are required to complete 20 units for graduation, up from
18 in 1972.[6]

In Florida, the Governor's Commission on Secondary Schools has recommended minimum graduation standards that would include three years of math, three of science and three of history and social science[7]—requirements considerably above the national average. Maine, Ohio, and Arizona have also considered proposals to increase state-imposed requirements for graduation.[8]

In the spring of 1983 a panel named by the Secretary of Education, The National Commission on Excellence in Education, called for "The New Basics." They would include four years of English, three years of mathematics, three years of science, three years of social studies, and one-half year of computer science.[9] For the first time, a national panel proposed a common curriculum for all schools.

What about electives?

Typically, about 55 percent of the students' four-year program is taken up with required courses, leaving eight to ten units for electives. This split between a "restricted" and an "open" curriculum reflects the continuing debate about how best to educate a large and diverse group of students. Should we tilt in the direction of an essential core or of student choice? The principal of a huge urban high school with 6,000 students vigorously stated the case for more electives.

> Sure we have a smorgasbord of electives, but it's essential. Our students range from National Merit winners to kids who can hardly read and write. Some go to Harvard and others are mechanics. It's just crazy to think that one curriculum can serve them all.[10]

In Illinois, more than 2,100 separate courses were being offered by 741 high schools that were sampled in 1977. Most courses were in nonacademic fields.[11] In another state, the principal at a large metropolitan high school where 165 different courses were offered told us: "We have courses here for every interest and ability and skill. There is something for everyone."[12]

At the fifteen high schools we visited, the number of electives ranged from 23 to 296. Brette High School, an urban academic school on the West Coast, has twenty courses in literature; fourteen in media (cinematography, drama, journalism, linguistics, mass media, public speaking, communications, and speed reading); five in composition; eight in sophomore-junior honors subjects, including The Adolescent in Literature, From Beowulf to Virginia Woolf, The Knight in Not-So-Shining Armor, and Continental Literature.[13]

At a suburban high school on the West Coast we found 247 curriculum choices, ranging from Shakespeare and Advanced Chemistry to Consumer Auto, Tots and Toddlers, Wilderness Survival, Gourmet Cuisine, Money Management, Baja Whalewatch, Office Assistant, and Bowling.[14]

At Rosemont High, in the Northeast—another top-notch academic school—the electives seem endless and the possibilities almost overwhelming. Twenty-three pages of the catalogue are devoted to career education, with courses in Accounting, Early Childhood Education, Food Services, Medical Careers, and Industrial Education. The foreign-language department has twenty-one pages in the catalogue, with courses ranging from Russian to Italian. The social studies department has fourteen pages, with such offerings as Women in Society and Afro-American History. The visual-arts curriculum includes drawing, painting, sculpture, printing, ceramics, cartooning, film making, and photography.[15]

Rosemont faculty express mixed feelings about curriculum proliferation, which began in the mid-sixties. Some view it as a worthy attempt "to respond to the diversity of students." Others see it as "a retreat from academic excellence." Still others see the thick catalogue as evidence of the school's unclear goals, and of an "unwillingness to decide what is most important."

In a nationwide survey, the number of seniors who feel high schools should place *more* emphasis on basic academic subjects has been growing—from 47 percent in 1972 to 67 percent in 1980.[16] Very often, however, we found that it was the academically outstanding schools that had the most electives, offering students a wide variety of upper-level courses for enrichment. The issue is not the number of electives—the so-called smorgasbord—but rather whether the school offers a solid academic core and whether students choose electives wisely.

How *do* students decide what they should and should not take? The answer: they do it casually, with little guidance. Small wonder. Guidance in most high schools is inadequate. On the average, each high school counselor must advise about 320 students,[17] helping them select programs, deal with personal problems, fill out forms and questionnaires, and choose colleges or jobs.

When students are asked to name the people who help them most in planning their academic programs, guidance counselors and teachers fall well behind mothers and peers (Table 12).

Curriculum decisions are shaped *most* decisively perhaps by the program or "track" in which a student is enrolled—academic, vocational, or general. At comprehensive high schools, the *academic* program is considered the most rigorous; it contains the greatest number of so-called "solids,"* and the aim is to prepare students for further education.

The *general* program is more open-ended, with few academic courses and great opportunity for electives. Significantly, "the percentage of students on the general track jumped from 12 percent in the late 1960s to 42.5 percent in the late 1970s."[18] At least two reasons are cited for this shift: First, a variety of "more attractive" courses were added to the curriculum, drawing students away from traditional academic subjects. Second, entrance requirements at many four-year colleges were lowered, and attendance increased at community colleges, where there were few, if any, requirements for admission. Thus, students soon discovered that even with a "general" course of study they could gain admission to all but the most highly selective higher-learning institutions.

*"Solids" are usually defined as the traditional academic subjects—English, mathematics, science, and foreign language.

Table 12 Sources of Curriculum Counseling

Question: How much have you talked to the following people about planning your school program?

	Great Deal		Somewhat		Seldom	
	Soph.	Sr.	Soph.	Sr.	Soph.	Sr.
Mother	38	45	50	43	13	12
Father	22	38	51	42	28	20
Peers	34	26	52	50	13	23
Teachers	5	15	34	43	61	42
Guidance counselor	7	11	41	39	51	50

Source: *High School and Beyond,* 1980. Public schools only, 10 percent sample. Totals may not equal 100 percent owing to rounding.

The *vocational* track is for students who plan to join the work force after graduation. Most vocational students complete a core of academic requirements, but they also are expected to complete about five or six job-related courses. About 11 percent of all high school students concentrate—take six or more units—in vocational education.[19] However, as we noted earlier, more than three-fourths of all students take at least *one* vocational course as an elective—typing or introductory shop, perhaps.

Vocational courses are usually grouped into categories:

Agriculture
Distribution and marketing
Health
Business and office occupations
Industrial arts
Trades and industry
Consumer and homemaking

One of these categories, trades and industry, is dominated by males. The other, business and office programs, enrolls mostly females. These two programs make up more than 50 percent of all vocational education enrollments.[20]

Daniel and Lauren Resnick, in a penetrating analysis of the influence of tracking on curriculum patterns, observed:

> . . . we have, but often fail to admit that we have, several different curriculum standards in operation simultaneously in our schools. Although everyone is expected to complete high school and to offer the requisite number of Carnegie units in order to receive a diploma, we have several different tracks or programs that students may follow—each with different sets of requirements. . . . Under these conditions there is no sensible way to address the question of curriculum standards in general.[21]

To take a closer look at the "different curriculum standards," about which the Resnicks write, we randomly chose the transcripts of three students who, in 1981, graduated from three widely differing schools. We analyze these transcripts here, not because they are representative of all programs, but because they reveal how sharply a high school education may differ from one student to another.

Predictably, all three transcripts had a core of courses: English or literature, science, mathematics, and social studies. But, even within these traditional subjects, course titles varied greatly. For example, in the freshman year, two students took English 9, while the third took Basic Communications. In mathematics, one student took Algebra 1, another took Pre-Algebra followed by Basic Algebra; the third enrolled in High School Math during the sophomore year.

Variations and paradoxes increase as one examines the transcripts more closely.

Transcript for Graduate A

Grade 9	Grade 10	Grade 11	Grade 12
English	Myths and Folklore	American Authors	Advanced Math 1
Algebra 1	Algebra 2	Geometry	Chemistry 1
Physical Science	Physical Science 2	Biology 1	Biology 2
Industrial Arts	Urban Studies	U.S. History	Sociology
General Office	Science Fiction	Metal Technology	Accounting 1
Physical Ed.	Driver Education	Typing 1	Technical Drafting 1
			Power Tools 1

This student took five science and four mathematics courses, U.S. History, three literature courses—Myths and Folklore, Science Fiction, and American Authors—and two social science courses—Urban Studies and Sociology. During the senior year the student had a full academic load. One assumes he or she is college bound. Yet there is no foreign language on the transcript and there are six vocational electives—including metal technology, technical drafting, and power tools.

Transcript for Graduate B

Grade 9	Grade 10	Grade 11	Grade 12
Basic Communications	Language Analysis	Types of Literature	Family Relations
American History	World History	Psychology 1	Foods 1
Pre-Algebra	Basic Algebra	Consumer Economics	Concert Choir
Physical Science	Creative	Accounting	Cadet Teacher
Vocational	Communications	Choir	
Homemaking	Child Development	Physical Ed.	
Typing 1	Record Keeping	Teacher's Aide	
Mixed Glee Club	Ceramics 1		
Physical Ed.	Glee Club		
Introduction to	Driver Education		
Business			

Graduate B took only one science course, Physical Science, and two math courses, Pre-Algebra and Basic Algebra. The student also took three English courses—Basic Communications, Creative Communications, and Language Analysis—but only one literature course, Types of Literature. The last two years were filled with Choir, Family Relations, Psychology, Consumer Economics. Note also that in the senior year this student took no academic courses. Interestingly, the student did take courses labeled Teacher's Aide, Child Development, and Cadet Teacher, suggesting he or she would like to be a teacher. At the same time, there is a heavy component of "practical" courses—Vocational Homemaking, Introduction to Business, Accounting, Record Keeping—suggesting an interest in other vocations. Again, no foreign language.

Transcript for Graduate C

Grade 9	Grade 10	Grade 11	Grade 12
English 9	English 10	American Literature	Composition
World History	High School Math	Composition	English 10
Psychology	Basic Science	U.S. History	American Literature
Horticulture	Health	Auto Mechanics 1	Values
Photography	Guidance	Metals 1	Team Sports
Woodshop	Team Sports	Team Sports	Soccer
Driver Education	Driver Training	Health	Guitar 1
		Graphic Arts 1	
		Architectural	
		Drafting 1	
		Service	

The transcript for graduate C presents still a different picture. Again the student shopped around: Horticulture, Photography, Woodshop, Auto Mechanics, Graphic Arts, Architectural Drafting. This student had only one mathematics course, something called High School Math, and one science course, Basic Science. In the freshman year, out of seven courses taken, four were in areas of "personal interest"—Horticulture, Photography, and the like. The sophomore year shows only three academic courses—English 10, Basic Science and High School Math. The trend continues. During the junior and senior years, the student was very busy taking Team Sports, Graphic Arts, Auto Mechanics, and Guitar. Again, no foreign language. Again no clear pattern.

Where, then, is the pattern?

During the past two years, we have heard much talk about raising academic standards, improving test scores, lengthening the school year. Many school people seem more concerned about how long students stay in school than they are about what students should know when they depart. We also have heard talk about adding another unit of science, another unit of math, or another unit of English to the required core, but we have heard little about the content of a high school education, about what it means to be an educated person.

More substance, not more time, is our most urgent problem, and in the following chapters we suggest a course sequence for all students. Our goal is not to impose a single curriculum on every school, but to underscore the point that what is taught in school determines what is learned.

6

LITERACY:
THE ESSENTIAL TOOL

The first curriculum priority is language. Our use of complex symbols separates human beings from all other forms of life. Language provides the connecting tissue that binds society together, allowing us to express feelings and ideas, and powerfully influence the attitudes of others. It is the most essential tool for learning. We recommend that high schools help all students develop the capacity to think critically and communicate effectively through the written and spoken word.

"Human beings combine in behavior as directly and unconsciously as do atoms," John Dewey said. "But participation in activities and sharing in results . . . demand *communication* as a prerequisite."[1] Only humans communicate in subtle and complex ways. Only humans find meaning in a few squiggly lines or in patterned utterances we call speech. Only humans create sentences that have not been heard or seen before, or describe a tall leafy object by using four abstract symbols: T-R-E-E. It is from this very activity that human society was formed.[2]

Language is linked to thought. Philosophers and linguists have long debated the precise ways the two are joined.[3] We do not propose to pursue that finely-shaded argument here. We do affirm, however, that thought and language are inextricably connected, and that, as students become proficient in self-expression, the quality of their thinking also will improve. Morton Bloomfield writes:

Language is our all-encompassing medium, almost certainly the oldest means of communication and expression, one which is both central to and pervasive in the realm of all human thought. It is the basis of whatever social cohesion we can attain. . . . We cannot escape its influence even by silence. We need it to grasp things intellectually and to get others to do so. We cannot avoid it even when we talk about it. To a large extent it defines our very humanity.[4]

When we speak of language we first mean the mastery of *English.* We acknowledge the richness of other languages and cultures, and later in this report we propose the study of a second language for all students. Still, for those living in the United States, the effective use of English is absolutely crucial. Those who do *not* become proficient in the primary language of the culture are enormously disadvantaged in school and out of school, as well.

How is the mastery of English to be accomplished?

The process begins early. No school is needed to teach a child to speak. The typical three-year-old has a vocabulary of a thousand words or more. Children, when they are very young, can use complex language that involves an intricate system of grammar.[5] They begin to master, almost miraculously it seems, the symbol system of the culture.

Schools should build on the remarkable language skills a child already has acquired. Unfortunately, reading programs in the primary grades often seem to assume that children come to school with limited language and that decoding skills can be separated from comprehension. An approach to reading that builds on the child's own language experience offers a rich alternative that can at once continue language development and build confidence as well.[6] Once young learners have become actively involved in the writing and reading of their own thoughts, they are ready to consider seriously the ideas and writing conventions of others.

In the early grades, students should learn to read and comprehend the main ideas in a written work. They should learn to write standard English sentences with correct structure, verb forms, punctuation, word choice, and spelling. In elementary school, students also should learn to organize their thoughts around a topic, and present ideas orally, both in casual discussion and in more formal presentations. In one suburban midwestern elementary school, first graders annually write and produce their own collections of poems and stories. They even hold a publishers' tea to introduce their creative efforts to parents and friends.

The language development of each child should be carefully monitored. Records of his or her proficiency in the use of oral and written English should be maintained and passed from grade to grade. If a student is not making satisfactory progress, special tutoring should be provided.

In Looscan School, a neighborhood elementary school in Houston, Texas, 96 percent of the children are Hispanic and 85 percent qualify for free or reduced-cost breakfasts and lunch. A dedicated principal, Herminia Uresti, has been instrumental in raising, impressively, the reading level of children in the early school years.

When asked how she accounted for student progress, Ms. Uresti said that she had no magic formula. "We simply expect that every child can perform, and they do. It is very important to have high expectations. Many think that because children come from impoverished homes they have no intellectual abilities. That is simply not the case."[7]

To help teachers accomplish their mission in teaching basic skills, Ms. Uresti does not permit office disruptions that distract from the teacher's time. "There is much paper work connected with teaching. I don't ask the teachers to do it. I do it myself, or I have my office staff take care of the paper work. The teacher's time must be spent in teaching; we permit as few interruptions as possible."[8]

Attendance is also stressed—to children and to parents. Last year, Looscan had a 97.5 percent attendance rate, higher than for any other school in the district. The climate for learning is established by a principal who, in turn, supports the teacher.

Not all students are as well served as those at Looscan School. Today, many come to high school pathetically ill prepared. Some, quite literally, are unable to read or write with even minimum proficiency. Such inadequacy cannot be ignored.

Schools that pass language-deficient students from one grade to another without providing special help perpetrate a cruel hoax. One failure leads to another; students become embarrassed, hostile, and confused; they fall farther and farther behind and eventually drop out or get a piece of paper that is worthless. It is better to assess language proficiency at the start of high school, when something can be done, than at the end, when it is too late.

Therefore, we recommend that a formal assessment of English-language proficiency be made for individual students the year before they go to high school.

The intensive assessment we envision should be based upon *all* of the pertinent records that are available; for example, accumulated teacher descriptions and evaluations of the student's reading, writing, and oral language use; samples of writing, audiotapes of oral language, results of informal reading and writing inventories, and, if used within the schools, results of standardized tests or locally designed language examinations.

Students who are judged by their eighth-grade teachers to have difficulty with reading, writing, or speaking must be identified. A remediation program must be developed. A pre–high school summer program directed at the particular difficulties should be provided for these students. For those who continue to need assistance beyond the summer session, an intensive program should be offered during the initial term of high school with continuing assistance available thereafter, if necessary.

As part of its assessment program, East Stroudsburg High School in Pennsylvania administers an English vocabulary and reading comprehension examination every spring to all incoming eighth-grade students. Of the 250 or so entering freshmen, about 60 who are language deficient are placed in a program for which they receive credit.

Five East Stroudsburg teachers work with these students in a special interdisciplinary program. They teach small classes, of eight to ten students each, in their subject areas—history, English, science, and math. They also focus on reading and writing skills. Students may spend up to two years in the program and then go on to the regular eleventh-grade classes, where, to date, they appear to be holding their own. Robert Stokes, East Stroudsburg coordinator of this special education program, is confident that, for many students, language deficiencies have been overcome and potential dropouts have stayed in school.[9]

During high school, every student—not just those with problems—should learn to write more clearly, read with greater comprehension, listen with more discrimination, speak with more precision, and, through critical thinking, develop the capacity to apply old knowledge to new concepts.[10] Patricia Albjerg Graham, Dean of the Harvard University School of Education, writes: "Literacy is essential both for the individual and the society in the late twentieth century, and the high school is the institution with the unique responsibility to assure it."[11] Therefore, we also recommend that high schools give priority to language study, requiring of all freshmen a one-year basic English course, with emphasis on writing.

Today, the average high school student spends more time studying English than any other subject. The typical student takes three or more courses labeled "English." But what does it mean to "take a course" in English? At Rosemont, a suburban high school in an upper-class community, four years (eight semesters) of English are required. However, students can meet this mandate by selecting courses from over thirty different offerings.

The English offerings at Rosemont High include Approaches to Composition, Responding to Literature, Options in English, Points of View, Literature on Trial, Adolescent Literature, Romeo and Juliet, and Expository Writing. An impressive list of courses, to be sure. Yet, Rosemont's English program has no agreed-upon priorities. The only requirement is that each semester all students "take a course in English."

A more unsettling problem in today's schools, perhaps, is the neglect of writing.

Clear writing leads to clear thinking; clear thinking is the basis of clear writing. Perhaps more than any other form of communication, writing holds us responsible for our words and ultimately makes us more thoughtful human beings.

Specific knowledge is conveyed in specific language, and unless the student communicates clearly what he has learned, thoughts will remain vague and imprecise. Creativity will be lost. Donald Graves, Professor of English Education at the University of New Hampshire, says: "In reading, everything is provided . . . in writing, the learner must supply everything."[12]

During our visits, only infrequently did we find writing being taught. Occasionally, writing assignments were given, but often papers were returned late with only brief comments in the margin. One student observed: "A good teacher writes a comment on the bottom of an assignment that shows you she has graded your work as carefully as you have written it."

An excuse given for the failure to teach writing is that the results are hard to measure. The pressure is on to teach the skills that can be counted and reported. One teacher said:

> We are so hung up on reporting measured gains to the community on nationally normed tests that we ignore teaching those areas where it can't be done. How do you say, "Susie has improved six months in the quality of her writing"? We test them to death in reading and math . . . but that's all.[13]

The most frequent reason given for the failure to teach writing is the extraordinary demand it places on the teacher's time. Today, most English teachers meet five classes daily, with 25 to 30 students each. If the teacher gives one writing assignment every week to each student, he or she spends, at a minimum, more than 20 hours correcting papers. The arithmetic is simple: 125 papers times 10 minutes to correct, critique, and mark each one equals at least 1,250 minutes—or 20.8 hours—for one assignment.

One English teacher, who left public school teaching, explained the drain on her personal life:

> I loved teaching high school. It was enormously gratifying, but tremendously enervating. The work just wore me out to a nub. My students loved to argue, and they loved to write. If I didn't return their themes within a week, they were terribly disappointed. When I did, they were as excited as if I had brought them a wonderful gift. But I was correcting papers all the time. I would take my sons to their 4-H meetings and sit and correct papers; I played bridge and corrected papers; I carried papers with me when friends invited me to dinner. I was totally enslaved by those papers. I had a class load of 130 students. Ninety percent of them showed dramatic improvement in writing at the end of the year. But I thought I was going to die.[14]

Teaching students to write clearly and effectively should be a central objective of the school. But this goal cannot be magically accomplished. Time must be provided to assure that the task is adequately performed. Teachers must have time not only to assign writing but also to critique carefully what students write. We recommend that those who teach basic English have no more than twenty students in each class, and no more than two such classes should be included within the regular teacher's load.

A well-taught basic English course will help students become better writers. But, unless the effort is reinforced by other teachers, the gains will be diluted if not reversed. In a recent study of high school writing in the United States,[15] it was found in most non-English courses that writing assignments were rarely given. Students' written responses were restricted to multiple-choice answers, filling in blanks, or short-answer statements on the quizzes. Good writing must be taught in every class.

The high school curriculum should also include a study of the spoken word. As humans, we first use sounds to communicate our feelings. Very early, we combine phonemes orally to express complex ideas. In our verbal culture we speak much more than we write. We use the telephone more frequently than we send letters. Talk is everywhere. Throughout our lives we judge others, and we ourselves are judged, by what is said. We need to be as precise in speaking as we are in writing. Therefore, we recommend that high schools give priority to oral communication, requiring all students to complete a course in speaking and listening.

The study of the spoken word—or *rhetoric* as it was once called—historically has been an essential part of education. The importance of speech is reflected in the classic works of Aristotle and Cicero and in the central position it once held in the curriculum of the schools. In the first public high school—the Boston English Classical School—Declamation was required every year. And in their second year all students had a course called Forensic Discussions. In 1856, at Woodward High School in Cincinnati all students were required to take courses called Declamations, Rhetoric, and Reading. In their senior year all students presented original addresses once every three weeks.[16] Today, speech is rarely a requirement for graduation.

The one-semester speech course we propose would include group discussion, formal debate, public speaking, and reading literature aloud. Again, the goal is not just effective self-expression; it also is reflective thinking. Students' oral comments must also be accompanied by careful analysis and critique by teachers.

Listening should be included, too. Today's young people are bombarded by messages. They should be taught to evaluate what they hear, to understand how ideas can be clarified or distorted, and to explore how the accuracy and reliability of an oral message can be tested.

We urge that speech, like writing, be taught in every class. At one school we visited, students in a literature class debated a question from a Shakespearean play: *Resolved that John would be a better heir apparent than Hal.* A civics class staged a mock trial that focused on constitutional rights. Students in a biology class thoughtfully discussed recent DNA discoveries, and, in a logic course, students were examining the reliability of proof. Good communication was a part of every course.

In the end, speaking and listening should be something more than the mere exchange of information. Communication, at its best, should lead to genuine understanding. Wayne Booth of the University of Chicago puts it this way:

> When we are working together at our best, we repudiate . . . the warfare of fixed positions; instead we try out our reasons on each other, to see where we might come out. We practice a rhetoric of inquiry.[17]

All too often, our efforts to speak and listen to each other seem to be a vicious spiral, moving downward. "But we have all experienced moments," Booth said, "when the spiral moved upward, when one party's effort to listen and speak just a little bit better produced a similar response, making it possible to try a bit harder —and on up the spiral to moments of genuine understanding."[18]

Language defines our humanity. It is the means by which we cope socially and succeed educationally. The advent of the information age raises to new levels of urgency the need for all students to be effective in their use of the written and the spoken word. The mastery of English is the first and most essential goal of education.

7

THE CURRICULUM
HAS A CORE

The second curriculum priority is a core of common learning—
a program of required courses in literature, the arts, foreign language, history, civics, science, mathematics, technology, health—to
extend the knowledge and broaden the perspective of every student.

Since *Sputnik* orbited into space, it has become dramatically
apparent that we are all custodians of a single planet. When drought
ravages the Sahara, when war in Indochina creates hundreds of
thousands of refugees, neither our compassion nor our analytic
intelligence can be bounded by a dotted line on a political map. We
are beginning to understand that hunger and human rights affect
alliances as decisively as weapons and treaties. These global changes
must be understood by every student.

There are a host of compelling reasons for global thinking.
Television and satellites nibble away at our parochialism. The
American economy is linked to Tokyo and Düsseldorf, yet to trace
that connection is an exercise only the tiniest fraction can perform.
Dwarfing all other concerns, the mushroom cloud hangs ominously
over our world consciousness.

Today's high school curriculum barely reflects the global view.
The world has shrunk, yet American young people remain shockingly ignorant about our own heritage and about the heritage of
other nations. Students cannot identify world leaders or the capitals

of other countries at a time when the destinies of all nations are interlocked.

The globe has changed. If the high schools are to educate students about their world, new curriculum priorities must be set. If a school district is incapable of naming the things it wants high school graduates to know, if a community is unable to define the culture it wants high school graduates to inherit, if education cannot help students see relationships beyond their own personal ones, then each new generation will remain dangerously ignorant, and its capacity to live confidently and responsibly will be diminished.

What, then, do we see as the basic curriculum for all students? Broadly defined, it is a study of those consequential ideas, experiences, and traditions common to all of us by virtue of our membership in the human family at a particular moment in history. These shared experiences include our use of symbols, our sense of history, our membership in groups and institutions, our relationship to nature, our need for well-being, and our growing dependence on technology.

These themes are not totally unfamiliar. They are based, in large part, on traditional academic subjects. Together they form a core curriculum that enlarges one's vision, and they are, we believe, appropriate for every student—not just the college bound. Therefore, we recommend that the high school help all students learn about their human heritage, and the interdependent world in which they live, through a core of common learning based upon those consequential experiences common to all people.

Shared Symbols: The Cultural Connection

Reading, writing, speaking, and listening—along with computation—are the basic tools of education. But the mastery of language means more than acquiring these essential skills. During high school all students should move toward cultural literacy.[1] They should discover how language is a part of culture, probably the most important part. They should learn about the variety of ways civilization is sustained and enriched through a shared use of symbols.

Literature. As a first step we recommend that all students, through a study of literature, discover our common literary heritage and learn about the power and beauty of the written word.

At the turn of the century, there was, in this country, what amounted to a core curriculum in literature. In more than 25 percent of the public schools, the following works were included: *The Merchant of Venice, Julius Caesar,* "First Bunker Hill Oration," *The Sketch Book, Evangeline,* "The Vision of Sir Launfal," "Snow-Bound," *Macbeth, The Lady of the Lake, Hamlet,* "The Deserted Village," "Gray's Elegy," "Thanatopsis," *As You Like It.* [2] Today, most students take at least one literature course to meet the English graduation requirements, but rarely do they encounter, in depth, enduring works of literature.

We do not propose a national great books curriculum. We do propose, however, a one-year literature course in which all students discover that creative writers are, as Abrams said, both the mirror and the lamp [3] of the time. Through comedies and tragedies of ancient Greek playwrights, the plays of Shakespeare, as well as the work of contemporary authors, students should be introduced to basic human questions and dilemmas and be inspired to return to great literature time and time again.

In one school we visited, a group of high school teachers spoke of using literature to help students better understand life's deeper meanings. A teacher with master's degrees in both English literature and psychology said:

> My background in literature is more useful [than my psychology background] in helping students understand human motivations and in making them more sensitive people. . . . They need to feel, through literature, a relationship and kinship with the human family. [4]

Many literature classes we visited were not inspired. Language skills, not great literature, were being taught. Poetry was used to teach punctuation. Course guides spoke only vaguely about the contributions of great writers. Rarely were great books listed as required reading.

Still more discouraging was the inclination to introduce only "gifted" students to great literature. At Garfield High, college preparatory students were reading Milton's *Paradise Lost* and e.e. cummings's "in Just-spring." These treasures were not being taught to students in the general or vocational program.

Literature addresses the emotional part of the human experience. It provides another perspective on historical events, telling us what matters and what has mattered to people in the past. Literature transmits from generation to generation enduring spiritual and ethical values. As an art form, literature can bring delight and re-creation. As a vehicle for illustrating moral behavior by specific examples (Job, Odysseus, Oedipus, Hamlet, Billy Budd, Captain Queeg) it speaks to all. As great literature speaks to all people, it must be available to all students.

The Arts. From the dawn of civilization, men and women have used music, dance, and the visual arts to transmit the heritage of a people and express human joys and sorrows. They are the means by which a civilization can be measured. It is no accident that dictators, who seek to control the minds and hearts of men, suppress not just the written and spoken word, but music, dance, and the visual arts, as well.

Murray Sidlin, the conductor of the New Haven Symphony, said:

> When words are no longer adequate, when our passion is greater than we are able to express in a usual manner, people turn to art. Some people go to the canvas and paint; some stand up and dance. But we all go beyond our normal means of communicating and *this* is the common human experience for all people on this planet.[5]

The arts are an essential part of the human experience. They are not a frill. We recommend that all students study the arts to discover how human beings use nonverbal symbols and communicate not only with words but through music, dance, and the visual arts.

During our school visits, we found the arts to be shamefully neglected. Courses in the arts were the last to come and the first to go. While some school districts had organized magnet schools for talented students, only one comprehensive high school we visited included art as a requirement for graduation. Nationwide, it is only rarely required.

A few schools do give priority to the arts. In one music appreciation class, students were playing instruments, trying out a composition, engaging in animated discussions about a musical theme. The combination of performance, experimentation, and interpretation demonstrated how exciting and rewarding the arts can be for students when they are actively involved.

We conclude that the arts not only give expression to the profound urgings of the human spirit; they also validate our feelings in a world that deadens feeling. Now, more than ever, all people need to see clearly, hear acutely, and feel sensitively through the arts. These skills are no longer just desirable. They are essential if we are to survive together with civility and joy.

Foreign Language. In an increasingly interdependent world, foreign language study must be a vital part of the core of common learning. We recommend that all students become familiar with the language of another culture. Such studies should ideally begin in elementary school, and at least two years of foreign language study should be required of all high school students.

The President's Commission on Foreign Language and International Studies reported that the study of foreign languages peaked a long time ago, in 1915, when 36 percent of all high school students studied another language (Table 13). During the 1960s, almost all colleges dropped foreign language requirements, with the result that

**Table 13 High School Enrollments in Foreign Languages
(1890 to 1980)**

	1890	1915	1955	1960	1965	1970	1974	1980
Percent enrolled	16	36	20	23	24	23	18	15

Source: S. Frederick Starr, "Foreign Languages in the American School," in U.S. Department of Health, Education, and Welfare/Office of Education, *President's Commission on Foreign Language and International Studies: Background Papers and Studies* (Washington, D.C.: U.S. Government Printing Office, 1979), p. 10.

high school language programs continued to decline. Today, only about 15 percent of American high school students study a foreign language—down from 24 percent in 1965. The commission also noted that only one out of twenty high school students studies French, German, or Russian beyond the second year.

Still more distressing is the fact that very few of those who *do* take a foreign language reach even a minimum level of reading, writing, or speaking proficiency. Indeed, two-thirds of the students in foreign language study are in a first-year program. And, based on past patterns, only 4 percent of the first-year Spanish and German students are likely to proceed to the fourth year. French, on the other hand, does better. In this language, 52 percent stay the course.[6]

James A. Perkins, chairman of the President's Commission on Foreign Language and International Studies, states the problem clearly: ". . . the hard and brutal fact is that our programs and institutions for education and training for foreign language and international understanding are both currently inadequate and actually falling further behind."[7]

Our own school visits confirmed the low priority of foreign language study. At one school, budget cuts made it necessary to consolidate all German instruction. Students, regardless of the level, were taught in one class. The teacher could barely cope with the fifty-three students.

Today, a foreign language requirement is being reintroduced by many colleges and schools to "tighten academic standards." But more than a token effort must be made. All students should not only "learn about" a foreign language but be proficient in its use. To achieve this goal, difficult issues must be faced.

First, the study of a second language should begin long before students come to high school. While there is no "right" time to learn a language,[8] research, experience, and common sense suggest that language study should begin early—by the fourth grade and preferably before—and it should be sustained.

Further, the method of foreign language teaching must improve. There is no "best" way to teach a second language. However, the current practice of devoting 40–50 minutes a day to such study with little time for intensive conversation is, for most students, insufficient. Larger blocks of time should be arranged. Some high schools have placed two language periods back-to-back. At other schools there are "language tables" in the cafeteria. Still others schedule weekend retreats during which all communication is in a second language.

Finally, there is the question of *which* foreign language should be offered. Today, nearly 15 percent of all families change their place of residence each year.[9] Students need continuity in language study as they move from one school to another. Since it is not possible for every school to offer every language at every level, some nationwide priorities must be set.

By the year 2000, the United States could be home to the world's fifth-largest population of persons of Hispanic origin.[10] Our future as a nation increasingly will be linked to our neighbors to the South. While some schools may choose to offer a variety of languages to reflect local traditions and ethnic interests, it does seem reasonable for all schools in the United States to offer Spanish. It is already the most frequently offered second language in the public schools.

The Perspective of History

As humans, we recall the past and anticipate the future. An understanding of one's heritage and the heritage of others—

the study of history—is an essential part of common learning.

In an age when family disruption, geographic mobility, techno-logical change, and the fast-paced electronic media so often seem to make everything but the fleeting moment remote and irrelevant, the study of history can strengthen awareness that there is a larger reality beyond the present. At a time when the sources of fear and anxiety are many, and, indeed, when human survival itself has be-come problematic, a sense of continuity with the past can provide a kind of lifeline across the scary chasm of our contemporary situa-tion.

United States History. By the time students reach high school, they will have encountered, more than once, the broad outlines of our country's history. They will have—or should have—encountered important persons and learned about political leaders who have had an impact on their times. They will have surveyed events that were turning points in the shaping of the nation. This basic knowledge should be well covered during the first eight years of school.

The study of American history should be continued and en-riched in high school. Specifically, we recommend that all high school students deepen their understanding of our national heritage through a study of United States history, with special emphasis on the people, ideas, and issues that have shaped the nation.

United States history is required for graduation from every one of the high schools included in our study, and it is the *one* social studies course uniformly required by most states. However, stu-dents often retrace superficially the chronology of American his-tory, reviewing material they have or should have studied in the early grades, with students complaining, "We never make it past World War I."

We propose a one-year United States history course that would involve an understanding of chronology at a deeper level. Such a course might include an investigation of how a single community emerged, or a study of the lives of a few influential leaders—artists, reformers, explorers who helped shape the nation. Primary sources, such as autobiographies, published diaries, and collections of letters, should be used.

Another approach to the study of American history would be to take a contemporary issue of great consequence, trace it to its roots, and look at the political, social, and economic forces that were at work. Today's environmental concern in the United States might be contrasted with earlier periods of expansion and resource exploitation. Today's immigration patterns might be compared with other great migration periods in the nation's life. Whatever the approach, students need a far deeper understanding of the central themes and dilemmas that continue to influence American life.

Western Civilization. Beyond American history lies the long sweep of Western Civilization, embodying a rich tradition of thought, culture, and political experimentation upon which our own nation has drawn in countless ways. We recommend that all students learn about the roots of our national heritage and traditions through a study of Western Civilization.

A one-year Western Civilization course, prepared as a part of the core of common learning, should help all students understand how early Near Eastern beliefs influence our moral and religious ideas today, how ideas about democracy flourished in early Greece, how our own standards of beauty were shaped by the European Renaissance, and how philosophers and revolutionaries of the Western world have influenced our traditions of government and law. We are a people with deep roots, sharing with over one billion others —the Russians included—an important cultural history.

Through a study of Western Civilization, students can come to understand more fully the organization of human communities, from tribes to city-states and ultimately to our contemporary nation-states, with their distinctive languages, cultures, and world views. Such a course will enable students to gain a sense of humility as well as personal enlightenment as they examine historical and literary works, from *The Egyptian Book of the Dead* to Plato's *Republic* to Cicero's *Orations* to Shakespeare's *King Lear,* to name a few.

Such a course, when well presented, will record moments of high achievement as well as dark chapters in our history. The Holocaust, for example, needs to remain a part of our shared remembrance of human failure and the capacity that exists for the destruction of human life and dignity. Students need to face the enduring strengths and fragile conditions that exist in our contemporary society and become fully aware of the web that we call civilization and how easily it can be torn asunder.

Non-Western Studies. A 1982 census placed the population of China at 1,008,175,288—nearly one-fourth of the earth's total.[11] With more billions in Africa, the Middle East, Latin America, and other parts of Asia, the student of the 1980s is part of a world in which the United States' population, and even that of the United States and Western Europe together, are a distinct minority.

The history curriculum must extend beyond American history and Western Civilization to include non-Western studies. Specifically, we recommend that all students discover the connectedness of the human experience and the richness of other cultures through an in-depth study of a non-Western nation.

Courses in non-Western civilization are now offered as electives at many high schools. As an alternate approach, we suggest a one-semester required course in which students study, in considerable detail, a single non-Western *nation*—Thailand, Japan, or the Ivory Coast, for example. The curriculum should place the nation in its own historical context and explore the civilization of which it is a part. Regardless of the approach, high schools simply must do a better job of reflecting the full diversity of the human experience and help students put their own heritage in perspective.

At present, such study is woefully neglected. We found that only two states, New York and North Carolina, mandate non-Western studies. It is essential that all students learn about the history of non-Western cultures as they take their places in a world of diverse peoples, whose concerns and very destinies have become intertwined in such complex and subtle ways.

Membership in Groups and Institutions

"We do not make a world of our own," Ralph Waldo Emerson observed nearly 150 years ago, "but fall into institutions already made, and have to accommodate ourselves to them."[12] Institutions are a fact of life. They touch almost every aspect of our being—economic, educational, familial, political, and religious. We are born into institutions; we pass much of our lives in institutions; and institutions are involved when we die.

Today, public trust in institutions is low, and alienation from them is high. Yet they cannot be abandoned. Institutions provide arrangements through which daily transactions are conducted, interpersonal relationships are nurtured, and social structure is maintained. All students, as a central goal of education, should learn about their social memberships and how groups and institutions shape their lives.

Civics. Many institutions might profitably be studied—the family, volunteer organizations, social agencies, for example. However, we propose that knowing about government and how it functions is critically important. Specifically, we recommend that a course in American government—traditionally called civics—be required of all students, with focus on the traditions of democratic thought, the shaping of our own governmental structures, and political and social issues we confront today.

When Thomas Jefferson was asked if mass opinion could be trusted, he responded, "I know no safe depository of the ultimate powers of the society but the people themselves; and if we think them not enlightened enough to exercise their control with a wholesome discretion, the remedy is not to take it from them, but to *inform their discretion* by education."[13]

The Jeffersonian vision of grassroots democracy that so captured the imagination of Alexis de Tocqueville when he visited America in the 1830s[14] seems increasingly utopian today. As early as 1922, Walter Lippmann warned that public ignorance of increasingly complex problems was democracy's greatest challenge.[15] Issues now facing the electorate have become enormously complex, and government seems increasingly remote.

Civics used to be a mainstay in the high school; recently it has declined. Civic illiteracy is spreading, and unless we find better ways to educate ourselves as citizens, we run the risk of drifting unwittingly into a new kind of Dark Age—a time when, increasingly, specialists will control knowledge and the decision-making process. In this confusion, citizens would make critical decisions, not on the basis of what they know, but on the basis of blind belief in one or another set of professed experts.

In our proposed one-year course on American government, students might be introduced to classic political thinkers from Plato and Locke to John Adams and James Madison. Also, students should study the Declaration of Independence, the Constitution, and the *Federalist Papers.* Equally important, students should study government today and how it works. Each student might take one contested issue now before Congress, a state legislature or community governmental body, reporting in depth on the history of the issue, points of conflict, and plausible resolutions.

In a course in government and law at Sands High School, a large suburban institution in the Southeast, students observed courtroom proceedings. They also interviewed jurists and state prosecutors. Legislators and the head of the state's attorney's office were invited to the class. For one project, students worked to get a street next to their school renamed. They lobbied the city council, secured citizen support, and filed appropriate papers. The city commission was responsive. The name of the street was changed.

Civics is an important part of the core of common learning. In a world where human survival is at stake, ignorance about government and how it functions is not an acceptable alternative.

Science and the Natural World

The study of science introduces students to the processes of discovery—what we call the scientific method—and reveals how such procedures can be applied to many disciplines and to their own lives, too. Through science, students learn to gather data, consider causal relationships, and discover how, through observation and testing, theories are found, refined, and sometimes discarded. A study of science is an essential part of the core of common learning.

Karl R. Popper has reminded us that "Science is not a system of certain, or well-established, statements; nor is it a system which steadily advances towards a state of finality. . . . *We do not know, we can only guess.* And our guesses are guided by . . . faith in laws, in regularities which we can uncover—discover."[16]

It is through the study of science that students discover the elegant underlying patterns of the natural world and learn that, in some manner, all elements of nature are related. Lewis Thomas, in his Phi Beta Kappa Oration at Harvard University, observed:

> There are no solitary, free-living creatures: Every form of life is dependent on other forms. . . . We should go warily into the future, looking for ways to be more useful, listening more carefully for the signals, watching our step, and having an eye out for partners.[17]

With these purposes in mind, we recommend that all students study science, focusing on its processes and its uses, and, through such a study, learn about the world of nature of which they are a part.

A 1980 study found that 75 percent of public high school seniors reported taking two years or less of science.[18] For most high school students, this means ninth-grade general science or environmental science and tenth-grade biology. Chemistry and physics account for only 37 percent and 22 percent, respectively, of twelfth-grade secondary-school science enrollments.[19]

We suggest a two-year science sequence that would include basic courses in the biological and physical sciences. These courses should be taught in a way that gives students an understanding of the principles of science that transcend the disciplines. The search for general principles of science can be, if not properly done, a superficial exercise. But, if carefully designed, an interdisciplinary view will give all students—both specialists and nonspecialists—a greater understanding of the meaning of science and the scientific process.

Advanced science study also should be available. Later in this report we discuss an elective cluster sequence for students who wish to complete upper-level courses in biology, chemistry, or physics to prepare themselves for professional work in science, engineering, and the new technologies. And in Chapter 14 we propose residential schools for outstanding science students.

Not all students are budding scientists, but becoming a responsible citizen in the last decade of the twentieth century means that everyone must become scientifically literate. Having a substantial knowledge of scientific facts and processes, and understanding more about the interdependent world in which we live, are essential parts of the core of common learning.

The Study of Mathematics

When reflecting upon the value of their education, some people say, "I haven't used algebra since I got out of high school." Others have nothing but high praise for the teacher who lit in them the flame of interest in mathematics that opened a new realm of understanding and a whole new set of vocational and leisure-time options.

Since mathematics is a sequential discipline in which previously gained insights and skills form the basis for continued learning, training in mathematics should begin early and progress steadily. A fitful and fragmented approach will not do. Therefore, schools should provide students an early opportunity to discover their interests and ability in mathematics by giving them first-hand exposure to the subject.

Specifically, in elementary school all students should become skilled in the fundamentals of arithmetic. They should be able to add, subtract, multiply, and divide; and, in a larger sense, they should understand the problem-solving process. To assure that a solid foundation has been laid, we recommend that a formal assessment of mathematics proficiency be made for individual students the year before they come to high school. Again, the goal is to determine if special assistance is needed, identify weaknesses, and give students the help they need to succeed. As was the case for language, students identified as needing assistance should be enrolled in a special summer program with continuing assistance as needed.

In high school, all students should expand their capacity to think quantitatively and to make intelligent decisions regarding situations involving measurable quantities. Specifically, we recommend that all high schools require a two-year mathematics sequence for graduation and that additional courses be provided for students who qualify to take them.

Through a study of mathematics, all students should develop quantitative perception. The aim should be to give students the ability to use mathematics to solve problems on their own. In one classroom, students were asked to find the weight of a brick after measuring its length, width, and height, and being given the value of its density in pounds per cubic inch. The exchange went something like this:

> *Teacher:* "Who can tell me the weight of the brick?"
> *Student:* "1016 pounds." (*Looking at his paper*)
> *Teacher:* "Lift the brick. Now, how much does it weigh?"
> *Student:* (*Again looking at his paper*) "1016 pounds."[20]

The student had failed to make the connection between the problem and real life. Calculations were unrelated to common sense. This example was not an isolated incident. Time after time we witnessed the use of numbers with little or no thought given to implications and applications.

For students who will become scientists and engineers, the need for thorough training in the theory and skills of mathematics is obvious. And mathematical insight is becoming an increasingly important component for success in many other vocations as well. Students planning to move into professions and vocations requiring it should study calculus by the time they leave high school. Specialty schools in mathematics and science are proposed in a subsequent chapter of this report.

For all students the goal should be to develop the ability to identify practical problems, structure them systematically, and find appropriate solutions.

The Impact of Technology

Thomas Carlyle once described man as "a tool-using animal."[21] While some lower forms of life awkwardly use sticks and stones, only humans fashion complex tools, using them for both betterment and destruction. In a recent essay, Professors N. Bruce Hannay and Robert McGinn put it this way: "Man attempts *through technology* to overcome his shortcomings and his vulnerability by extending his limited capacities. He thus enhances his power, which in turn often enables him to survive, and, on occasion, even to thrive."[22]

As early as the sixteenth century, Francis Bacon urged craftsmen to acquire greater scientific knowledge. And, during the past two centuries, technology has been based more and more on science. Today, the two are joined.

Oscar Handlin writes powerfully and perceptively of the evolution of technology and of its intimacy with science:

The ways of doing, which became technology, unfolded continuously from the experience of the past. Man the tinkerer had always sought to spare himself labor; and tradition in this respect was not entirely static. . . . The first machines of the eighteenth and the nineteenth centuries were simply extensions of familiar techniques. . . . The machines, whether of wood or iron, were not totally strange. The waterwheels, the great drive shafts and pulleys that dominated these plants, embodied no essentially new principles. . . . Technology, however, made it difficult thus to isolate science from life. As the nineteenth century drew to a close, the new knowledge invaded industry, changed the machine and altered the nature of the factory. . . . The drive shafts and the pulleys were no longer visible. Power was transmitted through wires and tubes— often hidden—and the whole was covered up and shielded so that the machine gave the appearance of being self-contained and autonomous.[23]

In the twentieth century, we have the magic of jet aircraft, atomic power, space shuttles, robotics, the artificial heart, satellites, and computers. Today, any telephone in the United States can be linked to over 500 million other phones throughout the world. Any one of these phones can be used to establish interconnections between giant mainframe computers miles apart, and can be used to transmit voice, text, and visual data all around the world. Through technology we are all connected.

We recommend that all students study technology: the history of man's use of tools, how science and technology have been joined, and the ethical and social issues technology has raised. During this proposed one-semester course, a student might well look at one technological advance—the telephone, the automobile, television, or the minicomputer, for example—trace its development, and examine the positive and negative impact it has on our lives today. In examining the pros and cons of technology, students might contrast the utopian world described by H. G. Wells in *The Shape of Things to Come* with Aldous Huxley's *Brave New World* and George Orwell's *1984.*

We are quite frankly disappointed that none of the schools we visited required a study of technology. More disturbing still is the current inclination to equate technology with computers. Today, there is a rush to buy more hardware, to get Apples or Tandys into the schools with little thought as to how they will be used and what larger educational purposes will be served.

We do not deny that the computer will be extraordinarily important in the lives of students. Nor do we deny the value of the computer as a tool for learning, a matter we discuss in Chapter 11. However, teaching every student to use a computer is not the first priority of education. The great urgency is not "computer literacy" but "technology literacy," the need for students to see how society is being reshaped by our inventions, just as tools of earlier eras changed the course of history. The challenge is not learning *how* to use the latest piece of hardware but asking *when* and *why* it should be used.

In a splendid essay, Professor Jeremy Bernstein writes of the necessity of educating students about technology and its relationship to science. He says:

> We live in a complex, dangerous and fascinating world. Science has played a role in creating the dangers, and one hopes that it will aid in creating ways of dealing with these dangers. But most of these problems cannot, and will not, be dealt with by scientists alone. We need all the help we can get, and this help has got to come from a scientifically literate general public. Ignorance of science and technology is becoming the ultimate self-indulgent luxury.[24]

It is increasingly important for all students to explore the critical role technology has played throughout history and develop the capacity to make responsible judgments about its use.

Health

Healthy "lifestyles" are in vogue; still, many young people appear shockingly ignorant about their bodies. Alcohol abuse is rising, particularly among youths.[25] Teenage pregnancies increase.[26] New, intractable forms of frightening diseases have become national epidemics.

Clearly, no knowledge is more crucial than knowledge about health. Without it, no other life goal can be successfully achieved. Therefore, we recommend that all students study health, learning about the human body, how it changes over the life cycle, what nourishes it and diminishes it, and how a healthy body contributes to emotional well-being.

Many high schools are responding to these health concerns. Within traditional physical education, biology, and home economics courses can be found "mini-units" on health problems. Often, however, such courses offer warnings, but healthy living and "wellness" are neglected.

Some schools are introducing students to the larger picture. They are moving beyond mini-units to full-blown health courses required for all. This year, Broward County, Florida, made Health a one-half unit requirement for all sophomores in its twenty-two high schools. The course covers a wide range of topics: alcohol and drug abuse; sex education and communicable disease; nutrition and diet; skin, health, and dental care; first aid; mental health; and aging and dying.

Josephine Powell, a health educator who has taught for twenty years at Hollywood's McArthur High, says many students have very little knowledge about their bodies and the life cycle. In one unit on aging and death, tenth graders learn about the changing dietary and sleep needs of older people and about the concerns of the dying. Students are encouraged to visit elderly relatives and neighbors. One student reported: "I have an aunt who is dying, and I really do understand better what she is going through."

Curriculum materials used in Broward County include "modules," created by the Education Development Center (EDC) in Newton, Massachusetts, and by local teachers. Modules bear such titles as "Accepting My Body," "Thinking About Feelings," "Being

Fit," "Handling Stress," "Environmental Health," and "Preventing Injuries." Lincoln, Nebraska, high schools now require a half-semester unit in Human Behavior that uses EDC materials on aging, nutrition, and dealing with stress. Another unit is Fitness and Wellness.

Unfortunately, too few teachers specialize in health education. Too frequently such courses are assigned to physical education teachers who tend to have very limited background in this field.

We conclude that a course in lifetime fitness should be a part of the high school core of common learning. When health is threatened it leaps to the top of our personal agenda; it is central to our well-being and survival, and the study of health must become a priority in the schools.

The Meaning of Vocation

Today, too many young people grow up believing that things "just happen." Services are provided; goods are on the shelves; food is on the table—almost magically, it seems. Today, few teenagers see the connection between production and consumption, or, as in the early days, between planting and harvesting the crops, between cutting lumber and building shelter, between damming streams and grinding corn. We recommend that all students complete a seminar on work, examining its importance in the lives of all of us, and preparing themselves to make responsible life choices of their own.

Some high schools have tried to introduce students to the world of work; the results, however, have been largely disappointing. "Career days" have been offered. They have been largely show-and-tell, with pitchmen giving students a shallow view of the meaning of vocation. The historical, social, and economic aspects of work that would justify the program as a serious academic study often have been lacking.

The one-semester study of work we propose would ask how attitudes toward work have changed through the years. How do they differ from one culture to another? What determines the status and rewards of different forms of work? In addition, students should learn about changes in the economy, job opportunities that are emerging, and those that are declining. Such a curriculum might also include a study of several work-related institutions and an in-depth investigation of one specific occupation.

The course on work would be a requirement within the academic core. While it might be a formal course, less formal arrangements might be appropriate as well. A series of occasional seminars, for example, might be arranged for students during their junior and senior years. A student might study a particular career as an independent project. Whatever the pattern, emphasizing the dignity and significance of work should be an important goal of a high school education.

From Courses to Coherence

A word of warning. Beefing up traditional academic courses, while essential, is not sufficient. When students are required to take another course in language or science or history, they may be introduced to a slice of these specialties with little thought given as to how the separate subjects are connected or how collectively they relate to the larger world.

The current instructional program reflects the compartmentalized view of curriculum. Students study world history at 10 A.M., economics at 1 P.M., biology at 9, health at 2. They are taught literature in one room, civics in another; fine arts on the second floor; French on the third. While we recognize the integrity of the disciplines, we also believe their current state of splendid isolation gives students a narrow and even skewed vision of both knowledge and the realities of the world.

In our day-to-day affairs, politics and economics are often indistinguishable. There is a philosophy of art and an art to philosophy.

The geography of nations often determines their history, just as history often determines their geography. Students, however, seldom develop a clear understanding of these connections.

Therefore, in addition to tightening requirements, we must bring a new interdisciplinary vision into the classroom and the total program of the school. The content of the core curriculum must extend beyond the specialties to touch larger, more transcendent issues.

Teachers must play a key role in making these connections between the disciplines. They must view the curriculum in a more coherent way. We cannot expect students to see relationships that teachers do not see. Teachers also should work together more collaboratively.

Students, too, must begin to seek out connections between the disciplines. It is one thing to teach students that the world is a complicated place; it is another—and more lasting—lesson for them to discover it on their own. Specifically, we recommend that all students, during their senior year, complete what we choose to call the Senior Independent Project, a written report that focuses on a significant contemporary issue one that draws upon the various fields of academic study that have made up the student's program. This assignment is part of core requirements. Students will receive one-half unit credit.

We envision that each classroom teacher will be responsible for working with a small number of students, assisting them in appropriate ways with this requirement.

Asking students to submit a senior project as a requirement for graduation is not unfamiliar. Such a project is frequently found at selected academic high schools. In addition, some alternative schools —the St. Paul Open School is an example—require students to complete a senior project. In St. Paul, students focus on a single topic or prepare a comprehensive summary of their high school educational experience—the activities they engaged in, significant books they read, the cultural events that were enriching, how their lives were changed. In a more modest way, the Board of Regents in New York State requires that all students demonstrate their proficiency in writing before receiving a diploma.

In the New York examination, topics assigned include a short report on subjects such as "Life in Contemporary Egypt," "The Early Life of a Senior Citizen," "Law Enforcement in the City," "Energy Problems Today," and "The Best Invention Ever." These topics only hint at the broad range of subjects students might select. We suggest still larger themes, such as "The Information Age," "The People and Pollution," "Travel Then and Now," and "The New Immigrants."

At first blush, such a culminating activity sounds like a senior thesis, one only honors students can complete. We are confident, however, that if education is effective, every high school graduate will be able to gather information from a range of sources, organize important ideas, think carefully about an issue, and, with clarity, put his or her thoughts on paper. The seminar project will, of course, vary in length and complexity from one student to another; still, such an arrangement is, we believe, the minimum we should expect of an educated person.

In the preceding pages, we have prescribed a core of common learning. The aim is to provide education of high quality for all students.

The pattern we propose would expand the number of required courses from one-half to about two-thirds of the total units required for graduation. In addition to the traditional English, mathematics, and science courses, we give added priority to foreign language, technology, civics, non-Western studies, the arts, the importance of health, and the meaning of work. Finally, we propose an independent project to help students move from courses to coherence. The proposed curriculum may be summarized as follows:

Our Proposed Core of Common Learning

	Academic units
Language, 5 units	
Basic English: Writing	1
Speech	½
Literature	1
Foreign Language	2
Arts	½
History, 2½ units	
U.S. History	1
Western Civilization	1
Non-Western Studies	½
Civics, 1 unit	1
Science, 2 units	
Physical science	1
Biological science	1
Mathematics	2
Technology	½
Health	½
Seminar on work	½
Senior Independent Project	½
TOTAL	14½

To be prepared to live in our interdependent, interconnected, complex world, students must be well informed. They also must have the ability to bring together information from ideas across the disciplines, organize their thoughts, reach conclusions, and, in the end, use knowledge wisely. To expect less is to underestimate the capacity of students and diminish the significance of education.

8

TRANSITION:
TO WORK AND LEARNING

Moving from high school to college or to work involves choices for which most students are not well prepared. Some wander about almost aimlessly. Others are put on tracks that may be inappropriate and that close off future options.

Schooling should prepare all students for a life of work and learning. This means solid grounding in the basic skills, a common core of learning, a cluster of elective courses, and student assessment and counseling to smooth the transition to jobs and higher education.

The Rites of Passage

The rites of passage into adulthood are not well defined. Driving a car, getting a social security card, registering to vote, and cashing the first paycheck are important milestones.

But the clearest step to adulthood, perhaps, comes at high school graduation. Some young people leave home and move into places of their own. To their delight, no one will be there to set hours, establish rules of behavior, or nag them. But they will also have to feed themselves, do their own laundry, and get themselves out of bed. Perforce, they will grow up.

By their junior year, students have already sampled adult life.

They are biologically mature. Frequently they hold jobs and spend a lot of money. In 1982, 3.3 million sixteen- to nineteen-year-olds —over 30 percent of the age group—had part-time jobs. About 80 percent worked in the service and fast food industries.[1] McDonald's arch has become an important passageway to adulthood in America.

In 1982, almost 3 million public high school graduates were handed their diplomas.[2] Nearly 60 percent went on to higher education. For these college-going students the passage was quite well defined. About 686,000 (39 percent) attended two-year institutions; 400,000 (23 percent) went to universities; and 655,000 (38 percent) enrolled in other four-year institutions.[3]

Graduates not going on to college had options that were less well defined—and less promising. In 1982, unemployment for sixteen- to twenty-four-year-olds was about 9 percent for college graduates, 17 percent for high school graduates, and 32 percent for dropouts.[4]

Work: Prospects and Preparation

What are the prospects for those who go directly to work? And which of our young people are most likely to get the available jobs?

First, those who have worked while in high school are likely candidates. Before graduation, roughly half of the graduates who do not go directly to college will have made employment commitments, and nearly one-third of them will work for the same employer they worked for as students.[5]

Family background also counts. Prospects for getting and keeping jobs are better for young people whose family income is above the poverty level and whose parents are well educated.[6] Having a friend or a relative in the firm that does the hiring also increases prospects for employment.[7]

Race is a factor, too. With the exception of college graduates, unemployment among black youth is twice as high as that among whites.[8]

How do students prepare for the world of work?

About 11 percent of all high school students concentrate in vocational education—taking six or more such courses. Another 18 percent take three vocational courses, while 78 percent of high school students take at least one vocational course, usually to satisfy a special interest or just to fill out the requirements for graduation.[9] A few students attend specialized vocational high schools or they go to regional vocational schools part time. However, more than 90 percent of all vocational courses are offered at comprehensive high schools where academic and vocational programs are combined.[10]

Vocational courses—auto mechanics, secretarial studies, metal shop, construction—are often quite popular with students. One student put it this way: "Most courses don't mean much to me. I'm not very interested in what we're supposed to study. In shop we talk about things that are a part of our lives every day. And when you're finished with a class you really can see what you've done."[11]

Parents like vocational courses, too. In a recent survey, one-fourth of all parents indicated that vocational preparation should be emphasized by the high school. And nearly 80 percent rated that goal as "very important," a close second to intellectual development, which was rated "very important" by 89 percent.[12]

Some school officials believe that vocational courses are what keep kids in school. The principal of a 5,000-student urban high school told us, "I'm convinced that if we cut out our vocational program, our dropout rate would skyrocket. It would shoot up 25 percent almost overnight."[13]

Holding students in school is, of course, a worthy goal. With a high school diploma, job prospects are enhanced, and many vocational students, sometime in their lives, go on to some form of postsecondary education.[14] But when it comes to preparing students for a *specific* job and putting them on the first rung of the career ladder, the results of vocational education are largely disappointing.

Vocational Education: An Unfulfilled Promise

Many factors have caused us to doubt the value of traditional vocational education. The first is its tenuous link to job opportunities. Time and time again, we heard school officials praise their vocational programs; yet, when pressed about the employment patterns of their graduates, these same administrators became defensive. Most high schools have little or no information about what their vocational-education graduates are doing. And when information is provided, it is largely anecdotal—and discouraging.

At one large urban vocational high school in the South, we talked to the head of the auto-mechanics program, one of the most popular in the school. We asked how many graduates get auto-mechanics jobs. His reply: "Oh, about three out of ten. And then two of those three will probably pump gas more than they will work on cars. But the kids really like the program. They love to tune their engines."[15]

A recent comprehensive survey confirmed our informal observations. The study concluded that job prospects for graduates of vocational programs are not much better, overall, than they are for students in the nonspecialized curriculum. There is, the survey reports, essentially no difference in employment advantages between male graduates of high school trade, industry, and business programs, on the one hand, and male general education graduates on the other.[16]

The one exception is "secretarial science." Studies reveal that female graduates of commercial-business programs (who do not go on for more education) have higher levels of employment than do young women who graduate from the general studies program. But even this advantage seems to decrease as time passes.[17]

One explanation for the failure of vocational education to deliver job opportunities is simply the lack of resources. Few comprehensive high schools can offer a full range of programs to match job options beyond the campus. Assuming an enrollment of 600 or fewer students, no more than 300 would be juniors and seniors— the levels where vocational specialization usually takes place. If 11 percent of these students concentrate in vocational education (taking six or more courses), this means only about 30 students would be so enrolled. At best, such schools can offer only a handful of vocational courses to match even a fraction of the jobs in the economy. Indeed, less than half of all high school seniors attend schools that offer five or more vocational programs.[18]

Even big schools are rarely able to offer a full range of vocational courses with well-trained staff and up-to-date equipment. One study of four large comprehensive urban high schools summarized the issue succinctly:

> The problems faced by the comprehensive high schools were noticed with such regularity . . . that one cannot begin but wonder whether this institution has begun to outlive its original purpose. Especially with regard to vocational education, instruction must now be so specialized and the necessary equipment must be so sophisticated that it is difficult to create complete vocational programs in all of the high schools of the city.[19]

Over 20 percent of all urban high schools concede that their vocational facilities and equipment are in need of major repair or replacement.[20] In an auto-mechanics class we visited, students were tuning decade-old engines. A print shop looked as if nothing had changed in print technology since 1950. One "commercial" teacher at a suburban high school told us: "Our school doesn't even have electric typewriters although most employers expect our graduates to use a word processor."[21]

Not only are existing programs restricted, but high schools increasingly are unable to keep up with emerging labor-market patterns. According to the latest Bureau of Labor Statistics (BLS) projections, aero-astronautic engineers, data processors, machine mechanics, and computer systems analysts, operators, and programmers will be among the fastest-growing job categories between now and the 1990s.[22] Current programs are ill-equipped to prepare students for such occupations.

Moreover, it has been predicted that the emerging "glamour" occupations will, in fact, account for only 7 percent of the new jobs in America.[23] One report concludes that by 1990 the United States will need three times as many new janitors and sextons (600,000) as new computer system analysts (200,000). Total new jobs in the same period for computer programmers (150,000) are less than one-fifth the projected growth in fast food workers and kitchen helpers (800,000).[24]

Increasingly, it appears, high school vocational programs will be either irrelevant or inadequate. At one end will be low-paying, dead-end jobs for which formal education will not be required and to which precious school time should not be given. Skills of a hospital orderly or of a fast food service worker should be learned on the job, not in school. At the other end will be high-tech jobs that require *more* technical training than most high schools can provide.

Another problem: vocational students are often academically short-changed. This is, in fact, the most serious issue presented by the current tracking pattern. Job training is being acquired at the high cost of a quality education. And options for the future are restricted.

The most successful programs we visited were not at comprehensive high schools but at specialized vocational schools. In the best of these, vocational curriculum choices were broad, equipment was up-to-date, and teachers were well-trained. But even here the academic offerings frequently were weak. One vocational school in the Southeast offers no foreign languages, no math above Algebra I, and only two literature classes. "There is no reason to offer academic courses," one teacher said, "because no one here will go to college."[25]

A teacher at a Western vocational school said that "students in the construction trades shouldn't spend too much time on academics. It's not their thing. It should be 80 to 90 percent hands-on and 10 to 20 percent class work."[26] And at another vocational school a teacher complained bitterly that the school was "nothing more than a dumping ground."

The picture at comprehensive high schools was especially discouraging. During our visits, we heard repeatedly that "voc-ed" is the place to send less gifted students who are "able to work with their hands rather than their heads." One vocational teacher told us: "They [the counselors] are sending us kids who are not really interested and are failing in school, so they put them in the vocational classes to strengthen their needed credits."[27]

Some vocational teachers *do* have high aspirations for their students. One spoke movingly of his desire to have students "vocationally *and* academically" prepared. And an English teacher at a large comprehensive high school has an excellent reputation among her colleagues precisely because she is capable of teaching effectively in the nonacademic program. Says one admirer:

> We all knew that she was extraordinary in working with the articulate, bright kids. Their facile minds could play with ideas. But then she managed to do a bang-up job with a bunch of "basic" students, and we said, "Now we *know* she is a fine teacher."[28]

An energetic and committed science teacher chooses to teach basic biology. "I love it," he exclaims. "It doesn't mean students get watered-down biology. What I teach they get in Standard and Honors. But it means that I have to work harder."[29]

At one big-city comprehensive high school, a new English teacher was advised, "Don't bother preparing anything for the vocational kids. They don't belong in school. Those kids need boxing gloves, not books." The teacher told us she was so offended by the attitudes of colleagues that she took, as a major challenge, the teaching of literature to a so-called nonacademic class. The results she reported are at once pathetic and inspiring.

I decided I would give them the identical reading list that I gave my college prep kids. On opening day I told them that our first unit will be "poetry." After a stunned moment's silence, the boys began to laugh and call to each other with remarks like, "Hey man, didya hear her? Poetry! That's for them college kids. Hey, we're no Einsteins." I paid no attention to their words, although I recognized their embarrassment. I did a lot of reading to them, and eventually they got caught up in the material. And we talked a lot about meaning. They obviously knew a great deal about human feelings and problems. Once I asked, after reading Poe's "Raven" with them, if the raven was a symbol for something else. The boy who never took off his black leather jacket, considered by the other teachers as the worst of the lot, volunteered: "I think the raven is like a haunting memory. It just won't go away." That year they read Hawthorne and Melville, and Shakespeare. I almost cried when I saw them walking in the hall with their Shakespeare turned so that the whole world could see that they were reading "Othello."[30]

More frequently, however, we found low academic standards and a stigma attached to teaching nonacademic students, many of whom were in vocational education. One administrator describes the tracking in his school as "insidious and discriminatory." As he puts it:

> The initial assignment is critical and it occurs in elementary school. It completely determines what the student will come away with. Some students come into school, get lost in a nonacademic life— do nothing, learn nothing, just hang around for four years.[31]

According to John Goodlad's *Study of Schooling,* students in low tracks are exposed to far less challenging curricular material and less effective instructional practices. The knowledge provided to these students [in low-track classes] "was typically basic literacy or computation material on topics oriented to everyday life and work. Activities and skills listed by teachers usually required only low level cognitive processes." Further, "effective instructional practices were found to be more characteristic of high than of low track classes."[32]

A case in point is our visit to a low-track English class at Ridge-field High, a class labeled "Achievement in English." The teacher read aloud for the entire period while students followed along in paperbacks. The book was *Rumblefish* by S. E. Hinton, a story of teenage gangs and motorcycles. The choice was an obvious attempt to be relevant, but the students looked bored. Eight followed along uninterestedly; the rest either stared ahead blankly, or slouched down—dozing, it appeared. Occasional laughter was heard when four-letter words or references to drugs were read. The teacher stopped to ask only two questions, both trivial. After class she explained: "These students can't read and I think the best I can do for them is to show them someone who enjoys reading and is enthusiastic. Of course, I hate this kind of writing—all those simple sentences —but it's all right for these kids."[33]

A Single Track

Putting students into boxes can no longer be defended. To call some students "academic" and others "nonacademic" has a powerful and, in some instances, devastating impact on how teachers think about the students and how students think about themselves. We say to some, "You're the intellectual leaders; you will go on to further education. You're the thinkers, not the workers." To others we say, "You will *not* go on to college; you're not an academic." Students are divided between those who think and those who work, when, in fact, life for all of us is a blend of both.

Indeed, looking to the year 2000, we conclude that twelve years of schooling will be insufficient. Today's graduates will change jobs several times; new skills will be required; new citizenship obligations will be confronted. Of necessity, education will be lifelong. Therefore, we recommend that the current three-track system— academic, vocational, and general—be abolished. It should be replaced by a single-track program—one that provides a core education for all students plus a pattern of electives, keeping options open for both work and further education.

Eliminating the vocational track does not mean abolishing all vocational courses. Indeed, many of these courses are enriching and useful. They provide excellent options for a wide range of students and should be strengthened, not diminished. What we would eliminate are discriminatory labels and a tracking pattern that assume some students need no further education and that cut off their future options. We would also eliminate the narrow "marketable" skills courses that have little intellectual substance, courses that give students "hands-on" experience while denying them a decent education.

What then is the single track that would be appropriate for all students?

All students should have a command of English as described in Chapter 6. The basic skills are needed for college; they are needed for the workplace too. In a recent survey, more than 65 percent of the companies questioned said that basic skills deficiencies now limit the job advancement of their high-school-graduate employees. And 35 percent were forced to offer a basic skills remedial program of their own. Half of the companies surveyed identified writing as a problem among employees.[34] More than half of the American businesses surveyed also said speaking and listening were serious problems. Employees were unable to follow verbal instructions and could not express ideas effectively. Repeatedly, both academic and business leaders have urged high schools to give priority to the skills of language.

All students—not just the college bound—should also complete a core of common learning. Specifically, the curriculum we propose in Chapter 7 would give all students the credits and knowledge they would need both for college admission and for work. Further, the core curriculum would help all students perform their social and civic obligations. While students may tackle these core courses in different ways, the basic content of the core should be the same for all. No student should suddenly wake up to discover that a college option has been foreclosed because a science or math or foreign language requirement has not been met. And no student should discover as an adult that he or she is ill-equipped to participate in the debate on consequential public issues or unable to act responsibly in community affairs.

Elective Clusters: The Transition School

Beyond literacy and the core of common learning, we also propose that all students—through a carefully selected cluster of electives—be given an opportunity to pursue their own unique aptitudes and interests. Specifically, we recommend that the last two years of high school be considered a "transition school," a program in which half the time is devoted to completing the common core and the other half to a program of "elective clusters."

"Elective clusters" would be a carefully planned program for each student. Such a program would include five or six courses that would permit advanced study in selected academic subjects or the exploration of career options—or a combination of both. Clusters might range from health services to the arts, from computers to science, from mathematics or a foreign language to office management. Here is where specialized upper-level academic courses and quality vocational offerings would appropriately fit.

A few high schools may be able to offer a full range of elective clusters—fifteen to twenty perhaps—to match the interests of their students. For most, however, this is not possible today and it will be less possible in the future. Many comprehensive high schools are getting smaller. Budgets have been tightened. Teachers have been laid off, and elective courses in both academic and vocational programs have been dropped. In spite of the talk about the smorgasbord of electives, the truth is that at many schools students will have fewer, not more, elective choices in the days ahead.

At one high school we visited—a large suburban institution in the Southwest—enrollment dropped from 2,400 to 1,600 students in five years. Upper-division science, mathematics, and English electives were cut, and in nonacademic areas only the sports programs were kept because of parent pressure. The principal put the problem simply: "I'd love to offer clusters of electives for our students, but I've had to fire most of the teachers who offer the special upper-level courses."[35] A California high school we visited has felt the impact of Proposition 13. Staff cutback meant eliminating twenty-four advanced courses in language, science, and computer education.

Clearly, if high schools are to offer advanced academic study and career exploration, they must recognize they cannot do it all. High schools must become "connected" institutions, creating networks and specialty schools, drawing upon resources beyond the campus. Part-time lecturers from business and industry and other professionals should be used. And students themselves must be given more responsibility for their education. New teachers, new locations, and new technology are important.

In a large city in a Rocky Mountain state we visited a "regional vocational school." Students from twelve different high schools in six separate districts participate in the program. They take their core academic courses at their home schools and then complete upper-level courses at nine separate specialty schools spread over the southern section of the city. Most of the specialty courses are vocational, but the idea of a network could apply to academic studies too.

"Satellite concept" was the phrase mentioned most frequently when we asked teachers and administrators to explain how the "regional" school functioned. "It's like a separate high school with special concentrations at different sites."[36] "The only difference from a regular high school," one teacher said, "is that our classrooms are not under one roof."[37]

In the most rural of North Dakota's school communities, a portable classroom program brings special teachers and equipment to the school for a term and then moves on. The woodworking van, for example, is parked at a school for eight to twelve weeks, during which time students receive intensive instruction. In a school district in Massachusetts, a portable classroom moves computers from school to school. We propose a portable classroom program in both career-related courses and in other fields—the arts, foreign languages, science, and computers—to bring to schools for a term specially-equipped vans accompanied by well-qualified teachers.

In De Witt Clinton High School in the Bronx, New York, a program in health care is being offered to students in cooperation with two nearby hospitals. In Minneapolis, Minnesota, and in Houston, Texas, a network of specialty schools have been developed district-wide.

The Cleveland Museum of Art inaugurated, in 1974, the nation's first museum-based advanced-placement program in art history. Several hundred high school juniors and seniors have taken the two-semester course, with more than three-quarters of them receiving college credit.

The St. Louis, Missouri, Botanical Garden offers a model science-education program. In a three-week seminar session, high school students learn to organize and analyze information. They select a science project that can have an impact on the environment.

The New Haven Education Center for the Arts in Connecticut offers classes in four areas of the arts—music, dance, the visual arts, and theater—to students from fifteen school systems in the New Haven area. The classes are offered four days for ten hours a week and are taught by professionals in each field.

We recommend that the transition years include independent study, time with mentors, early college study or apprenticeship experience off the campus. Such arrangements would make it possible for students to participate in what Lawrence A. Cremin refers to as the "Ecology of Education," combining learning places, old and new.[38]

Guidance: A Critical Need

As graduation day approaches, many high schoolers experience a great deal of uncertainty about what to do next. In one national survey about 10 percent of high school seniors were still undecided about whether or not they should go on to college.[39] At Prairie View High School in the central plains we chatted with students about the future. Almost half had no specific plans. The rest had more-or-less well-shaped notions of what they wanted to do.[40]

- "I'm going to college and have a teaching career; be happy." (11th-grade girl)

- "I want to go to college and major in P.E. to be a P.E. teacher. I'll get married, but I'll wait awhile." (11th-grade boy)

- "I don't think I'll go to college. I'll never make it in math. I'm thinking about the Air Force." (12th-grade girl)

- "I'll just keep working at a nursing home. Maybe I'll be a vocational agriculture teacher. I may end up getting married at the end of high school." (11th-grade girl)

- "I'll go to college. I don't know what I'll go into yet. I want to see the world." (12th-grade boy)

- "I think I'll join the Army. It's at least better than hanging around the house." (12th-grade boy)

- "I'd like to get a master's degree. I may go into computer programming. I plan to stay single for a while. (10th-grade girl)

Where do students turn for advice as they consider future options? The obvious place is the guidance office. But often this leads only to frustration. At every school we visited, the counselors were shockingly overloaded. They had little time to talk to students about career choices or even to stay informed themselves. At Sands High School in the Southeast, John Pierovich, one of four counselors, starts his day on the run. "I begin seeing students at 7:15. I'll meet twenty to twenty-five every day plus two or three parents each day."[41] Pierovich is responsible for 450 students in all.

At eight one morning at DeSoto High, a parent sat with her child in the guidance office, waiting to see a counselor. None was present, explained the secretary, because they were giving tests that morning. Soon one of the counselors happened to appear. After being introduced to the parent, he confirmed the situation. "We're tied up with tests this morning. I couldn't see you until eleven." The parent said she couldn't wait and left with her daughter.[42]

One student at a West Coast high school complained, "You have to know what you want before you go to the counselor. If you're really smart at this school you get college prep. Otherwise they stick you with wood shop. They don't tell you of the array of options you have if you don't go to college."

Vocational students occasionally get fragments of advice about job prospects, but, more often, they are on their own. Although high school counselors seem somewhat more confident in helping students who are college bound, very often this means talking about how to get into competitive colleges.

Our conclusion: The American high school must develop a more adequate system of student counseling. Specifically, we recommend that guidance services be significantly expanded; that no counselor should have a caseload of more than one hundred students. Moreover, we recommend that school districts provide a referral service to community agencies for those students needing more frequent and sustained professional assistance.

Assessment: High School and Beyond

Today, the most dramatic rite of passage for many students is taking the SAT. Every year, about a million high school students —those who are college bound—sit for two and a half hours with soft-lead pencil in hand, marking up the SAT score sheets administered by the College Entrance Examination Board.

During our school visits we found that the SAT was the most important and most traumatic evaluation time in the lives of many students. One student told us that "the SAT pressure around here is terrific. We're told that if we do lousy, good colleges will reject us. We won't be able to go to college."

The SAT was developed at a time when many believed an instrument could be prepared to measure "aptitude"—a relatively constant set of intellectual characteristics and abilities not seriously affected by previous education. Now substantial evidence suggests that this early faith was misplaced. Today it is generally acknowledged that the SAT does not measure aptitude, nor is it directly linked to the curriculum in the schools. Still, the nation has mistakenly come to view the SAT as a reliable report card on the nation's schools.

The SAT also was created at a time when the quality of high schools was extremely uneven, and when ethnic and racial intolerance was a harsh reality in the admission procedure. The SAT sought to make the process of student selection more accurate and equitable. And SAT scores were given considerable weight in selecting students. Today, the majority of higher learning institutions are not highly selective, and there are few that use the SAT as the primary criterion for choosing students.

Moreover, the SAT is not very helpful in predicting how a student is likely to do in college. When used alone, the SAT is somewhat better than random selection in predicting academic success. When the SAT score and high school grades are combined, the accuracy of predicting success in college modestly increases. Still, we are concerned about the inflated attention given the SAT at a time when colleges are less inclined to screen students out. We are also concerned that this major testing effort is limited to the college bound. We conclude, therefore, that while the SAT has performed a useful purpose in the past, it will have a decreasingly important role to play in the years ahead.

There is an urgent need, currently unmet by the SAT, for a

more effective assessment and guidance program that will give colleges and universities a more realistic portrait of what students have learned during their high school years—not to screen students out but to help them find colleges that fit them best.

There is also an urgent need to help noncollege students figure out where they should go and what they should do. It is ironic that those who need the most help get the least. Frequently noncollege students get only snippets of information about job possibilities from family or friends or other students or counselors at school. It is unacceptable to focus our elaborate testing and assessment system only on those moving to higher education while neglecting the other 40 to 50 percent who even more urgently need guidance.

We recommend that a new Student Achievement and Advisement Test (SAAT) be developed to serve the needs of *all* students as they make the transition from school to work and further education.

The goal of the new assessment program would be to evaluate the *academic* achievement of the student—linking it to the core curriculum that the student studied. The goal also would be to provide *advisement*, helping students make decisions more intelligently about their futures—again, not to screen students out of options, but to help them move on with confidence to college and to jobs.

The College Board now offers achievement tests in specific subject areas. With some modification, these could form the basis for at least the achievement portion of the new evaluation program. The National Assessment for Educational Progress also offers a model for the type of evaluation we propose. Further, we are encouraged that the College Board recently has released a thoughtful report on what a college-bound high school student should know. This provides a beginning, we believe, for the linking of education and evaluation.

This new assessment instrument would be only one part of a larger, more comprehensive student evaluation program. The full assessment program should include carefully constructed teacher evaluations, student-prepared portfolios containing academic and vocational work samples, a student interest inventory, as well as the Senior Independent Project described in Chapter 7.

One final point. Each year, millions of graduates are handed diplomas, and then, except for an occasional class reunion, the school-student connection snaps. High schools remain ignorant about the long-term performance of their students. A few schools do keep track of the colleges their graduates attend—but even then they know virtually nothing about whether they succeed or fail. They know even less about what happens to those who go to work.

We conclude that high schools must become better informed about how their students do after graduation. They should discover where students go and whether they succeed or fail. Specifically, we recommend that every high school periodically survey its graduates, to assess the long-range performance of students.

There are good examples of what we have in mind. Warren Consolidated School District in Michigan and Duval County, Florida, both survey high school graduates annually. The state of Ohio has conducted one five-year follow-up survey of high school graduates and is beginning a second. Oregon surveys vocational graduates every three years. Follow-up surveys of high school graduates are also made in New York, North Carolina, Texas, and Wyoming.

One teacher in Tennessee considered the need for reliable information about the graduates of her school so urgent that she conducted a survey of vocational graduates on her own. But the practice is by no means general. Frequently, high schools lack the resources to carry out this essential function. More than hit-or-miss arrangements are required.

Since 1970, the United States Department of Education—in a program called "High School and Beyond"—has periodically surveyed graduates from a sample of high schools across the nation. We propose that this national survey be expanded. Specifically, we recommend that the U.S. Department of Education, working through state education departments, survey a sample of graduates from all high schools, at four-year intervals, to learn about their post–high school placement and experience. Such information should be made available to the participating schools and be used to understand statewide and national patterns, too.

It is difficult to imagine how schools can make informed judgments about the effectiveness of their programs without finding out how their graduates are doing. A systematic program of post–high school reporting of student progress is urgently required.

To keep the career options open and insure a smooth transition to work and further education, we must put all students on a single track—one that provides for them basic skills, a core of common learning, and a cluster of electives to serve individual aptitudes and interests. Such a program will ensure that all young people realize their full potential. No goal is more important to the future of the nation.

Chart 8 High School: A Proposed Four-Year Program

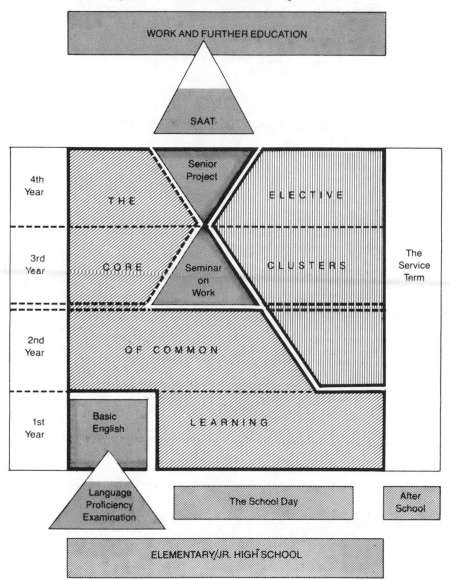

PART IV

THE HEART
OF THE MATTER

9

INSTRUCTION:
A TIME TO LEARN

For about six hours every day, students and teachers live in classrooms. Not much larger than a spacious living room, the typical classroom accommodates thirty or more students. At most, each student occupies about four square feet of space, *not* taking into account chairs, desks, and tables.[1] Desks are typically placed in rows, often according to a seating plan so the teacher can quickly spot who is missing, who is acting up, and who is asking for attention. The claims of order compete with the claims of freedom.

The chairs are no longer bolted down, and the floors are now apt to be vinyl rather than wood, but no matter how modern it is, a visitor from an earlier era would have little trouble recognizing that he was in a classroom. In front is the teacher's desk. Just behind there is a blackboard or its more modern counterpart, "the greenboard."

Just as the arrangement of space is standardized in the American classroom, so is the use of time. If ideas are to be thoughtfully examined, time must be wisely used. Time is the student's treasure. However, what occurs in the classroom is often a welter of routine procedures and outside interruptions that come to dominate the life of students and teachers alike and, in the end, restrict learning. Time becomes an end in itself.

Within the average fifty-four-minute period, the teacher must take attendance, make announcements, and do numerous bookkeeping chores. One teacher describes the problem:

Time is the currency of teaching. We barter with time. Every day we make small concessions, small tradeoffs, but, in the end, we know it's going to defeat us. After all, how many times are we actually able to cover World War I in our history courses before the year is out? We always laugh a little about that, but the truth is the sense of the clock ticking is one of the most oppressive features of teaching.[2]

The school day fares scarcely better: in a large number of schools, a steady stream of assemblies, announcements, pep rallies, and other nonacademic activities take up precious time, leaving teachers frustrated. At one school we visited, a class was interrupted on three separate occasions by trivial announcements. We agree with the teacher who said in exasperation that "the first step in improving the American high school is to unplug the PA system."

In a crowded setting, a typical high school teacher must manage twenty-five to forty students each class period. He or she must maintain control, teach a prescribed course of study, engage the students, pay attention to student differences, and determine through tests and questioning how well students have learned the material presented. Few teachers are brilliant lecturers or exceptionally skilled in give-and-take discussions. Almost all find it difficult to sustain a high level of performance five or six periods every day.

Most teachers feel their work is negatively influenced by students who are unmotivated, by parents who are nonsupporting, by administrators who saddle them with trivial tasks (study halls, hall duty) or burdensome paper work, by schools that permit students to "slide through with any course just as long as they meet A.D.A. [Average Daily Attendance] expectations."[3]

One teacher talked of feeling powerless, an expression that we heard time and time again:

> There is no teacher input into the curriculum, the scheduling, the goals, or the rules at this school. I'm allowed to make suggestions, but I don't think that anyone ever pays any attention. Even if they are implemented, I don't think it's because I suggested something.[4]

Teachers do not usually decide how many students and which ones will be in their classes, how long the school day or the class period will be, the format and content of the report card, or even what grades or subjects will be taught. And, in all too many cases, teachers are forced to prepare their students for tests that are unrelated or perhaps inappropriate to the curriculum of the school.

Also, teachers in most settings have little say in the selection of the textbooks they must use. Today seventeen states, most in the South or Southwest, have a centralized system for the selection of textbooks for students in all schools and all grades.[5] In four more states, multiple textbook series are adopted by the state, and local districts can choose from as many as six alternatives in any one discipline. But, again, that decision is usually made in the central office and not by teachers in a particular school. At the extreme, in one of the schools we studied, teachers not only were told what textbooks to use, but also were handed a detailed lesson plan for each day. That they lacked much commitment to teaching is understandable.

Most textbooks present students with a highly simplified view of reality and practically no insight into the methods by which the information has been gathered and facts distilled. Moreover, textbooks seldom communicate to students the richness and excitement of original works. When students are privileged to read the primary sources, they meet authors personally and discover events first hand. We recommend, therefore, that the use of original sources be expanded.

We further recommend that states ease their control over the selection of textbooks and transfer more authority to the district and local school system. Teachers should have a far greater voice in selecting materials appropriate to their own subject areas. In the event of conflict, school boards should act as arbitrators. The result of these changes, we believe, will be to introduce richer instructional materials into the classroom.

Given teachers' lack of control over so many factors crucial to instruction, it is perhaps little wonder that few view themselves as professionals with professional responsibilities. And, given the heavy load and tyranny of time, it is hardly surprising that most teachers fall back on fairly standard procedures: lecturing, question-and-answer, recitation, seat work, and homework. After all, these are the practices that teachers are familiar with from their own school days, and they demand little imagination. Further, as many teachers told us, "there is no expectation that we do much more."

One teacher admitted her frustration and her compromises:

In world history classes, I used to give more essays and more assignments where students had to write out their ideas. But in terms of time, I've been reduced to giving multiple choice and matching quizzes. And so I have to share part of the blame. There was tremendous pressure on me the first year. On Thanksgiving I was grading papers no matter where I went. On Christmas, I was preparing my lectures—so it just became a problem of time. I didn't want to spend all that extra time away from my family.[6]

Or, from another teacher:

We have all compromised on our values. Inside the classroom, students will work for me or I see to it that they don't stay there. But I don't give them nearly as much homework as I would like because I have been beaten down; too many simply will not do it.[7]

"Beaten down" by some of the students and unsupported by the parents, many teachers have entered into an unwritten, unspoken, corrupting contract that promises a light work load in exchange for cooperation in the classroom. Both the teacher and the students get what they want. Order in the classroom is preserved, and students neither have to work too hard nor are too distracted from their own preoccupations. All of this at the expense of a challenging and demanding education.

Consider one ninth-grade English class that was typical of others we observed. The bell rings at 10 A.M. The roll is called. Then come such matters as late slips, excused and inexcused absences, problems about uncompleted homework.

The teacher begins the class by handing back a grammar test dealing with subject, object, and verb identification. She briefly reviews the test, giving the correct answer to each question. She then collects the papers, announcing that she will give the test over again and average the two scores.

After the papers are collected, the teacher instructs all students to "turn to page 24, read the poem on that page, and answer the accompanying questions, in complete sentences, in your notebook."

At this point, students begin to cluster together. As it turns out, few have brought textbooks to class. The teacher complains: "I specifically asked you to bring your texts on Friday." She then warns that she is going to give a test on the poem they've been asked to read. Her final instructions are to read the poem twice and then answer the questions.

One student, clearly stalling for time, asks if they will have time to do it all. The teacher explains that she will grade them on what they have done. The students remain restless. Sensing this, the teacher urges them to get to work and suggests that "if you don't have a text, you can sit with someone else as long as you don't talk or read aloud. Otherwise you will not be able to complete the assignment."

Very few students work alone. Those in clusters begin to talk. Realizing that the class has not yet settled down, the teacher once again goes over the rules for working together. One of the rules, she reiterates, is that they cannot talk or read aloud.

By now the teacher is beginning to be exasperated. "We've wasted almost five minutes going over a simple rule that you are not to talk or read aloud," she exclaims. But her show of impatience doesn't seem to work either, so she begins to single out individuals and implore them to get to work.

"Joe, get busy," she warns. Joe replies that he is busy. "Are you being rude?" "No, ma'am," Joe answers. But the teacher is still not quite sure, and she gives Joe a brief lecture on impudence.

It is now 10:25. Almost thirty minutes of instructional time has been lost. Prose and poetry will have to wait.

In a world history course, students go over the worksheets on the Middle Ages they completed earlier. For the next thirty minutes, the teacher lectures on the following topics: Reasons Constantinople was a good location for a capital, differences between the Greek Orthodox religion and the religion of the Western world, and characteristics of Gothic church architecture.

Each of these topics might represent at least one class period in its own right. The challenge of the teacher seems to be to cover the material, to carry students from medievalism to the present, within the next five months.

At various points throughout the lecture, the teacher reads from the text, obviously assuming that the students hadn't read the book or that, if they had, they didn't understand it. Fragments of information, unexamined and unanalyzed, are what is being transmitted here. There is no time for student questions. Instead, the teacher, using an overhead projector, has carefully outlined the key points, which the students assiduously copy down. Curiously, there are no pictures or photographs to illustrate Gothic church architecture.

Students suffer from information overload—not to mention boredom. Some pass notes to each other; others doze in the heat of the afternoon, heads down on the desk. Nevertheless, the teacher believes it has been a successful class. He has "covered the material," and there have been no serious disruptions.

Most discussion in classrooms, when it occurs, calls for simple recall (What were the provisions of the Treaty of 1763?) or the application of an idea (Use the periodic table to find an atomic number). Occasionally students are asked to develop explanations (If we were to release ammonia in one corner of the room, why is it possible to smell it in the opposite corner?). But serious intellectual discussion is rare.

In a chemistry class, a teacher who has some of the school's ablest students used questioning as just another way of telling.[8]

Teacher: (Working from an overhead projector) Does anyone have an idea of how to go on from moles to molecules?

Student: Multiply.

Teacher: Okay, multiply. (The teacher then writes out a formula on the overhead projector.) Now, how would you change from grams to molecules? (He writes on the overhead projector "G to molecules.")

Student: We haven't done this.

Teacher: If you look at step one [a previously given formula], it will tell you how to go from grams to moles, and then, if you put moles to molecules, you can get the answer, or, if you want, you can go the reverse.

These vignettes of the American classroom raise disturbing questions about how instruction relates to the professed goals of education. How, for example, can the relatively passive and docile roles of students prepare them to participate as informed, active, and questioning citizens? How can the regimented schedule and the routinized atmosphere of classrooms prepare students for independence as adults? Not least, how can we produce critical and creative thinking throughout a student's life when we so systematically discourage individuality in the classroom?

In most schools, we found that teacher expectations of students varied dramatically from class to class. Some teachers held high expectations for all their students; others expected little. This was illustrated by great variations in the intellectual intensity of classrooms, the amount of homework required, and the grading procedures used. In fact, among the schools we visited, confusion on the matter of standards was as great as was confusion over goals. We conclude that until there is a consensus on student performance among educators and parents, individual schools will find it extremely difficult to improve the quality of instruction.

In one suburban school we met bright college-bound students

who told us: "Most classes don't get us to think. In most of the large classes the teacher just teaches to the middle, so we aren't challenged. We just do the work and take a test. The teachers may be doing the best they can, but that's not good enough."[9] A high school sophomore summed up the general sentiment this way: "We work hard, but we can handle it. We need to work more. We would like more challenges. We need more writing. We don't want more busy work, but we'd like to have harder work, not just being told what to do, but being told how."[10]

As Mortimer Adler observes,

> There is little joy in most of the learning they [students] are now compelled to do. Too much of it is make-believe, in which neither teacher nor pupil can take a lively interest. Without some joy in learning—a joy that arises from hard work well done and from the participation of one's mind in a common task—basic schooling cannot initiate the young into the life of learning, let alone give them the skill and the incentive to engage in it further.[11]

Adler, in the provocative and widely discussed *Paideia Proposal*, goes on to describe three teaching styles to achieve three education goals: lecturing, to transmit information; coaching, to teach a skill; and Socratic questioning, to enlarge understanding.[12] Adler's conclusion is that "all genuine learning is active, not passive. It involves the use of the mind, not just the memory. It is a process of discovery in which the student is the main agent, not the teacher."[13]

John Goodlad, at the University of California, Los Angeles, found that barely 5 percent of instructional time in the schools is spent on direct questioning and less than 1 percent is devoted to open questioning that calls for higher-level student skills beyond memory.[14]

> From questionnaires filled out by students and from extensive classroom observations it becomes apparent that the range of pedagogical procedures employed, particularly in the academic

subjects, is very narrow. . . . The teaching observed in our current study [*A Study of Schooling*] was characteristically telling or questioning students, reading textbooks, completing workbooks and worksheets, and giving quizzes. This pattern became increasingly dominant with the progression upward from primary to secondary classes.[15]

There is a place in the classrooms for telling or lecturing, especially when the goal is the acquiring of organized knowledge. Teachers who can lecture well should do so. There is a place, too, for questions and answers, for structured review and drill. But there comes a time when probing questions should be asked, when the teacher should direct the student's mind from the familiar to that which is less well known but no less important. Socratic questioning is indeed the hallmark of certain great teachers. By this means students proceed from the obvious to the subtle, from easy assumptions to supporting evidence.

Much of what the teacher must do to succeed in teaching is a matter of common sense—careful planning for each lesson, educational goals for each day's work, pacing and timing, love of the subject matter, and respect for the students. Clarity in procedures, discipline in carrying through, and the careful measurement of accomplishments are essential elements in the formula for success.

We are almost embarrassed that so much about good pedagogy is so familiar, but, at the same time, we are encouraged by this realization. There remain some old-fashioned yet enduring qualities in human relationships that still work—command of the material to be taught, contagious enthusiasm for the work to be done, optimism about the potential of the students (teachers are quite properly eternal optimists), and human sensitivity, that is, integrity and warmth as a human being. When we think of a great teacher, most often we remember a person whose technical skills were matched by the qualities we associate with a good and trusted friend.

When good teaching does work—as it does every day in many schools—the results are brilliant and enduring. Rosemont High School is a large suburban high school in the Northeast. When you walk through the halls during class periods and peer through open doors, students are attentive and busy. Most teachers feel confident enough to leave their doors open. The educational setting seems lively—and highly accessible. Teachers share ideas with other teachers and often work together on curriculum projects across the disciplines. Teachers here have a shared sense of purpose. They value their lives in this teaching community.

At Rosemont, there are many types of teachers with many different styles of teaching. A typing class is energetically engaged in pounding the keys, working against the teacher's stop watch. In a physics laboratory, small groups of students work collectively on an experiment, while the teacher circulates around the room offering encouragement and clarification. Students in a U.S. history class lead a lively discussion, with the teacher in the background.

The visitor at Rosemont is surprised not to hear the harsh sounds of bells signaling the beginning and end of class periods. Despite the absence of bells, classes started on time. Rosemont students show surprise when asked about the lack of bells. Says one, in mock alarm, "This isn't a prison, you know! We're not Pavlov's dogs!"

The seriousness of purpose is not limited to courses for bright, academic students. In a reading class for those with learning disabilities, the room is noiseless as students work individually at their seats. The teacher insists upon quiet and helps students focus on their assignments. When their attention wanders, she directs them back to the task; when they become discouraged and begin to turn off, she supports them and re-engages them in their work.

When one student begins to be disruptive and distracts his classmates from their reading, the teacher will not tolerate it. With only a few minutes left to go in the class period, Christopher resists getting another assignment from the teacher, insisting, "But it's only four minutes left." The teacher responds firmly: "I know, but you have to do something in those four minutes. Hurry up or you'll only have three minutes left!" When Randy approaches the teacher for approval because he has gotten a perfect score on an exercise, the teacher pushes him to do more challenging work: "Randy, if you got 100 percent, it was too easy. Did you feel it was too easy?"

Certainly there are those at Rosemont who slip through unnoticed and unchallenged. Not all teaching is at a high level. One hears the typical student complaints about teachers who are uninspired, tedious, and boring. But standards for teaching and learning seem high across the full range of academic abilities.

Even more impressive were those "star" teachers we encountered: the Constitutional History teacher who has developed an innovative curriculum using primary sources and original documents and has created a teaching style that uses role playing; the English teacher who has developed a course called The Art of the Essay, in which students write and critique each other's work.

In a large mathematics class of more than forty students, the teacher demanded creativity and individual participation. The students were excitedly engaged in their own personally constructed strategies and arguments, with the teacher doing all he could to keep up with the various approaches.

In an American literature class at Rosemont High School the desks are in a circle. Many students in this class have learning disabilities and have had difficulty focusing their attention.

At the beginning of the class, the teacher returns their papers and warns, "Now, folks, don't panic. Some of you got low grades, but consider this a quiz. This is like the core of a paper, beginning ideas. . . . If you have a low grade, it is a sign that there has been a misunderstanding."

She clarifies the next day's assignment. "You will need to develop a thesis statement, and that means it must be a debatable idea or opinion, not a factual statement. Here are some pitfalls for a debatable statement: it can be too huge and expansive [she offers an example]; it can be so obvious that only a ninny would debate it.

Virginia Woolf says a writer is one who sticks his neck out . . . takes a firm stand with some intellectual risk and then backs it up with evidence."

Today, the discussion is on *Death of a Salesman;* the focus is on Willie's decision to commit suicide, and the teacher encourages students to talk to one another rather than direct all their comments to her. She pushes for participation. To one girl who is having difficulty penetrating the barrage of comments, the teacher says quietly, "Assert yourself . . . get in there . . . you have something to say."

When the conversation begins to lose direction, the teacher breaks in. "We have a whole lot of separate ideas on the floor. Let's take a few minutes of silence to sort these out. . . . If you can't remember anyone's ideas except your own, you haven't been listening. . . . I have heard at least fifteen explanations for Willie's suicide. . . . See if you can reconstruct it."

The class grows quiet as students begin to write ideas down. The teacher walks around the room, encouraging students who seem stuck or discouraged and restating her question for greater clarity. Then she offers a clue to the whole class: "See if you can remember Cynthia's question; it was a turning point in the discussion." She didn't give an answer, only a question.

After several minutes of silent contemplation, the teacher says, "Let's combine our reasoning," and students immediately begin to offer reasons for Willie's suicide:

"He wanted to quit a world where nothing was going right for him."

"He felt he had failed terribly and was a disgrace to those who loved him."

"He wanted to have people pay homage to him at the funeral."

"He had only half achieved his dream."

The contributions are energetic and fast-paced. When the exchanges become heated and confused, the teacher intervenes with a tentative and thoughtful voice, "Let me ask you a very hard question. What happens when a dream you've lived by turns out to be a lie? How do you feel about that? Or are you too young?" The responses are charged and unrestrained.

One girl speaks with passion: "People shouldn't circle their lives around one idea." Another disagrees: "But it is not just one idea, it is their whole reason for being." A third comments, "There is always a danger in being too committed, too closed. . . . You should have one or two goals. You should choose. . . . You don't have to die with one ideal." The discussion becomes argumentative, but not hostile.

The teacher does not direct them toward a tidy conclusion. They are struggling with unanswerable questions, profound dilemmas, and she wants to encourage them in the struggle. She wants them to recognize Willie's pain.

Class is over. Students leave troubled, reflective, and inspired.

10

TEACHERS:
RENEWING THE PROFESSION

This nation has always been ambivalent about teachers. Dan Lortie, Professor of Sociology at the University of Chicago, put his finger on the problem: "Teaching . . . is . . . honored and disdained, praised as 'dedicated service,' lampooned as 'easy work.' . . . Teaching from its inception in America has occupied a special but shadowed social standing . . . *Real* regard shown for those who taught has never matched *professed* regard."[1]

Today, teaching occupies an even more "shadowed place" in the public's esteem. In just twelve years, from 1969 to 1981, the number of parents who said they would like to have their children become teachers in the public schools dropped from 75 to 46 percent.[2] Seventy-one percent of the senior high school teachers sampled in another survey indicated that public attitudes toward schools had a negative effect on their job satisfaction.[3] And a science teacher who left the profession in disgust after twenty years told us that if his daughter elects teaching as a profession he will not pay for her education.[4]

Whenever schools are discussed, teachers are blamed for much of what is wrong. While there are inept teachers in the public schools, concentrating only on the weakest teachers misses an essential point. Whatever is wrong with America's public schools cannot be fixed without the help of those teachers already in the classrooms. Most of them will be there for years to come, and such teachers must be viewed as part of the solution, not the problem.

Surveys reveal that teachers are deeply troubled, not only about salaries, but also about their loss of status, the bureaucratic pressures, a negative public image, the lack of recognition and rewards. To talk about recruiting better students into teaching without first examining the current circumstances that discourage teachers is simply a diversion. The push for excellence in education must begin by confronting those conditions that drive good teachers from the classroom in the first place.

The Conditions of Teaching

Sometime between 6 and 8 A.M. each weekday morning, about 970,000 public high school teachers arrive at school.[5] If they are late, it is rare. One of the hallmarks of the American school is that it starts and stops on time. Visit any high school and you are struck not just by the emphasis placed on punctuality, but by the way time dominates. Clocks are everywhere. Bells ring to announce the beginning and end of every segment of the day.

Many people think teachers have soft, undemanding jobs. One parent told us, "I'm not sure what they have to complain about. After all, it's an easy life. The hours are good—nine to three—and you get the summer off."

The reality is different. The average high school teacher not only teaches five or six classes a day, but has only 54 minutes of in-school preparation time.[6] Teachers are often responsible for three different levels of a single course. Outside the classroom, teachers must review subject matter, prepare lesson plans, correct and grade papers, make out report cards, and counsel students.

Moreover, in some schools, budget cuts have made it necessary for teachers to prepare for their classes at night, early in the morning, or over a brief lunch break. Occasionally, they are assigned courses for which they are not prepared. One teacher told us:

It's not unusual for me to be teaching a course that I know very little about. I could manage it if I had some time to do some background reading. But there is no preparation time here; the day is jammed. So any digging into the subject that I do, I have to do at night. But then that gives me little time to grade reports or handle the paper work for other classes. I often wonder if I'll ever catch up.[7]

Teachers also are required to perform menial tasks—supervise lunchrooms, police hallways, and chaperone student activities—when the time could be better used for instruction or planning. The majority of these chores are viewed by teachers as babysitting or security-related and as reducing their professional image. "I would like to use my duty periods for tutoring," one teacher told us, "and have the kids guard the halls. They don't do it here because they don't want kids in the position of being the security force."[8]

In addition, clerical burdens must be assumed. One teacher estimated that he spends three to four hours each week on paper work, not counting the reading of students' papers. As we went from school to school, we heard a steady drumbeat of complaints about these distracting duties:

We have more busywork because the computer [in the central office] wants something. We spend a lot of time on ID's, passes, and cut slips.

People in charge of teachers are more interested in promoting the organization of the school. Clerical work should be done by clerks. The office should handle "tardies" and cuts, we should have computerized programming.

The paper work is unbelievable. If you even have to discipline a student it has to be fully recorded, dated, and submitted. You just ignore lots of things.

At one high school, teachers must turn in lesson plans each week. This district requirement is enforced by the principal, who assigns his two assistant principals the responsibility of reviewing these plans. The assistant principals, in turn, complained that paper work keeps them from "more important matters."

At this same school, teachers also must keep elaborate student attendance records. There is a district policy that students who have been absent without permission more than six times during a semester may not receive credit for the course. Teachers must make written reports to the counselors, then write to parents notifying them that their child missed class. As one teacher explained it:

> There is a lot of paper work. That is one of the things that competes for my time. You have to check roll in homeroom and then you have to see if anyone is tardy. You have to fill out a report for that. In second period, you have to fill out an attendance report that is audited for average daily attendance. You have to keep those records in your grade book. Then, if a student is absent three times you have to list him on a special form that goes to the principal with your lesson plans. And you have to call the student. On the fourth day, you have to send a letter to the student's parents, and send another form into the office when the student is absent the sixth time. I think that is a lot of time that surely could come from some other source, like from the attendance office. It is an every period activity.[9]

Counseling students—while far more important than paper work—also consumes a lot of the teacher's time. The average pupil-counselor ratio in American high schools is 319 to 1,[10] but in one of the schools we visited the ratio was 600 to 1. In such situations, students may see their counselors only once a year and then only briefly. Where, then, do students turn for help?

"They turn to us," one teacher told us.

> I think the counselors try to help the kids, but there just aren't enough of them. So the kids come to us. We help them select courses; we give them advice about future careers or what college they should go to. Often they're in trouble at home or even with the police. When a kid has a real problem, you can't tell him you don't have the time to give him help or advice. The truth is you don't have the time. But you somehow find it. It comes with the territory, with being a teacher. But the whole situation is really

cockeyed. It's not fair to kids; it's not fair to counselors; and it's not fair to teachers.[11]

Strikingly, while performing these myriad duties, teachers spend little time in the company of other adults. This one condition may, in fact, separate teaching from most other professions. It is even more arresting when we consider that, in the average high school, a teacher inhabits the same building as 62 other classroom teachers and 11 other full-time professional staff members such as librarians, guidance counselors, and principals—usually within close distances.[12]

And yet, teachers feel isolated. The combination of the self-contained classroom and a heavy teaching schedule gives teachers few opportunities to share common problems or sustain an intellectual life. One teacher describes it this way: "I don't know what it's like in business or industry. It may be the same. I don't know how friendly co-workers are, how honest they are. It just seems that in teaching . . . you do your thing in your class, and you leave, and you don't talk to anyone about it."[13] Another teacher, when asked with whom he discussed his teaching, responded, "My wife."[14]

There are other harsh facts. Teachers frequently have no permanent classroom—or even a desk—of their own. They usually have no pleasant place to take a break or have lunch with colleagues, let alone with friends from outside the school. In some schools, floors are dirty, windows grimy, and restroom facilities less than satisfactory.

Far more serious, teaching materials often are in short supply. Here is how one teacher in an urban school describes it:

> I sometimes wonder how we're able to teach at all. A lot of times there aren't enough textbooks to go around; the library here is totally inadequate; and the science teachers complain that the labs aren't equipped and are out-of-date. We're always running short on supplies. Last year we were out of mimeograph paper for a month, and once we even ran out of chalk. After a while you learn to be resourceful. But it's still frustrating to try to teach under these

conditions. I mean, talk about teaching the basics! We don't even have the basics to teach with.[15]

The threat of physical violence in the schools has received considerable attention. The problem is, in fact, very real. Teachers in some schools do not feel safe in the halls, in the parking lots, or even in the classrooms. A recent *New York Times* poll of over five thousand randomly selected teachers revealed that one-third of New York City teachers and one-fourth of those elsewhere said they had been assaulted. Forty percent reported that violence is a daily concern.[16]

In 1981, more than one-third (36 percent) of the high school teachers said they would not or "probably" would not go into teaching if they had it to do over again. This is almost twice as many (19 percent) as felt that way in 1976, and almost three times as many (13 percent) as felt that way in 1971.[17]

In sum, the teacher's world is often frustrating, frequently demeaning, and sometimes dangerous. The result for many teachers is a sense of alienation, apathy, and what is now fashionably called "teacher burnout." We propose that the following steps be taken to improve the working conditions of the teacher:

First, we recommend that high school teachers have no more than four formal class meetings. They also should be responsible one period each day for small seminars and for helping students with independent projects.

Second, we recommend that teachers have a minimum of sixty minutes each school day for class preparation. The current catch-as-catch-can "arrangement" is simply not good enough.

Third, teachers should be exempt from routine monitoring of halls and lunch rooms. School clerical staff and parent and student volunteers should assume such noninstructional duties.

Another way to improve the working conditions of the teacher is to improve the intellectual climate of the school. Robert Schaefer, former dean, Teachers College, Columbia University, maintains that the school must be organized as a "center of inquiry," where teachers are "freed to inquire into the nature of what and how they are teaching."[18]

We affirm Schaefer's interest in liberating the creative talents of the teachers. Teachers should feel that innovations in the classroom will be recognized and supported by "the system," that teachers are expected to be not only accountable but creative and imaginative, as well. Good ideas should be rewarded. To achieve this goal, we recommend that a Teacher Excellence Fund be established in every school—a competitive grants program to enable teachers to design and carry out a special professional project. One teacher may plan a weekend seminar with students, another may propose a lecture series for his or her class, still another may want support to prepare a new lesson plan.

This idea has already been successfully introduced by the St. Louis Metropolitan Teacher Center. Mini-grants were given to develop projects, ranging from the production of a slide program on Japanese culture for an Asian history course to the preparation of individualized assignments for students in theater and drama classes. The Director of the St. Louis Teacher Center reports that the mini-grant program also "promotes the professional growth of teachers."[19]

A variety of small moves also can be made to improve the working conditions of teachers—making lounge areas more attractive, ensuring that teachers have adequate supplies, having a Xerox that works, encouraging teachers to get together to discuss professional issues—a step that would help to reduce teacher isolation.

Far more difficult is the issue of teacher safety. At a minimum, every school should have a fair, clearly stated, widely understood code of conduct. In addition, principals and other administrators have an obligation to see that standards of discipline are consistently and fairly enforced throughout the school, that disruptive students are promptly removed from the classroom, and that teachers are supported in the maintenance of discipline.

The issue of safety in the school is a community one, as well. City authorities, law enforcement officials, parents, and citizens all have a role to play in reducing vandalism and crime outside the building and in assuring safe access to the school. Learning cannot occur in a climate of threats, fear, and intimidation.

Improving working conditions is, we believe, at the center of our effort to improve teaching. We cannot expect teachers to exhibit a high degree of professional competence when they are accorded such a low degree of professional treatment in their workaday world. Nor can we expect to attract the best and brightest into teaching when they have had twelve years of opportunity to observe first hand the daily frustrations and petty humiliations that many teachers must endure. As Donna Kerr at the Institute for Advanced Study, Princeton, observes: "There is a disturbing duplicity in a society that itself fails to create the conditions that would foster teaching competence and then complains of incompetent teachers. Our teaching corps can be no more competent than we make it."[20]

Recognition and Rewards

The next way to renew teaching is to give good teachers adequate recognition and rewards. A teacher at Ridgefield High spoke sadly about the lack of recognition:

> You rarely get any thank you—you sometimes do from students. It is a rarity that you get any kind of thank you from the community, superintendent, school board, or administrators. There is no positive reinforcement for anything you do. There are no pats on the back. There's no reward system, no bonuses. You know, it makes me very ill sometimes when you look at somebody who's given 35 years of service to a school district and they leave and they are not recognized for any contribution.[21]

In his 1975 study *Schoolteacher,* Professor Dan Lortie talks about three kinds of rewards for teachers: psychic, extrinsic, and ancillary. Extrinsic rewards are those that take the form of "earnings" of different kinds: financial compensation, to be sure, but also status, prestige, and "power over others." Ancillary rewards include security, spare time, convenient schedules, freedom from rivalry, and a subjective sense that what one is doing is "appropriate" for himself or herself—what we have just described as the working conditions of the teacher.[22]

Psychic rewards come from the satisfaction of reaching students and helping them learn, the chance to work with young people, the opportunity to associate with other teachers, to study, and to read. Three-fourths (76.5 percent) of the teachers in Lortie's sample said "psychic" rewards are most important, and within that category the vast majority (86.1 percent) said "the times I know that I have 'reached' a student or group of students and they have learned" mattered most.[23] As one teacher told us: "My rewards are seeing kids succeed, finally understanding something, or reading a book for the first time; being the play director and getting close to kids; having kids ask me questions."[24]

Today, psychic rewards appear to be harder to come by. Teachers say, for example, that many of today's students "don't like to study anymore," "aren't interested in learning," "won't do homework," "don't seem to care about school."[25] In 1980, 73 percent of senior high school teachers replied that "student attitudes toward learning had a *negative* effect on their job satisfaction."[26]

One teacher complained:

> I'm not receiving the same positive response from my students. In the past, I felt more like a coach to my students, helping them achieve the highest level of skills they're capable of. But I've felt more in an adversarial position recently and I don't know why. It's almost as if they say, "I defy you to teach me." I had one class of students last year with a dozen chronic behavior problems. I dreaded dealing with that class every day. It affected my whole life.[27]

Another complaint we frequently heard was that students are no longer motivated to learn. One teacher with twenty years experience told us:

When you accept the role of being a teacher, your satisfaction comes when you know you've helped and served. Satisfaction in teaching is having a student come back saying, "I learned something." Being around young people is a reward in itself. But those rewards are getting fewer. . . . My major problem is how to motivate students who don't care about themselves. And my biggest frustration is their "what's the difference" attitude. Those who do care seem to be dwindling every year. You know, how many kids ever come back to say "thanks"?[28]

Even more devastating, is the subtle disrespect many adults have for teachers. Teachers told us:

I go places around town collecting items for my various courses and I'm almost embarrassed to say that I'm a teacher. It's people's view of teachers as goof-offs—that they get the summer off—that really hurts.[29]

I work as a meat-cutter in the summer at one of the nearby butcher shops, and I don't usually tell them I'm a teacher. One butcher finally found out that I was a full-time teacher and his comment to me was, "Man, that's a dead-end job. You must be a real dummy."[30]

Weekends I wait on tables at a sandwich shop to make extra money, but I don't tell anyone that I'm a teacher. They talk a lot about the school district and have only negative attitudes toward the schools. When I listen to them, it makes me feel really small to be a teacher.[31]

The time has come to reaffirm the centrality of teaching, to support good teachers and give them the recognition they deserve. Students and parents have the most frequent opportunities for extending such recognition. A student's "thank you" for making a difficult lesson clear, or a complimentary note from home, are simple examples, rendered special by the infrequency with which they occur. Prompt parent responses to teachers' requests for conferences, and public participation in school events also signal community support.

Outstanding teachers can be honored in both formal and informal ways.

Each year Trinity University in San Antonio, Texas, joins with local school districts to select and honor two teachers of the year. The honorees receive a citation, $2,000, and a "thank you" for a job well done. The teacher celebrations in San Antonio are citywide events with civic leaders joining in. These are more than occasions to honor individual teachers, they are also a time to honor public education.

Higher education has a special obligation, too. Several years ago, the Reverend Timothy Healy, S.J., of Georgetown University called fifteen Georgetown students, all graduates of the Bronx High School of Science, into his office. He asked who was the best high school teacher they had had. They agreed on the same person— quite quickly. Next spring, at commencement time, Father Healy said, "I would like to introduce a candidate for an honorary degree. He teaches at Bronx High School of Science. He is one of the great educators who has made Georgetown possible." The audience was deeply moved.

In 1959, an alumnus of Princeton University donated money to honor each year four outstanding teachers in the state of New Jersey. The winners are introduced and given special citations and cash prizes at commencement. Cash awards are also made to the libraries at the schools where the winners teach.

We propose that every college recognize an outstanding teacher every year, selecting perhaps an alumnus who has been an effective teacher in the public schools.

We also recommend that an outstanding teacher be honored annually in every school district, and that—statewide—the governor and the legislature in every state honor an outstanding teacher. Cash awards should be given as a part of such recognition.

Newspapers and other businesses in each community should adopt a teacher recognition program.

In May 1983, the Washington *Post* announced that beginning

in the fall of that year it would make twelve annual awards of $2,000 each to outstanding public school teachers throughout the metropolitan area.[32]

While these public demonstrations of support are significant, in the end, the greatest satisfaction will come as students and their parents convey directly to teachers their appreciation for a job well done.

The Payment of the Teachers

The third step in renewing the profession is improving teacher salaries. A teacher at a midwest high school said, "We are tremendously frustrated with pay. We are college graduates—we are professionals—we receive such a low salary in comparison." Another teacher put the problem in very personal terms:

> Utility bills, house notes, and car notes eat up a teacher's paycheck and you haven't even talked about putting clothes on your back or about doing your grocery shopping or paying doctor bills. So if a lot of us are disenchanted with the teaching profession, it's because we can't live on what we take home. I mean, how can you like what you are doing when it's not taking care of you?[33]

In 1981–82, the average starting salary for teachers with a bachelor's degree was $12,769. When average starting teachers' salaries are compared to starting salaries of other professionals with bachelor's degrees, the contrast is striking. For engineers, it is $22,368, and for computer scientists, $20,364. Equally important is the fact that the percentage increase for teachers since 1973 is lower than for the other professions (Table 14).

The average secondary school teacher salary nationwide was $19,142 in 1981–82. However, this group included clerical as well as professional employees. In addition, for other public employees it was $17,568. However, the percentage increase in salary over a ten-year period was slightly greater for government employees.

**Table 14 Average Starting Salaries of Public School Teachers Compared
with Salaries in Private Industry**

Position/Field	1973–74	1980–81	1981–82	Percent change 1981–82 over 1980–81	Percent change 1981–82 over 1973–74
Average minimum mean salary for teachers with bachelor's degree	$7,720	$11,758	$12,769	8.6	65.4
College graduates with bachelor's degree					
Engineering	$11,220	$20,136	$22,368	11.1	99.3
Accounting	$10,632	$15,720	$16,980	8.0	59.7
Sales-marketing	$9,660	$15,936	$17,220	8.1	78.3
Business admin.	$8,796	$14,100	$16,200	14.9	84.2
Liberal arts	$8,808	$13,296	$15,444	16.2	75.3
Chemistry	$10,308	$17,124	$19,536	14.1	89.5
Math-statistics	$10,020	$17,604	$18,600	5.7	85.6
Economics-finance	$9,624	$14,472	$16,884	16.7	75.4
Computer sciences	N/A	$17,712	$20,364	15.0	N/A
Other fields	$9,696	$17,544	$20,028	14.2	106.6

Source: 1973–74: National Education Association, *Prices, Budgets, Salary and Income* (Washington,
D.C.: National Education Association, February 1981), p. 20; all other data: National Educa-
tion Association, *Prices, Budgets, Salary and Income* (Washington, D.C.: National Education
Association, February 1983), p. 22.

There is great variation in average teachers' salaries from state
to state (Table 15).

By 1982–83 the average salaries for secondary school teachers
had risen to $21,100 from the prior year. Again, however, the na-
tional averages mask state differences. They range from a high of
$34,154 in Alaska to a low of $14,571 in Mississippi (Table 16).

For many teachers moonlighting has become essential.
Throughout the nation, 11.1 percent of teachers admit to holding
jobs after school hours, though many authorities believe the actual
figure to be much higher.[34] In fact, a 1982 survey of Texas teachers
revealed that 29 percent moonlight during the school year (versus
22 percent in 1980). Thirty-six percent hold extra summer jobs,
compared to only 30 percent in 1980. The average pay earned
through moonlighting was $3,189.[35]

Table 15 Average Salaries Paid Full-Time Employees of State and Local Governments Compared with Average Salaries Paid Teachers, 1971–82

State	Government Employees			Teachers		
	1971	1981	% increase	1971–72	1981–82	% increase
Alabama	$6,744	$14,220	110.9	$7,737	$15,600	101.6
Alaska	$13,236	$28,728	117.0	$14,124	$31,924	126.0*
Arizona	$9,072	$19,104	110.6	$9,915	$18,014	81.7
Arkansas	$5,964	$12,936	116.9	$6,843	$14,506	112.0
California	$10,908	$22,428	105.6	$11,417	$22,755	99.3
Colorado	$8,256	$18,504	124.1	$9,264	$19,577	111.3
Connecticut	$9,780	$16,884	72.6	$10,295	$18,880	83.4*
Delaware	$8,172	$16,320	102.2	$10,420	$19,290	85.1
Florida	$7,740	$15,456	99.7	$8,935	$16,780	87.8
Georgia	$6,684	$13,884	107.7	$7,926	$16,363	106.4
Hawaii	$9,432	$10,072	94.8	$10,320	$22,542	118.4*
Idaho	$6,888	$15,252	121.6	$7,392	$10,401	121.9*
Illinois	$9,672	$19,164	98.1	$10,624	$21,020	97.9
Indiana	$7,908	$15,612	97.4	$9,755	$18,622	90.9
Iowa	$8,088	$16,728	106.8	$9,207	$17,989	95.4
Kansas	$7,260	$14,988	106.4	$8,251	$16,712	102.5
Kentucky	$7,152	$15,108	111.2	$7,362	$17,290	134.9*
Louisiana	$6,984	$14,964	114.3	$8,767	$18,500	111.0
Maine	$7,044	$14,400	104.4	$8,545	$15,105	76.8
Maryland	$9,192	$18,504	101.3	$10,463	$21,210	101.9*
Massachusetts	$9,264	$17,280	86.5	$10,176	$18,787	84.6
Michigan	$10,524	$21,480	104.1	$11,620	$22,351	92.3
Minnesota	$9,384	$17,976	91.6	$10,219	$19,907	94.8*
Mississippi	$5,724	$12,420	117.0	$6,530	$14,135	116.5
Missouri	$7,644	$14,448	89.0	$8,688	$16,413	88.9
Montana	$7,620	$16,188	112.4	$8,514	$17,770	108.7
Nebraska	$7,224	$15,492	114.5	$8,454	$16,570	96.0
Nevada	$8,952	$18,696	108.8	$10,200	$20,105	97.1
New Hampshire	$7,560	$14,424	90.8	$8,453	$14,701	73.9
New Jersey	$9,564	$18,276	91.1	$10,725	$19,910	85.6
New Mexico	$7,188	$15,432	114.7	$8,238	$18,690	126.9*
New York	$10,404	$20,088	93.1	$11,830	$23,437	98.1*
North Carolina	$7,968	$14,784	85.5	$8,593	$16,947	97.2*
North Dakota	$7,452	$18,360	146.4	$7,587	$17,686	133.1
Ohio	$8,412	$16,548	97.1	$8,772	$18,550	111.5*
Oklahoma	$6,828	$14,292	109.3	$7,647	$16,210	112.0*
Oregon	$8,844	$18,540	109.6	$9,485	$20,305	114.1*
Pennsylvania	$8,484	$17,400	105.1	$9,903	$19,482	96.7
Rhode Island	$8,448	$18,720	121.6	$9,910	$21,659	118.6

Table 15   Average Salaries Paid Full-Time Employees of State and Local Governments Compared with Average Salaries Paid Teachers, 1971–82
(continued)

State	Government Employees			Teachers		
	1971	1981	% increase	1971–72	1981–82	% increase
South Carolina	$6,528	$14,304	119.1	$7,355	$15,170	106.3
South Dakota	$6,888	$14,124	105.1	$7,678	$14,717	91.7
Tennessee	$6,780	$14,664	116.3	$7,990	$16,285	103.8
Texas	$7,164	$15,984	123.1	$8,472	$17,582	107.5
Utah	$7,896	$16,476	108.7	$8,460	$18,152	114.6*
Vermont	$8,040	$14,844	84.6	$8,462	$14,715	73.9
Virginia	$7,656	$15,876	107.4	$9,084	$17,008	87.2
Washington	$9,396	$20,700	120.3	$10,175	$22,954	125.6*
West Virginia	$6,888	$14,472	110.1	$8,103	$17,129	111.4*
Wisconsin	$9,204	$18,360	99.5	$10,016	$19,387	93.6
Wyoming	$7,368	$18,300	148.4	$9,234	$21,249	130.1
United States	$8,760	$17,568	100.5	$9,705	$19,142	97.2

*Percentage increase in salary from 1971 to 1981 higher for teachers than for these state and local government employees.

Source: National Education Association, Prices, Budgets, Salary and Income (Washington, D.C.: National Education Association, February 1983), p. 18.

Selling tickets, mowing lawns, babysitting, and waiting tables are the kinds of work they do. And 68 percent of the teachers surveyed said the outside work interfered with their teaching. The phenomenon of moonlighting was nicely captured in a recent cartoon that pictured two young people looking at a street vendor selling fruit. One said, "Why don't you buy an apple for your teacher?" The other replied, "That *is* my teacher."[36]

Our society pays for what it values. Unless teacher salaries become more commensurate with those of other professions, teacher status cannot be raised; able students cannot be recruited. Therefore, we urge that, as a national goal, salary averages for teachers be increased by at least 25 percent beyond the rate of inflation over the next three years, with immediate entry-level increases.

Most school systems increase a teacher's salary when he or she gets a graduate degree or earns more college credits. However, very

Table 16   Public Elementary-Secondary Teachers' Salaries

	1972–73		1982–83		Percent change Elem.	Percent change Sec.
	Elem.	Sec.	Elem.	Sec.		
50 States and D.C.	$9,823	$10,460	$20,042	$21,100	104.0	101.7
Alabama	$8,024	$8,184	$17,400	$18,000	116.8	119.9
Alaska	$14,549	$14,409	$33,784	$34,154*	132.2	137.0
Arizona	$10,155	$11,160	$18,637	$19,318	83.5	73.1†
Arkansas	$7,209	$7,508	$14,789	$15,548	105.1	107.1
California	$11,360	$12,350	$23,240	$24,538	104.6	98.7†
Colorado	$9,589	$9,963	$20,267	$21,453	111.4	115.3
Connecticut	$10,300	$11,000	$20,700	$20,800	101.0	89.1†
Delaware	$10,430	$10,770	$20,062	$21,166	92.3	96.5
District of Columbia	N/A	N/A	$26,068	$26,021	—	—
Florida	$9,100	$9,400	$18,720	$18,124	105.7	92.8†
Georgia	$7,910	$8,613	$17,111	$17,847	116.2	107.2†
Hawaii	$10,660	$10,750	$25,335	$24,024	137.7	123.4†
Idaho	$7,491	$7,803	$16,892	$18,255	125.5	133.9
Illinois	$10,700	$11,865	$21,747	$24,242	103.2	104.3
Indiana	$9,600	$10,120	$19,657	$20,483	104.8	102.4†
Iowa	$9,101	$10,213	$17,978	$19,361	97.5	89.6†
Kansas	$8,329	$8,669	$18,213	$18,385	118.7	112.1†
Kentucky	$7,660	$8,075	$17,850	$19,150	133.0	137.2
Louisiana	$8,933	$9,297	$18,810	$19,690	110.6	111.8
Maine	$8,699	$9,424	$15,288	$16,604	75.7	76.2
Maryland	$10,910	$11,417	$21,780	$23,142	99.6	102.7
Massachusetts	$10,440	$10,600	$18,781	$19,165	79.9	80.8
Michigan	$11,600	$12,200	$23,732	$24,217	104.6	98.5
Minnesota	$9,789	$11,231	$21,450	$23,068	119.4	105.4
Mississippi	$6,787	$7,100	$14,049	$14,571	107.0	105.2†
Missouri	$8,917	$9,271	$17,268	$18,173	93.7	96.0
Montana	$8,461	$9,696	$18,786	$20,314	122.0	105.5†
Nebraska	$8,200	$9,300	$16,650	$18,173	103.0	95.4†
Nevada	$10,721	$11,030	$20,585	$21,306	92.0	93.2
New Hampshire	$8,890	$9,238	$15,250	$15,471	71.5	67.5†
New Jersey	$11,050	$11,460	$21,244	$22,175	92.3	93.5
New Mexico	$8,368	$8,537	$20,290	$21,000	142.5	146.0
New York	$12,040	$12,700	$24,300	$25,700	101.8	102.4
North Carolina	$8,877	$9,454	$17,847	$17,754*	101.0	91.1†
North Dakota	$7,762	$8,664	$17,680	$19,110	127.8	120.6†
Ohio	$9,100	$9,650	$19,850	$21,020	118.1	117.8†
Oklahoma	$7,750	$8,000	$17,660	$18,600	127.9	132.5
Oregon	$9,412	$9,720	$21,872	$23,136	132.4	138.0

Table 16 Public Elementary-Secondary Teachers' Salaries *(continued)*

	1972–73		1982–83		Percent change Elem.	Percent change Sec.
	Elem.	Sec.	Elem.	Sec.		
Pennsylvania	$10,400	$10,800	$20,500	$21,300	97.1	97.2
Rhode Island	$10,200	$10,498	$24,070	$22,154*	136.0	111.0†
South Carolina	$7,890	$8,175	$15,890	$17,040	101.4	108.4
South Dakota	$7,638	$8,253	$15,386	$15,988	101.4	93.7†
Tennessee	$8,040	$8,700	$17,369	$17,517	116.0	101.3†
Texas	$8,735	$8,735	$19,000	$20,100	117.5	130.1
Utah	$8,500	$8,610	$19,078	$20,615	124.4	139.4
Vermont	$8,380	$8,890	$14,877	$15,778	113.3	77.5†
Virginia	$9,268	$10,033	$18,020	$19,655	94.2	95.9
Washington	$10,215	$10,988	$22,977	$23,923	124.9	117.7†
West Virginia	$7,968	$8,430	$17,290	$17,479	117.0	107.2
Wisconsin	$10,130	$10,737	$20,480	$21,470	102.2	100.0†
Wyoming	$9,300	$9,700	$22,740	$24,293	144.5	150.4

*Secondary school teachers' salaries less than those of elementary school teachers in these states.

†Secondary school teachers' salaries increased less than those of elementary school teachers from 1972–73 to 1982–83 in these states.

Source: National Education Association, *Estimates of School Statistics* 1982–1983 (Washington, D.C.: National Education Association, January 1983), p. 35; and National Education Association, *Estimates of School Statistics,* 1972–73 (Washington, D.C.: National Education Association, 1973), p. 31.

few provide for sabbaticals, study leaves, or exchanges with other schools, much less for opportunities to spend a semester or a year gaining new perspective and breadth by doing something altogether different.

Many conscientious teachers manage to find time during evenings, weekends, and vacations to read professional journals, attend conferences, and otherwise try to keep up. But the sad fact is that such activities often compete for time with daily classroom responsibilities and with the teacher's need to augment his or her income with outside employment.

We propose that a two-week Teacher Professional Development Term be added to the school year, with appropriate compensation. This would be a time for study, a period to improve instruction, and an opportunity to expand knowledge. The planning of such a term should be largely controlled by teachers at the school or district level. Local colleges should be actively involved.

We recommend that every five years teachers be eligible to receive a special contract with extra pay to match to support a Summer Study Term. To qualify and to compete for this extended contract, each teacher would prepare a study plan. Such a plan would be subject to review and approval both by peer panels and by the school and district administrations.

Finally, we propose that every school establish a Teacher Travel Fund. An informal survey of selected math and science teachers on Long Island revealed that their most urgent need was not higher salaries but contact with colleagues in their profession.[37] Most high schools provide no money to help teachers work on professional projects and no funds for sending teachers to regional or state or national conferences or for bringing scholar-colleagues to the school. The fund we propose would make it possible for teachers, based on competitive application, to travel occasionally to keep current in their fields—a practice that is commonplace and expected in other professions.

Recruiting Teachers

We now turn to the issue of the recruitment of new teachers. We cannot hope to attract good candidates into teaching until conditions change. We are convinced, however, that as working conditions improve—from more recognition and better pay to continuing education—the nation's classrooms will become more attractive to outstanding students.

Teaching has never been a haven for the most gifted students. Fifty years ago, an examination revealed that the standardized test scores of students in education were lower than those of most other majors.[38] Twenty years ago almost half a million male college students took the Selective Service College Qualification Test; education majors scored the lowest.[39] Nearly thirty years ago James

Koerner concluded from his study of teacher education that, by about any academic standard that can be applied, students in teacher training programs are among the least able on the campus. . . .[40]

Even today, those who enter teaching come from the lower half of their college classes. From 1972 to 1982, SAT verbal scores for high school seniors planning to become education majors dropped steadily from 418 to 394—a loss of 24 points. SAT math scores during this period fell from 449 to 419—a 30 point drop.[41] (The comparable national averages: verbal scores dropped from 453 in 1972 to 426 in 1982, a 27 point slide; math scores declined from 484 in 1972 to 467 in 1980, a 17 point drop.)[42]

Recently, teacher education students scored lowest of all college students in an examination of international literacy.[43] Further, of nineteen fields of study reported by the American College Testing Program, education students were in seventeenth place in math scores, and fourteenth place in English.[44]

Not only do poor students enter the profession, but those who leave teaching often are the ones the school can least afford to lose. A study of Wisconsin high school graduates who became teachers revealed that 40 percent had left teaching after five years. Based on ability grouping, 72.9 percent of the low ability students were still in teaching compared to only 59 percent of the most able students.[45]

We cannot adequately prepare the coming generation if the least able students enter the profession. Teaching must become a top priority and gifted students must be recruited.

The process should begin in high school. Some years ago, when teachers were in short supply, schools frequently organized clubs and activities for students interested in teaching. In recent years such activity has declined. We recommend that every high school establish a "cadet" teacher program. High school teachers should identify gifted students and make opportunities for them to present information to classmates, tutor students needing special help, and meet with outstanding school and college teachers. For a young person to be told by a respected adult that he or she could be a great teacher may well have a profound impact on the career choice of that student.

The Houston School District is developing a magnet school for prospective teachers—a place where high school students interested in teaching as a career can get a "feel" for the profession. While students at the magnet school will complete a solid academic program, they also can do classroom observation and have the opportunity to work with outstanding college teachers.

Further, recruiting teachers means involving higher education too. There is at many colleges a shocking bias against preparing students to teach in public schools. While administrators and professors complain loudly about precollege education, they often fail to recognize that the problem frequently begins at home. Professors who work with schools are not rewarded and students who want to teach are often told that this would be a big mistake.

At one prestigious Ivy League university, a student interested in teaching said: "We are under tremendous pressure all around to constantly justify our choice of a career. Professors want to know why we are taking this course, and most of the other students think we are crazy. There is no money in teaching, especially in a public school."

There is, quite frankly, a lot of hypocrisy at work when colleges call for "excellence in the school" while spending several hundred million dollars every year recruiting athletes and spending virtually no time or money recruiting prospective teachers. To correct this curious imbalance, we suggest that the nation's colleges and universities consider giving full-tuition scholarships to the top 5 percent of their gifted students who plan to teach in public education. Such scholarships would begin when students are admitted to the teacher preparation program at the beginning of the junior year.

If higher education leaders wish to be part of the solution—rather than the problem—they must speak with conviction about the significance and the dignity of teaching and become actively involved at the local level in support of public schools.

There is a federal role as well. In 1957, the federal government approved an emergency scholarship program to recruit teachers in science and mathematics. In 1972, Congress established the National Health Service Corps to improve health care in areas with a shortage of medical personnel. For those in the program, federally funded scholarships were provided.[46]

Today, there is a national crisis in teaching, one that calls for a national response. Specifically, we propose a National Teacher Service, especially for teachers in science and mathematics, that would enable young people to enlist in the cause of education as they might enlist in the military or join the Peace Corps. This would be a publicly funded tuition scholarship program for students in the top third of their high school graduating classes. Those admitted to the National Teacher Service would be expected to complete successfully an academic program and teach a minimum of three years in the public schools.

The Schooling of the Teacher

Recruiting able students is only the beginning. The next step is to teach prospective teachers well.

Today's high school teachers have had much formal education —nearly six out of ten have earned master's degrees or more—but many complain bitterly about their education. One teacher's reaction was typical:

> Some of the courses were interesting. But none of them really prepared me for that first day or even that first year. You walk into class and you're suddenly facing forty teenagers, and it's a sink or swim situation. That's when I really began to learn to teach. Some of the other teachers gave me pointers. But mainly I was on my own. I've learned a lot in ten years about teaching, but it was on-the-job training. I won't say teacher education is a total waste of time, but it wasn't much help either.[47]

The schooling of teachers must improve. We propose the following five-step program:

First, during the first two years of college, all prospective teachers should complete a core of common learning, one that parallels, in broad outline, the high school core curriculum proposed in Chapter 7 of this report. Liberal arts departments on the campus bear a heavy responsibility in preparing teachers who will be broadly educated and well equipped to teach. Non-education professors often forget that three-fourths of a prospective teacher's time is spent, not in education, but in the school of arts and sciences.

Second, all teacher candidates should be carefully selected. Formal admission to teacher education should occur at the beginning of the junior year when students begin a three-year teacher preparation sequence, and only students who have a cumulative college grade point average of 3.0 (B) or better and who have strong supportive recommendations from two professors who taught them in required courses should be admitted.

Third, once admitted to the program, the teacher candidate should devote the junior and senior years primarily to the completion of a major in an academic discipline and classroom observation. Sadly, high school teachers often are not well prepared in the subjects they plan to teach and many of the so-called academic majors are soft programs that have no depth. In 1981, half of the new teachers employed to teach mathematics and science in high schools were uncertified to teach in those subjects.[48] In Maryland, it is possible to become a history teacher with only six semester hours of American history.[49] Simply stated, prospective teachers should major in an academic subject, not in education.

Fourth, after grounding in the core curriculum and a solid academic major, every prospective teacher should have a "fifth year" of instructional and apprenticeship experience. This year would include a core of courses to meet the special needs of teachers. While many speak disparagingly of teacher education courses, we conclude there is important information uniquely relevant to teachers. The following four-course sequence is proposed.

- The first: *Schooling in America.* All teachers should be well informed about the roots of education in the nation, how the public schools began, how they grew, and how their mission was expanded. Prospective teachers should be informed as well about current issues confronting public education.

- The second: *Learning Theory and Research.* All teacher education students should study theories of learning, the ways teachers teach and students learn, and examine also the findings of current psychological and physiological research bearing on these themes.

- The third: *The Teaching of Writing.* This report gives high priority to language. Writing is an essential skill for self-expression and the means by which critical thinking also will be taught. Every teacher should be prepared to help students write better. The skills involved in the teaching of writing should be well understood by all teachers.

- The fourth: *The Use of Technology.* In Chapter 11, we discuss the significance of technology, how classroom instruction can be enormously enriched by the electronic teachers. For this potential to be fulfilled, however, teachers must learn more about the possibilities and the limits of the new teaching tools. A course on technology and education—including the use of computers—should be required of every prospective teacher.

The fifth year also should include classroom observation and teaching experience. This is the best way, we believe, to learn about students, and teaching too. Such experience does not mean sending new teachers into the classroom with a group of children, closing the door, crossing fingers, and hoping all goes well. Teachers often learn the hard way, to be sure, but working closely with senior teachers is absolutely crucial. Indeed, we suggest assigning prospective teachers to a "teacher team," even as a prospective doctor, during residency, is assigned to a medical team. In this way the student would have occasion to work closely with more experienced teachers skilled in different methods of instruction.

An additional activity for the fifth year of teacher education would be a series of one-day Common Learning Seminars in which students would meet outstanding arts and science scholar-teachers who would relate the knowledge of their fields to a contemporary political or social theme. The goal would be to help prospective teachers move across the disciplines, and better prepare themselves to teach the core of common learning to students in the schools. A minimum of six such seminars is proposed (Table 17).

Across the country, state legislatures, colleges and universities, and professional organizations are now revising teacher preparation programs. In Florida, teacher education students must have a composite score of 835 on the SAT or 17 on the ACT, and they must pass competency-based tests prior to graduation if they wish to obtain regular certification.[50] Also, full certification is not granted until the satisfactory completion of one year of school teaching.

Glassboro State College in New Jersey, along with many other colleges in the nation, now requires a 3.0 average in specific subject matter and a 2.5 average overall to get into the education program and to earn a certificate for teaching.[51]

In 1981, the Oklahoma legislature enacted a teacher education bill to raise standards for admission to colleges of education, to

Table 17   A Proposed Program for Teacher Preparation

Freshman-Sophomore Years	Junior-Senior Years	Fifth Year
A core curriculum	Admission to teacher education program on basis of B average and faculty recommendations	Classroom observation and teaching experience
	Academic major	Professional career courses Schooling in America Learning Theory & Research The Teaching of Writing The Use of Technology
	Classroom observation	Certification

require competency examinations in subject areas before graduation, to mandate an entry-year internship before certification, to monitor the performance of beginning teachers, and to require continuing education for teachers.[52]

In South Carolina, an "Educator Improvement Act" establishes an entrance-to-exit system to strengthen the training, employment, and evaluation of public educators.[53] And in 1978 the New Jersey Legislature established a commission to study the quality of teacher education programs.[54] The commission recommended that nearly half of the program for all education students should be in general education, distributed among arts, humanities, mathematics, and the natural, social, and technological sciences. The commission further recommended that every student be required to major in an academic discipline and that every prospective teacher take courses in the behavioral and social sciences.[55]

For years there has been a lively debate over how teachers should be prepared. The program proposed in this report is only one approach. We are convinced, however, that bold new reforms must be introduced if students are to be equipped adequately to teach the coming generation.

The Continuing Education of the Teacher

The next important way to strengthen teaching is to improve the continuing education of the teacher. Some teachers may be able to fit a program of continued education in around the edges, but we believe that a planned program should be a part of every teacher's professional life.

Schools currently provide an average of five or six "professional days" each year—occasions when teachers attend workshops and other professional meetings.

Unfortunately, "in-service training" is seldom more than an occasional day-long workshop in which teachers are lectured to by "experts." Too often, these authorities are long on process, short on substance, and know little about the classroom. Here is what one teacher had to say:

> Most teachers think workshops are a waste of time. . . . The actual intellectual curiosity of learning is gone out of so many people. It's partially because they have gone to so many workshops that are so useless. . . . They often take education courses at the nearby state university where the instructors are ex-principals and superintendents who are not such good teachers and haven't done much research. I took a course in supervision last year at the nearby state university taught by an ex-principal. He literally taught out of the textbook. He stood in front of the classroom and read the textbook with us.[56]

At local schools, staff development programs are often nonexistent, and programs frequently are weak. The time has come to recognize that continuing education must be an essential part of the professional life of every teacher. Every district should adopt a realistic continuing-education policy, one that serves all teachers and includes programs such as those earlier proposed. Excellence in education will be achieved only as we invest in the education of teachers in the classroom.

A Career Path for the Teacher

Two of the most troublesome aspects of the teaching profession are the lack of a career ladder and the leveling off of salaries. The irony is that to "get ahead" in teaching you must leave it. The notion seems to be that, if you are good, you will move out of the classroom and become a school counselor or principal—or a football coach. The lack of opportunity for advancement in teaching is in sharp contrast to other professions, where outstanding performance is rewarded.

Good teachers must be recognized and moved forward within the profession, not outside it. And salary increases should follow such recognition. Our proposals for structuring the teaching ca-

reer provide for such advancement at predictable stages of experience.

The career ladder we offer begins upon completion of the five-
year teacher preparation program. At this point, the prospective
teacher would be considered eligible to apply to a state teacher
licensure board for credentials. In most states, today, students who
complete a teacher preparation program and graduate from college
can get credentials from the State Education Agency. No further
step is required. Those who educate prospective teachers also control credentialing.

We propose that credentialing be separate after college preparation. To qualify for credentials, each candidate would submit written recommendations from a member of the faculty in his or her
academic major; a member of the faculty in his or her education
sequence; and a teacher who has supervised his or her school internship.

Before being credentialed, the candidate would also pass a written examinations in English proficiency and subject matter competence administered by a Board of Teacher Licensure to be established in every state. We would urge that the majority membership
on such boards be comprised of senior classroom teachers.

Once credentialed, a candidate would become an *associate
teacher.* For two years this teacher would work under the mentor-
ship of senior teachers. He or she would have a full teaching load.
During this time, however, there would be continuous assessment
and counseling by senior teachers to screen out individuals whose
performance is inadequate.

After two years, a candidate's performance would be more formally reviewed. The evaluation of the teacher would be based upon
testimony of the mentor, the written record, and testimony of other
school personnel, including students. Direct observations would be
crucial. Equally important are character, motivation, and, most especially, success in the classroom. If the review is favorable, the
associate teacher would be given full *teacher* status.

Table 18 Teacher Certification Process, by State: 1983

State	Approved Degree Program		In-State Graduates					Out-of-State Graduates								Fee
	Yes	No	Recommendation	Recommendation plus Transcript	State Exam	National Teacher Examination	Other	Transcript Evaluation	Evaluation plus Recommendation	Interstate Reciprocity Agreement	NCATE Program Approval	Equivalent Certificate	State Examination	National Teacher Examination	Other	
Alabama	X		X		X		X	X		X	X					$10
Alaska	X		X					X	X	X						$30
Arizona	X		X					X								$10
Arkansas*																
California	X		X					X	X	X				X		$40
Colorado	X			X				X								$15
Connecticut	X			X				X	X	X						$15
Delaware	X		X							X						
Florida	X			X				X	X	X						$12
Georgia	X											X				
Hawaii		X														
Idaho	X			X				X								$20
Illinois	X		X					X								$20
Indiana	X			X				X		X	X					$ 5
Iowa	X			X				X	X			X				$15
Kansas	X		X					X								$13
Kentucky	X		X					X	X	X	X					None
Louisiana	X							X	X		X				X	None
Maine	X		X					X		X						None
Maryland	X		X					X		X	X	X				$10
Massachusetts	X			X				X		X						$10
Michigan	X		X					X	X	X	X					None
Minnesota	X			X				X								$35
Mississippi	X		X					X								None
Missouri		X	X					X								
Montana	X		X					X	X	X						$20
Nebraska	X		X	X				X	X				X	X		$25
Nevada		X						X								$30
New Hampshire*																
New Jersey	X		X					X		X						$20
New Mexico	X		X	X				X								
New York	X		X					X		X						$10
North Carolina	X					X				X					X	$20
North Dakota	X		X							X						$ 5
Ohio	X		X	X						X						$ 2
Oklahoma		X	X	X	X			X	X							
Oregon	X		X							X						$25

TEACHERS: RENEWING THE PROFESSION / 181

Table 18   Teacher Certification Process, by State: 1983 (continued)

State	Approved Degree Program		In-State Graduates					Out-of-State Graduates								Fee
	Yes	No	Recommendation	Recommendation plus Transcript	State Exam	National Teacher Examination	Other	Transcript Evaluation	Evaluation plus Recommendation	Interstate Reciprocity Agreement	NCATE Program Approval	Equivalent Certificate	State Examination	National Teacher Examination	Other	
Pennsylvania	X		X					X		X						$15
Rhode Island*																
South Carolina*																
South Dakota	X		X					X	X	X						$10
Tennessee	X			X				X	X		X	X				$ 2
Texas	X		X							X						$17
Utah	X			X							X					$10
Vermont	X		X								X					$10
Virginia	X			X								X				
Washington	X			X				X		X						$15
West Virginia*																
Wisconsin	X		X					X								$30
Wyoming	X			X				X							X	

*States did not respond to survey.

Source: Data survey, Feistritzer Associates.

Moving to regular teacher status is a critically important step. Here is where poor teachers should be weeded out. This is the point where tenure would begin.

After at least three years of service and careful assessment by a master teachers panel, the rank of *senior teacher* could be achieved. Those not so designated would continue to hold the rank of teacher. Those advanced to senior teacher status would not only teach, they would also serve as "mentors" to associate teachers.

With each new professional rank, major salary increases should be provided. Such increases would be in addition to cost-of-living and merit pay earned within the ranks.

The notion of *senior teacher* has advocates and critics too. Those promoting the idea agree that outstanding teachers must be re-

Table 19 Proposed Career Ladder for Teachers

	Rank	Requirements
Step 1	Certification of eligibility	Completion of teacher education program
Step 2	Associate teacher	Credential granted by State Licensure Board on the basis of examination, faculty recommendations, academic record
Step 3	Teacher	State credential; three years as associate teacher, recommendation of review board including experienced teachers
Step 4	Senior teacher	State credential; three years as teacher; recommendation of review board including senior teachers

warded. Those opposed worry that such a program will be politicized—that benefits will be awarded for reasons other than good teaching. Such danger is real; however, we are convinced they would be reduced if effective and fair peer review procedures are introduced to protect the professional integrity of the program.

In summary, we urge that a clear career path for teachers be established and that the shaping and oversight of this program be controlled by teachers. Well administered, such a program would bring health to the profession, confidence to the public, and excellence to the classroom.

Part-time Practitioners

Finally, we suggest that outstanding professionals be recruited to teach part time in the nation's classrooms. Such teachers could serve in those fields where shortages exist and provide enrichment in other fields, as well.

Recently, differential pay scales have been proposed so that teachers in high-demand fields such as math and science could be kept in teaching. We reject this arrangement. Schools should resist practices that place certain teachers in a privileged position, not on the basis of performance, but on the basis of the subject taught. Further, today's shortage may be tomorrow's surplus.

Still, the dearth of good math and science teachers has reached crisis proportions. These shortages cannot be ignored. New patterns of employment must be explored. There is a vast reservoir of potential teaching talent outside the schools in these fields, professionals who, we believe, would be available on a temporary basis.

To tap this talent we recommend that school districts establish a lectureship program to permit highly qualified professionals to teach on a part-time basis. Such teachers would devote most of their time to their regular jobs—in business or government or law or medicine—while they also contribute significantly to education.

Second, school districts should look to recently retired college professors and business and industry personnel for persons who, with brief orientation, could teach part time in high-demand subjects.

Third, we recommend that school districts enter into partnerships with business and industry to form joint appointments. In this way, two-member teacher teams could be created. One member of the team might teach in school for a year or two while the other works at a nonschool job. Then the cycle should be reversed.

We also propose in-and-out teaching terms, permitting a professional to teach for one to three years, step out, and then return for another one-to-three-year term. This strategy is especially appropriate for those who may have special family obligations, as well as those who are in fields of high demand.

Finally, we urge that teacher certification be modified to make possible the issuance of part-time practitioner credentials to put in place the recommendations we propose.

While vigorously supporting a highly paid, fully professional teacher corps, we believe the time has come to enrich the school teaching force with outstanding professionals who serve part time. There are risks involved in such arrangements, but the potential benefits outweigh the perils.

We cannot expect students to shine unless we brighten the prospects for teachers. While far too many first-rate teachers have left the profession, many more remain. Our recommendations are aimed at keeping outstanding teachers in the classroom and attracting into teaching young persons worthy to be their successors. Given present conditions, these goals may appear to be unreal. But conditions can be altered. This is the time for the reform and renewal of the teaching profession. The nation cannot afford to let this special moment pass

We offer our recommendations with the conviction that teachers are professionals. If reforms such as those we have outlined were put in place, teachers would, we believe, *be regarded* as professionals, they would *be treated* as professionals, and they would *consider themselves* professionals. Above all, they would be better teachers and the quality of the school would be enhanced.

Everything we know about teachers suggests that they are able and willing to meet the challenges of rebuilding the profession. But they need tools and backing to do the job.

11

TECHNOLOGY: EXTENDING
THE TEACHER'S REACH

An important landmark was reached in 1982. That was the year *Time* magazine named, not a man of the year, but the computer "Machine of the Year."[1]

There was a time when communication was possible only in the present, when sounds were traded face to face, when messages were fleeting, and when only through memory could ideas be preserved.

Somewhere in the early dawn of history we had a revolution. First through squiggles of art on the walls of caves, and later through scratches on stones and on parchment, meanings could be vicariously experienced. Man's feelings and ideas could be passed along to someone else at a later time in a different place. This was the first revolution in communication: the invention of a visual, widely understood symbol system that could endure.

The second communication revolution began about five hundred years ago in Germany. The name Gutenberg has, quite rightly, acquired a monumental importance in our history. His invention of movable type gave birth to the age of mass communication, as it permitted multiple copies of written words to be transmitted to other places and to succeeding generations.

In 1844, the third communication revolution was ushered in by Samuel Morse's message "What hath God wrought!" The telegraph magnetically transmitted signals over great distances at great speed.

For the first time, the sending of messages was no longer constrained by the speed of man.

Now we are living in a new information age. Glossy full-page ads describe computers as the new electronic teachers and Congress has debated the value of giving an Apple to every teacher. The micro-millennium, as it has been called, touches every sector of our lives. Digital watches, hand-held calculators, microwave ovens, telephones, and miniature TV all depend upon the power of the silicon chip—a minute integrated circuit etched onto a fleck of silicon that controls the flow of "bits" of information.

Educators with long memories will say, "Here we go again." They recall that virtually every new piece of hardware introduced into the schools in the past three decades has been oversold, misused, and eventually discarded. "Technology breakthroughs" still fill school storerooms. They gather dust, unused after twenty years or more.

In the early 1950s, the so-called "teaching machines" were heralded as the miracle cure for education. These devices, educators were told, were the most important invention since the printing press. A stunning new world of learning was just around the corner. In 1966, a Stanford professor wrote that "one can predict that in a few more years millions of school children will have access to what Philip of Macedon's son Alexander enjoyed as a royal prerogative: the personal services of a tutor as well-informed and responsive as Aristotle."[2]

Teachers reacted with suspicion. The machines, they said, would dehumanize the classroom. As it turned out, their suspicions were well placed. Teaching machine materials were afflicted with a kind of behaviorist-industrial jargon—such as operant conditioning, contiguous association, and multimedia packages—that seemed strikingly out of place in the school. The miracle came and went.

Educational television of the 1950s fared little better. Foundations invested large sums of money in experimental programs. The entire school district of Hagerstown, Maryland, was wired for closed-circuit production and transmission of televised lessons by outstanding teachers. The novelty made an audible splash among the education-minded public, but students and teachers were less enthusiastic.

In one curious experiment known as the Midwest Airborne Television Project, a four-engined aircraft was kept circling (weather permitting) over a six-state area while transmitting televised lessons into the classrooms below. Cynics responded by referring to the experiment as "educational crop dusting," a term that aptly condensed the idea's fundamental flaws.

Some years later, Alvin Eurich, an early supporter of instructional television as director of the Ford Foundation's education program, wrote: "After a decade and more of intensive effort and the expenditure of hundreds of millions of dollars, television has *not* made a decisive impact on schools and colleges in this country."[3]

Then there was the talking typewriter—an early computerized device developed by O. M. K. Moore—that spelled out, in sound as well as type, the letters hit by children. The machine presumably taught them to read and write in a new and painless way. The few experimental models soon were discarded.

Another technological advance, language laboratories, were catapulted into classrooms after *Sputnik*. These electronic carrels were installed in schools from coast to coast, often with federal dollars. Frequently, they stood unused while students recited lessons to their teachers.

Perhaps the only tool that caught on was the overhead projector —a simple, manageable little box used to throw an image on the wall for the whole class to see.

Today, another technological tidal wave is sweeping over education. Computers are now in. The floppy disk has become the badge of progress. And no school district that wants to be "with it" can afford *not* to have at least one computer in each school. Educators seem confused about precisely what the new miracle machines will do. But the mood appears to be "Buy now, plan later."

A survey completed several years ago found that slightly more than one in every three public schools had at least one microcomputer or computer terminal available for instructional use by students.[4] Since then, school use of computers has been increasing at a dramatic rate.

Still, school use of computers is spotty and uneven. Math classes use computers more than other classes, and male students use them more than females. Further, while schools are eagerly acquiring computers, there are substantially fewer computers in schools that serve children from poor families than in schools serving more affluent households. A 1982 survey of public school districts concluded, "Schools with higher proportions of poverty level families are less likely . . . to use microcomputers than are the wealthiest schools." Although poorer school districts have increased the proportion of schools with microcomputers (12 percent to 18 percent), they are losing ground to the wealthier districts. In 1981 the percent difference between the wealthiest and poorest school districts with instructional computers was nearly 18 percent. A year later the gap had grown to slightly less than 26 percent.[5]

This last finding is particularly disturbing. It supports the claims of those who fear that the computer revolution in the schools may bypass disadvantaged students. Children of the well-to-do will have access to the new information channels while children from poor homes that do not have the latest personal computers, video recorders, and the like will remain information poor. They will fall further behind in the struggle for equal opportunity.

We found such inequities in our school visits. One beleaguered principal told us, "The first thing you have to remember is that we work in a business that is bankrupt. Look at the clocks. Nearly all of them tell a different time because we have no money to fix them." Talk of a technological revolution here would be almost laughable if it were not so sad. At this school, time has stopped. There is one small computer. The school does not have money for computer printouts, so both sides of the paper are used. Half the class must share a few terminals while the other half work on programming, and the teacher, quite literally, runs from one group to the other.[6]

On the other hand, DeSoto High School, a more affluent institution of eleven hundred students, has perhaps one of the most sophisticated administrative computer services in the country. There are eleven different printout reports on each student, from family background to class schedules, supported by a full-time data processor.[7]

While the administrative use of the computer has made its way into schools like DeSoto High, instructional uses of the new technology still involve relatively few students even in more affluent high schools. The staff of the National Science Foundation concluded in a 1982 report to Congress:

> There is, as yet, little evidence that the modern electronics revolution has had much impact on the formal educational system. . . . Realizing the full potential of those technologies in the classroom would necessitate a considerable restructuring . . . of educational strategies and methods.[8]

Technology and Its Content

Looking back, we can see that technology revolutions have come and gone in part because the hardware has been better than the content. Consider instructional television. Programs of twenty years ago were little more than "talking heads" that offered the worst features of classroom teaching and none of the excitement of the new medium. Little wonder teachers, students, and then the tube were turned off. *Sesame Street*, which so captured the eyes and ears of preschoolers, was one of the few exciting experiments that endured because the presentation was imaginative and because the content was substantial.

Sesame Street was the exception. A 1979 report found that school use of television was hampered by a paucity of high-quality programs and by outdated equipment—61 percent of the television sets in classroom use still were black-and-white.[9]

Once again, we have technology with little school-related content. Computer companies are aggressively marketing hardware and even giving sophisticated equipment to the schools while failing to help educate the teachers and failing to prepare first-rate material linked to school curricula or objectives.

Bonnie Brownstein, vice chairman of the educational advisory panel to the New York Academy of Sciences, criticizes much of the existing software for its failure to encourage original thinking. "You just buy a package," she said. "It's so controlled and organized that you don't have to use your own mind."[10]

Karen Sheingold, of the Bank Street College of Education, has added the criticism that computer-based instruction is often not related to the curriculum in the schools,[11] a point of view supported by a U.S. Department of Education study:

> Teachers want materials that will give students expanded practice for skill mastery and they want software that can give them more time to meet their students' instructional needs—literally to "free-up" time for teaching. But one only has to look at a sampling of these activities to raise questions about the content, the pedagogical approach, the formats, and even the errors in some of the programs that are being used. . . . We have a lot to learn.[12]

These warnings are not from people opposed to computers in the schools. On the contrary, they come from those who share the belief that, properly used, this new technology can help, even revolutionize, education. The point is, however, that all too much of today's computer instructional material resembles a book cover without pages. The technology is available—and increasingly affordable—but educational content that makes the investment worthwhile is largely lacking.

Hardware manufacturers view schools as a small portion of the total computer market. One estimate places the share at only 3 percent by 1985.[13] Firms are cautious about developing software for the modest school market, and yet, ironically, they are pushing computers on schools with full-scale ads and tax-writeoff proposals to Congress.

To improve computer material for education and to fulfill what we, quite frankly, believe to be a moral obligation, we recommend that every computer firm selling hardware to the schools also establish a special instructional-materials fund. Such a fund would be used in consultation with classroom teachers to develop high-quality, school-related programs. We also recommend that when schools consider the purchase of computer hardware they base their decision not only on the quality of the equipment but also on the quality of the instructional material available. In addition, districts should take into account the commitment of the company to invest—either alone or in collaboration with other companies—in the continued developing of instructional material for schools.

Further, teachers need to know that programming material is accurate and unbiased. They also need to be reassured that a software package has an educational value that cannot be achieved in other ways. It is strange that, while textbooks are endlessly scrutinized, it seems computer software is virtually ignored. Several educational journals are beginning to publish software reviews as an aid to teachers, but the efforts are only marginally helpful at best.

Therefore, we recommend that a national commission, comprised in part of outstanding classroom teachers, be named to evaluate the quality of computer software being prepared for classroom instruction. Recommendations from this commission regarding the value and use of such material should be made available to the schools. It would be appropriate, we feel, for the Secretary of Education to appoint such a national commission.

Technology and the Teacher

Another problem. Technology revolutions have also bypassed the schools because teachers have been bypassed in the process. Again, television is a case in point. There has been little or no training among teaching staff in the use of television. Indeed, only 17 percent of the nation's teachers have had *any* such training.[14] American Federation of Teachers Vice President Pat Daly put a very human face on this phenomenon:

> Teachers are much like other people. Things which are new and rather technical can intimidate them. It is difficult to change old habits, old patterns. It isn't going to be enough to bring an expensive piece of equipment before a faculty, give them a half hour of instruction on how it might be used, and then wheel it back to the media center and wait for the flood of reservations that should follow. A few teachers on the staff will accept it as a challenge and run the risk of falling flat on their faces as they experiment with it. Do you know what it is like to fiddle around ineptly with a piece of electronic gear before a class of 17-year-olds whose bedrooms resemble the testing laboratories at RCA?[15]

For technology to be used in schools, teachers must learn about the new equipment. They must discover how it works and become informed about its possibilities and its limits. In our proposed teacher education program, discussed in Chapter 10, a course in the new technology is included. For those teachers already in the classroom, we recommend that computer companies provide short-term summer seminars and perhaps scholarships for teachers to keep them up-to-date on the uses of technology as a teaching tool.

An experiment in Massachusetts is moving in the right direction. The Digital Equipment Corporation has joined with the Lexington and Lynnfield school districts to teach teachers about the new technology. Once trained, teachers return to their districts to develop video-disk–computer programs. The Digital Corporation has agreed to provide the equipment needed in the schools and market the materials developed by the teachers. Profits would return to the school districts to help support the new technology program.[16]

We also suggest that federal funds be used to educate teachers regarding technology and its uses. In more detail, we recommend that ten Technology Resource Centers be established on university campuses—one in each major region of the nation. These centers would assemble for demonstration the latest technology. They should also give top priority to the development of regional networks to provide computerized library service to all schools. Such networks should be launched with federal support.

Technology and School Goals

Having addressed the issue of technology and its content as well as technology and teachers, we now acknowledge that poor content and poor teaching are only symptoms of a larger problem. Technology revolutions have failed to touch the schools largely because purchases frequently have preceded planning. School administrators are eager to be "with it." Having TV instruction or teaching machines or language laboratories in the schools has been viewed as a flashy symbol of school leadership and success.

The pressure is intense. During our school visits we heard officials say that the first question many parents ask today is: "Do you have a computer in the school?" Here's how one school official put it:

> We have a list of problems in this district—budget cutbacks, declining test scores, a rising dropout rate, low teacher morale, and pockets of poor teaching. But there is a sense around here that computers are going to solve all of our woes. I know computers are supposed to be the wave of the future, but they represent the only nod in the direction of the future that we're making—at least in this district.[17]

Here is the essential point. The deliberate absence of a computer policy is itself a policy with major risks. We conclude that no school should buy computers, or any other expensive piece of hardware, until key questions have been asked—and answered. Why is this purchase being made? Is the software as good as the equipment? What educational objectives will be served? Which students will use the new equipment, when and why? Are teachers able to fit the technology and the software into the curriculum?

In searching for appropriate answers to these questions, we recommend that the following priorities be followed by schools as decisions are made about the purchase of computers:

Learning About Computers. The first priority is to teach all students *about* the technological revolution of which computers are a part— a point we discuss in Chapter 7, where the core curriculum is described. In the future, computers for the nonspecialist will be so convenient ("user-friendly" is the term) that little technical skill will be required. Few citizens of tomorrow will spend time at a computer keyboard or will write a computer program. Therefore, the first goal should not be hands-on experience for students. Rather, the urgent need is for students to learn about the social impact technology has played and will play in their lives.

All students should understand the extent to which the microchip controls transactions at work and increasingly at home, and they should discover the implications of a global communications network that makes it possible for messages instantaneously to span the earth. In short, the first obligation of the school is to put the technological revolution in perspective. Buying computers before this core educational program is solidly in place is to turn school priorities upside down.

For a small number of students, learning *about* computers also means advanced computer study. This upper-level program would teach computer language and specialized usage to those students who will need such skills in their future work as engineers or scientists or specialists in high-tech fields. At the Oxford, Massachusetts, high school, about forty students graduated in 1982 with two years of programming experience in three different computer languages. The school system prepared these students to gain a foothold in a local economy highly dependent on the latest technologies.

Learning with Computers. The second priority for the school is to make it possible for students to learn *with* the computers. Here we have in mind the use of computers to gather information, with students using terminals in the library or in classrooms for reference and bibliographic searches. Students at Lindbergh, Princeton, and Palisades Park high schools in New Jersey are using a personal computer connected by telephone lines to an electronic version of the *Academic American Encyclopedia,* which is exactly the same as the printed version consisting of twenty-one volumes and nine million words.[18] Such user-friendly equipment soon will make it possible for students to call up information with little knowledge about the technical aspects of computer programming or detailed equipment procedures.

Learning with computers also means helping students study specific subjects and improve their skill in areas such as writing or spelling or mathematics. Here, the computer may be especially important for remedial work. Today most computer programs are, in fact, designed for rote learning. They are what one educator described to us as "the new drill sergeant of the classroom." They stress recall of previously learned facts and can be very helpful as a tutor to individual students.

Learning from Computers. The third priority is to help all students learn *from* computers. Computer learning at its best is interactive. The most powerful teaching use of the computer occurs when students use technology to achieve high-order learning, when a student can, in a very real sense, "converse" with the computer and develop better thinking in the process. Ithiel de Sola Pool describes the possibilities of this new kind of schooling:

> Before the computer, every communications medium or device was essentially dumb. If it worked right, it delivered at the far end exactly the message that a human being had put in at the start. There could be noise or attenuation, the paper could tear, but the medium added nothing positive. What a human being put in, a human being could take out, and that was all. Now for the first time, the message that goes in is not necessarily the message that comes out. For the first time, thanks to digital logic, messages may be modified or even created in the machine.[19]

Looking down the road, we can see that the day may come when schools will have available to every student multimedia consoles with enriching programs, when students will move easily from the teacher to a console and back again, when the curriculum and the computer content will have been blended. Students at such a console could study the anatomy of the human body, conduct science experiments, design buildings, stress test the Brooklyn Bridge, or view, on the screen, the world's greatest art gallery.

Consoles now combine a personal computer with a video disk on which 54,000 pictures—in still form or in animation—can be stored and retrieved.[20] In science, mathematics, language, and the arts, possibilities for learning are almost endless.

But prospects for a technology revolution in education go far beyond computers. Cable television is moving into communities from coast to coast. Over ten years ago, the National Cable Television Association issued a statement supporting a plan whereby all cable systems would allot at least one channel to local school districts. Unfortunately, schools have not met the challenge. Cable channels assigned to education go unused.

There are exceptions. Irvine, California, teachers have available to them commercial instruction programs as well as locally produced minicourses on the school's cable network.[21] Community residents explain their hobbies; electrical engineers discuss the space shuttle; members of famous bands talk about the music industry; and math professors, physicists, and physicians share the latest developments in their fields.

Community involvement is encouraged by the very nature of Irvine's cable network: It is decentralized. Rather than using a single central studio, the Irvine network consists of thirty-one ministudios located in twenty-four schools, two colleges, City Hall, the school district's main office, two area museums, and the county public library.[22]

Cable television is also well-suited to in-service programs for teachers and administrators. In Danville, Illinois, videotapes of experienced teachers in the classroom are used to help orient new teachers.[23] *Central View,* a discussion show for educational shop talk, has been produced by the Wappingers Falls Central School District in New York.[24] And, again in Irvine, teachers use one piece of technology to learn about another: the district has produced in-service programs for teachers on its newly acquired microcomputers.[25]

If cable television allows teachers to become students, it also allows students to become teachers. High school students in Irvine tutor gifted elementary school students in math. Because 70 percent of local homeowners have cable television, elementary school kids can go home after school, turn on the TV, dial up the local high school, and get help from "homework tutors."[26]

We conclude that television offers a rich resource for the nation's public schools. And we recommend that school districts with access to a cable channel use the facility for school instruction and that a districtwide plan for such use be developed.

One further word. Both commercial and public broadcast companies also have an important role to play. The programs they offer can be distracting or enriching. These broadcasters have a profound social obligation to prepare television specials that supplement the curriculum in the schools. Specifically, we support the proposal made several years ago that all commercial television networks set aside prime-time hours every week to air programs for education and thereby indirectly enrich the school curriculum.

There are still other ways technology can extend the teacher's reach. Today we have a gold mine of materials on film and video cassettes. A single video disk will hold four reference works the size of the *Encyclopaedia Britannica* (one page per frame) or the entire contents of the Louvre in Paris. This new technology is making a stunning array of information available.

Consider the science series *Search for Solutions*. In each film of this video cassette series, science and scientists come to life. One segment reaches back to the Middle Ages, showing a group of monks as they observed what they believed to be an explosion on the sun. The film then leaps to modern science, with giant telescopes discovering—in fact—some past disturbance on the sun. The combination of the monks' illuminated manuscript with its eyewitness report and the corroboration, centuries later, by modern science permits students to ponder the continuity of observation and discovery, as well as the connection between speculation and proof.

Great musical performances have been broadcast "Live from Lincoln Center." Dramatization of the world's great literature is on film. Presidential speeches, Congressional debates, and summit meetings can now be seen and heard. These rich, exciting features should live on in classrooms from coast to coast. They should be seen by each new generation.

We recommend that a National Film Library be established with federal support. This resource center would secure outstanding film and television programs, both commercial and public offerings, index and edit them, and make them available for school use. One source for such material is the Museum of Broadcasting in New York City. These archival materials should not only be available for scholars, they should be available to students, too.

If we could tap the great music, the great literature, the great science, the illuminating history now on film to enrich great teaching in the schools, we could, we believe, within a decade have the best and most broadly educated generation in history.

In the summer of 1938, the essayist and novelist E. B. White sat in a darkened room and watched transfixed as a big electronic box began projecting eerie, shimmering images into the world. It was his first introduction to something called TV. E. B. White—who not only wrote *Charlotte's Web,* but also co-authored that great manual of clear communication *The Elements of Style*—said:

> I believe television is going to be the test of the modern world, and that in this new opportunity to see beyond the range of our vision we shall discover either a new and unbearable disturbance of the general peace, or a saving radiance in the sky. We shall stand or fall by television—of that I am quite sure.[27]

Whether the new electronic teachers, from TV to the computer, become a "saving radiance" in education or remain an "unbearable disturbance" will depend on whether we have learned the lesson of the past. It will also depend on whether programs are well prepared, whether teachers are made partners in the process, and, above all, whether schools have an education plan before they purchase equipment.

The challenge is not to view technology as the enemy; nor is it to convert the school into a video-game factory, competing with the local shopping center. Rather, the challenge is to build a partnership between traditional and nontraditional education, letting each do what it can do best.

The potential of technology is to free teachers from the rigidity of the syllabus and tap the imaginations of both teacher and student to an extent that has never been possible before. Today, teachers and school librarians can capture instructional materials—films, video cassettes, computer programs—and fit them appropriately into the curriculum. Such programs can help students study on their own.

In the long run, electronic teachers may provide exchanges of information, ideas, and experiences more effectively (certainly differently) than the traditional classroom or the teacher. The promise of the new technologies is to enrich the study of literature, science, mathematics, and the arts through words, pictures, and auditory messages. To achieve this goal, technology must be linked to school objectives.

Television can take students to the moon and to the bottom of the sea. Calculators can solve problems faster than the human brain. And computers can instantly retrieve millions of information bits. Word processors can help students write and edit. And the classroom of the future can be a place where the New York Philharmonic comes live from Lincoln Center.

But television, calculators, word processors, and computers can not make value judgments. They cannot teach students wisdom. That is the mission of the teacher, and the classroom must also be a place where the switches are turned off.

Above all, the classroom should be a place where students are helped to put their own lives in perspective, to sort out the bad from the good, the shoddy from that which is elegant and enduring. For this we need teachers, not computers.

12

SERVICE:
THE NEW CARNEGIE UNIT

I t is the end of lunch hour on a warm fall day at Ridgefield High. Students lounge on the front steps of the building, chatting easily in groups. Here and there are individual students alone, reading or merely skygazing. One or two couples stroll about the grounds deep in conversation.

Near the steps, a young girl, a junior, talks about her reactions to school.

> The classes are okay, I guess. Most of the time I find them pretty boring, but then I suppose that's the way school classes are sup-posed to be. What I like most about the place is the chance to be with my friends. It's nice to be a part of a group. I don't mean one of the clubs or groups the school runs. They're for the grinds. But an informal group of your own friends is great.
>
> Usually, we don't do too much. I mean, we just hang around together, sit together when we can in class and at lunch, and some-times meet after school, though most of us work. . . . This year I've been working at McDonald's so I can buy some new clothes and a stereo set. The work isn't all that hard or exciting, but still it makes me feel on my own and that I'm an adult person, that I'm doing something useful. In school, you never feel that way. Not ever.[1]

The current folklore has it that teenagers are selfish, lazy, and undisciplined. But that image does not square with the number of hours students work or the reasons they give for working: not only to have money to buy things, but also to feel useful and responsible. It does not fit with the growing popularity of religious sects, which demand discipline and provide purpose. It does not mesh with the conclusion George Gallup drew from a national youth survey well along in the "me decade": "The youth population has been mis-named the self-centered generation," Gallup said. "There's a strong desire to serve others. The problem we face in America today is not a lack of willingness to serve or to help others but to find the appropriate outlet for this."[2]

And the image of a lazy, self-indulgent generation does not jibe with Washington *Post* reporter Dan Morgan's interviews with young people all around the country. Morgan concludes:

> Society has not served this generation of Americans as generously as it seems. What's missing? Skeptical adults would be surprised by the answer from scores of young people: the lack of challenging responsibilities against which they can shape their character, their values and their commitment to society. A sense of purpose, of inspiration, of fruitful connections, not only to parents but also to other elements of the larger society. . . . [Young people] are deprived of responsibilities and cut off from real-life activities that are impor-tant to the adult community. They are waiting—waiting to be grown-up. And they are bored.[3]

"We have created what might be called 'compulsory youth,' " a Carnegie Council study declared, "a substantial time between dependence and independence, a twilight zone of uncertainty and ambiguity of status," during which youth "are often left largely to the guidance, companionship, and mercy of their peers and the electronic media."[4] A United States Office of Education report described our schools "as the social 'aging vats' that have isolated adolescents and delayed their learning adult roles, work habits, and skills."[5]

Former United States Commissioner of Education Harold Howe II spoke powerfully about the problem when he called American youth an island in our society. The message it receives from the adult world is, "We have no use in our economic system for you young people between the ages of 12 and 18, and precious little use in our community affairs. So we suggest you sit quietly, behave yourselves, and study hard in the schools we provide as a holding pen until we are ready to accept you into the adult world. The answer of American youth to this message, as well as that of the young people in other industrialized countries, is not printable in a polite speech to a polite audience. And youth has gone ahead to create its own culture with its own customs, its own music, and even its own language.[6]

Educators have, for decades, talked about building a sense of community in school, of helping to teach social and civic responsibility to all students. Here is what catalogues at schools we visited have to say:

> Social activities "help prepare young people for the physical and social problems faced by the rapidly growing and rapidly maturing student."[7]

> Student activities generally provide "ample opportunity for the development of understanding and cooperation among social and ethnic groups within the student body."[8]

> The student council "provides a laboratory for students to learn how to make wise, moral, and informed choices, and to carry them into action. Every school needs a program for developing and training both leaders and participants in student activities, so that democratic citizenship is learned through practice."[9]

> And not least, "In all activities, the development of democratic leadership and cooperative attitudes is a major objective."[10]

While this is what schools say they are trying to accomplish, in real life a quite different message often is conveyed both on and off the campus. Youth are considered feckless and irresponsible—forever adolescent. One teacher bluntly confessed his bias: "There's something almost primitive about adolescents. The more freedom you give them, the wilder their behavior gets." And one principal we interviewed talked sadly of the attitude of adults toward teenagers.

Adults drive past our high school quickly. Sometimes they avoid it entirely, particularly if they see groups of teenagers hanging around outside. I think they're illustrating something I've lately come to believe—that there's a fear of adolescents in this country. Few adults understand them, and most find them hard to like. What we do feel is that they must be controlled.[11]

Visit any high school, walk the corridors, check the bulletin board, look at the graffiti, have lunch in the cafeteria, listen to the public address system, and you will hear and see how students are controlled. Some have called this "the hidden curriculum." There is, in fact, nothing hidden about it. It is perfectly visible—and audible—to all.

It is homeroom time in a tenth-grade class. The booming voice of the assistant principal is suddenly heard on the P.A. system:

May I have your attention. Anyone who was not on time this morning must report to the principal's office with a late slip within the next half hour. If late slips are not turned in by then, you will be marked absent for the day. Also, anyone who was not here yesterday must turn in an absence slip. If you were late yesterday and do not have an excused absence, please see me immediately.

Next, I have to report more incidents of smoking in the third-floor men's room. That room, as a result, will be closed, and students will use the men's room on either the first or second floor. In case some of you have forgotten, let me repeat: students caught smoking anywhere in the building will face dismissal from school according to school regulations.

My next announcement is a disgrace to this school and to its student body. The north side of the building has, for the fifth time this year, been smeared with graffiti. Until the student who defaced the building comes forth and owns up, I'm taking the precaution of confining all students to the interior of the building during the school day until further notice.

Finally, I have to remind you again that you are not to linger in the halls between classes. At the sound of the bell, go promptly to your next class. Anyone caught in the halls after the last bell without a pass will report to me.[12]

Schools are places of strict boundaries, both physical and social. One student, sitting with us in the school cafeteria, explained the social geography of the room. "Of course there are cliques. There are cliques everywhere. Behind you are the jocks; over on the side of the room are the greasers, and in front of you are the preppies —white preppies, black preppies, Chinese preppies, preppies of all kinds. The preppies are the in group this year. Jocks, of course, are always in and greasers are always out."[13]

At another school a student told us, "The athletes are *the* group in the school. If you're not a jock, you've got very little status." And at another: "The really popular kids in this school are rich. For example, the ski club is the big club to belong to, but you have to be rich to be in it. Last year they went to Sun Valley, and you've really got to have pots of money to afford that."[14] At still another school, we heard that "Religious groups are very important here. If you don't join a Christian club, you're pretty much excluded socially."[15]

At most schools, students generally agreed that only rarely did a student belong to more than one group. In fact, belonging to one clique usually makes it impossible to join another.

Some students remain outsiders, staying on the periphery of school life, either because they choose not to join in or because circumstances prevent it. "I have to work after school," one student told us, "and so I'm not really part of any group, which may be why I've never felt very comfortable here."[16] Another student, clearly pained by his experience as an outsider, remarked, "I've never really been a part of any group. I suppose I don't have anything to offer.

It gets awfully lonely at times, but after a while you get to like being alone."[17]

Students are roughly divided into winners and losers. Such division may be in the classroom, where students compete with each other for the teacher's attention or praise, or through the grading system, or on the athletic field, or through acceptance or rejection by peers. Wherever it is, students quickly learn that they are in competition with each other. As a result, collaboration, cooperation, and giving assistance are often discouraged by the life of the school. One student described the dilemma this way: "I like to work, to study, but in this school you don't learn for the sake of learning, but so you can do better than the next person. It gets to be an unpleasant rat race after a while."[18]

As for extracurricular activities, these, too, seem to be part of the problem rather than part of the solution. At Sands High School, for example, we were told: "At 2:15 life quickly changes here. Depending on the student, three different things happen. One quarter of them remain at school, either for sports or clubs or performance groups; almost half of the students go to part-time jobs; the remainder go home or take off with friends." One student said the clubs were "for the plastic people" and added, "Personally, I get out of the school each day as quickly as I can."[19]

Nationwide, 53 percent of all students do *not* participate in any nonvarsity sport or athletic activity; 85 percent do *not* belong to pep clubs or take part in cheerleading, debating, or drama; more than 80 percent do *not* participate in either student government or the school newspaper; and over 78 percent are *not* members of chorus or dance, or band or orchestra activities.[20]

The location and size of school has something to do with how active students are in clubs and sports. Suburban schools, for example, have higher rates of participation than do either urban or rural schools. And students attending small schools (under 1500 students) are more active than pupils in larger ones.[21]

What is most revealing, however, is which students join out-of-class activities. Participation is highest among white, male, college-bound students. Minority groups have a lower participation rate than whites. Students with high grades are more apt to be involved than those with low grades. And students from middle-income families are more active in school programs than students from lower- and higher-income families.[22] One student summed it up: "Activities, they're for important people; there's nothing here for the ordinary student."[23]

Athletics may be the exception. In a recent Illinois survey, athletics was the most popular student activity, with 41 percent of students in the state participating in some form of physical program. Music came next, with 19 percent of students involved. Class-related activities were the third most popular, attracting 17 percent. Drama was fourth, with a 5 percent participation rate.[24]

The fact remains that too few students participate in school activities, and frequently they join not to serve but to promote their own special interests. One student candidly confessed: "You hear a lot about colleges looking for good students who are well-rounded. . . . You get the idea that it's important to join activities in order to show colleges that you're interested in something besides grades."[25]

And a Korean student, advising his younger cousin, was even more succinct. "If you want to get into Harvard, sign up for some extracurricular activities." A junior-year student offered this explanation: "Students don't join the French club to experience French culture but because Yale will be impressed."

At an academic high school we visited there are sixty-four separate clubs, squads, and teams.[26] Some students at the school belong to as many as five groups, a level of participation that is, itself, unusual. There is an astronomy club, an Asian society, a Latin cultural society, a West Indian club, and an Irish society. There are debating, math, swimming, gymnastics, handball, and track teams. Students can join a frisbee team, a photo squad, and an honors society. They edit twelve publications, including the newspaper, a biology journal, a feminist publication, a social studies journal, and a math journal. And yet students complain of feeling unfulfilled.

Today it is possible for American teenagers to finish high school yet never be asked to participate responsibly in life in or out of the school, never be encouraged to spend time with older people who may be lonely, to help a child who has not learned to read, to clean up the litter on the street, or even to do something meaningful at the school itself.

As for acting as small-scale democracies, student clubs and organizations seem more marked by exclusivity and class distinctions than by the democratic spirit. "We've failed to make them responsible for what they do or fail to do," says a former director of the California Conservation Corps. "We've made promises to them without exacting responsibility from them."[27]

A counselor at one school we visited declared, "Schools must help these kids find direction in life. We have an obligation to make students politically and socially aware, to show them how politics relates to them and to their community."[28]

And at a school in the Midwest we heard a parent speak passionately about enlarging the purposes of education. "In our topsy-turvy world," she said, "service is increasingly an essential goal. High school is the appropriate place to get students more involved."[29]

We conclude that during high school young people should be given opportunities to reach beyond themselves and feel more responsively engaged. They should be encouraged to participate in the communities of which they are a part. Therefore, we recommend that every high school student complete a service requirement—a new "Carnegie unit"—involving volunteer work in the community or at school.

The Carnegie unit, as historically defined, measures time spent in class—academic contact time. This new unit would put emphasis on time in service. The goal of the new Carnegie unit would be to help students see that they are not only autonomous individuals but also members of a larger community to which they are accountable. The program would tap an enormous source of unused talent and suggest to young people that they are needed. It would help break the isolation of the adolescent, bring young people into contact with the elderly, the sick, the poor, and the homeless, as well as acquaint them with neighborhood and governmental issues.

The service program we propose would work like this: During each of their four high school years, students would do volunteer work in or out of the school. They could tutor younger students; volunteer in the school cafeteria, office, audio-visual center; or maintain sports equipment and playing areas. They might also move beyond the school to libraries, parks, hospitals, museums, local government, nursing homes, day-care centers, synagogues, or churches.

The new Carnegie unit would not be bound rigidly by calendar or clock. The amount of time could vary. We suggest, however, that a student invest not less than 30 hours a year, a total of 120 hours over four years, in order to qualify for one Carnegie service unit. Students could fulfill this service requirement evenings, weekends, and during the summer.

The proposed service program will require careful supervision. Jerome Kagan, professor at Harvard University, writes:

> Acts of honesty, cooperation, and nurturance are public events that the staff of a school can tally and use to assign individual evaluations that are understood to be essential complements to subject mastery. We do not keep such records as faithfully as course grades, because we do not believe the schools should judge motives and behavioral attitude toward others; that is a task for the home and police department. But judging youth on standards for action and talent would make it possible for many more students to participate in, and identify with, the school community.[30]

In the spirit of this proposal, we recommend that students themselves be given responsibility to organize and monitor student service activities and to work with school officials in seeing that credit is appropriately assigned.

The idea of combining school and service is more than novel speculation. We present three examples of service programs that have some of the elements we have in mind.

Detroit city schools require students to complete two hundred hours of out-of-school experience between the ninth and twelfth grades, in order to graduate. Students may either work for pay or do volunteer work. The principal purpose of the program, according to Emeral Crosby, principal of Northern High School in Detroit, is to give students a greater understanding of "the world of work."[31]

Each student receives a card that must be signed by his or her supervisor, recording the number of hours worked or volunteered. Students in the inner city tend to complete their two hundred hours mainly at their places of employment. But many, especially students in upper grades, devote the time to service. Also, students in more affluent schools tend to engage in volunteer activities.

The places of service include hospitals, museums, convalescent homes, churches (teaching Sunday school or singing in the choir). The range of activities is broad, from tutoring children to helping elderly or disabled people (reading to them, raking leaves, helping to prepare a meal, running errands, and the like). Students accept the requirement of their service assignment with little complaint.

South Brunswick High School in New Jersey, a suburban school serving a middle-class community, has had, for the past ten years, a service program for all of its ten thousand students.[32] The program offers two types of experiences to the students: service and career. Service experiences are available in day-care centers, nursing homes, hospitals, nutrition sites, and other social service institutions. Career placements take interested students to such workplaces as an auto mechanic's shop or a gas station or a computer center, or to colleges where they may take courses or work as research aides.

Once a week, students meet in groups to review their individual experiences and to voice any questions or problems they have encountered.

The service requirement at South Brunswick was initially a practical response to overcrowding. To prevent the school from going on split sessions, students were in school four days a week. On a fifth day, they participated in the service or work program. Twenty percent of the students were off campus any given day. Over the ten-year period, the program has accumulated four hundred sponsors to which students can be assigned. They range from American Cyanamid and IBM to Tennyson's Florist.

School enrollments are now dropping, and overcrowding is no longer a problem. The administrator of the South Brunswick school is under pressure to drop the program. Some teachers feel that it is difficult to plan with 20 percent in service every day. Some parents want their children to spend more time in traditional classes. Further, the scheduling of student calendars and transportation is complicated, and many elect the career exploration option. Nevertheless, administrators at South Brunswick defend the program as a valuable learning experience.

Metro High School, a public high school in St. Louis, has 250 selected students; 65 percent are black, 35 percent are white.[33] Since Metro opened its doors in 1972, students have been required to work as volunteers in the community. Today the service requirement is sixty hours each year at a nonprofit agency within the city limits. Students can choose to volunteer after school, on weekends, or during the summer. If students have not completed the required service hours by the end of their senior year, they will not graduate.

This unusual schoolwide commitment to service originated with Metro's principal, Betty Wheeler, who feels that everyone has a debt to repay to the community. She tells the students, "As citizens you owe the community from which you come. You have special talent that you should share with others. The more talent you have the more responsibility you have to share."[34]

While most educators would not disagree with Wheeler's altruistic vision, few have gone to such lengths to implement a required program of service. She explains her initial motivation this way: "I had seen kids, especially here in the city, who felt 'The world owes me something, the city owes me something. I should get welfare, I should get this, I should get that,' simply because they live in St. Louis. And, you know, there should never be expectations like this. People need to learn that . . . we are here to help if we possibly can."[35]

Today at Metro everyone—including those students who are on welfare—gives, and all of them appear to receive far more than they give. A young student spoke enthusiastically about her job at the Division of Family Services and about what she learned in her first face-to-face encounter with hunger and poverty: "On the first day I had this lady, this young girl, she was about nineteen or twenty, and she had a little baby with her. . . . Her husband had run out on her. She didn't have any heat, any electricity, any gas, nothing. They were living on biscuits and gravy. She started crying. We've got people in there—I mean you wouldn't believe the conditions. They have been sleeping in the bus station, living out on the streets. You just don't believe that unless you see it. It was really an incredible experience."[36]

Some Metro volunteers work on special exhibits at St. Louis Art Museum and backstage on sets at the Theater Project Company, do displays and research at the Botanical Gardens, and act as guides at the McDonnell planetarium. Students do volunteer work in local hospitals, assisting in the office of admissions, in radiology, physical therapy, patient transportation, the intensive care unit, and the pharmacy.

One young man with longish hair, tight and faded blue jeans, and a street-wise expression on his face spoke movingly of what he learned while working on the "graveyard shift" (12 midnight to 7 A.M.) in the emergency room of a medical center: "I learned a lot this past summer. I learned how to deal with my own feelings. I learned how to cry. That was a big step. When a little three-year-old girl goes into seizures and they found out she had meningitis and died that morning, you learn to feel for people."[37]

For others, the joy of simply feeling needed is a significant experience. A tall broad-shouldered young man volunteered at a convalescent home and became a welcome friend to the patients. Still other Metro students teach at the YMCA, in their churches, or at elementary schools during summer sessions. Quite a few students find jobs within Metro High itself—tutoring and library, office, and maintenance jobs.

Although some Metro students felt juniors and seniors should be permitted to take paying jobs, every student we interviewed endorsed wholeheartedly the idea of service. One student summed up the commonly held belief that community service makes them better persons: "I learned a lot from it. Knowing that there are people out there who need help and helping them out gave me a lot of self-satisfaction."[38]

Students also report that community service provides opportunities for career exploration and work experience. The payoff is not the same for all students. Some get job experience, others explore careers.

At least one student felt the experience enhanced his college application: "If you're interested in getting a job while in college or whatever, then the fact that you worked as a volunteer is good. They'll say, 'You have some kind of experience. You're the type of person who will go out and do things to help improve yourself even though you don't get paid for it.' I think that it helps you out a lot."[39]

In the Metro service program each student is responsible to get his or her own volunteer assignment. The fact that students actually have to present and sell themselves to the agencies is, according to the principal, a major strength of the experience. In addition, one student earns her community service hours by assuming the overall responsibility for record keeping. According to this young woman, "Most of our students have been recorded [by employers] as doing excellent work because we put a lot in and we get a lot of training out of it—some people have left here with four hundred hours of service credit."

How might one account for such dedication? It may have something to do with the students who choose to attend Metro. It may also have something to do with the desire of many young people to be useful. We suspect, however, it has a great deal to do with a principal with a clear vision and serious expectations.

Mrs. Wheeler talked about her goals: "In our orientation every year we let [the students] know that they're going out and representing Metro. What they do could have lasting effects on what happens to all of us back at school. . . . Everybody does a good job. . . . These are standards that we expect you to keep up as a Metro student. People have done this for ten years and this is part of our curriculum."[40]

John Dewey wrote on one occasion: "A society is a number of people held together because they are working along common lines, in a common spirit, and with reference to common aims. . . . The radical reason that the present school cannot organize itself as a natural social unit is because just this element of common and productive activity is absent."[41]

A service term for all students will do much to help build a sense of community and common purpose within a school. In the end, the goal of service in the schools is to teach values—to help all students understand that to be fully human one must serve.

PART V

A SCHOOL
THAT WORKS

13

THE PRINCIPAL AS LEADER

It was late afternoon. The students and most teachers had left the building. As we walked along the corridor of a midwestern suburban school, the principal talked about his job: "I go almost every year to conventions for principals, and there's always a speech telling us we need to be educational leaders, not managers. It's a great idea. And yet the system doesn't allow you to be an educational leader. Everyone wants the power to run schools in one way or another—the central office, the unions, the board, the parents, the special-interest groups. What's left for the principal to decide isn't always very much. There's so little we have to control or to change. The power, the authority, is somewhere else, though not necessarily the responsibility."[1]

For years now, studies have been pointing to the pivotal role of the principal in bringing about more effective schools.[2] Our own field studies bear out these findings. In schools where achievement was high and where there was a clear sense of community, we found, invariably, that the principal made the difference. Like a symphony orchestra, the high school must be more than the sum of its parts. If the goals we set forth in this report are to be accomplished, strong leadership will be needed to pull together the separate elements in the school and make them work.

At Sequoia High School in the Northwest, a teacher told us, "Our administration is democratic. It consults, but it is hard to get a consensus. Our meetings are brief." Another teacher put it this way: "Our principal lays it on the line, but he offers good tries."[3]

Ron Young at Sands High School is credited by almost everyone as having led high schools with vitality and vision. Easygoing by nature, Young came to Sands nine years ago, just as the school was being transformed from a small all-white institution with an enrollment of 1,200 to a desegregated beehive of social change with 3,800 students, two-thirds of whom are black.

Before becoming a principal, Young was a mathematics teacher, a guidance counselor, and an assistant principal at both junior and senior high school levels.

Reactions to Ron Young's leadership were best typified by a mathematics teacher who has taught at two other county schools:

> I can't find fault with this school's administration. The biggest advantage for me teaching in this school is just that—the administration. It's very supportive. They treat you like a human being. You're here to do a job and you're trusted to do your job properly. If you don't, you hear about it. Until then, you're assumed to be O.K. I think most of the teachers feel this way. Turnover is very low here. Teachers throughout the country know about this school and many would like to transfer here."[4]

The average high school principal is male (only 7 percent are female), white (fewer than 5 percent identify themselves as members of minorities), and between the ages of forty and forty-nine (only 25 percent of principals are under forty). Before assuming their current jobs, they held one or more of the following positions: 54 percent were assistant principals at the secondary level, 35 percent were high school athletic directors, and 26 percent were junior or middle school principals or assistant principals. Fourteen percent had served at the elementary level and 18 percent had been counselors.[5]

The typical high school principal has been in his current job ten to fourteen years; he works between fifty and fifty-four hours a week[6] and earns $37,602 a year.[7]

How a principal gets a job is strikingly quixotic. Most principals are judged by a set of local and custom-bound criteria that may be as cloudy as anything existing in the contemporary job market. Here is how one study put it:

> Principals themselves often did not know exactly why they had been selected and placed at a particular school or what their *specific* mission at the school was to be. . . . Many of our principal respondents expressed very deep frustration and anger at the lack of information they had received about their own appointment. (Some even reported that they had learned that they had "won the race" by reading it in the local newspaper's announcement of the School Board meeting agenda, or by a "buddy's phone call!"). . . . Further, very well qualified appointees found their leadership undercut by such processes, which led teachers to regard their new principal as "just another administrative hack."[8]

Once appointed, the principal is expected to be all things to all people. He spends more than 65 percent of his work day in face-to-face interchanges with staff, faculty, and pupils.[9] Principals spend an additional 8 percent of their day on the telephone. In one recent study, principals identified program development and personnel as their first and second priorities, but they reported spending far more actual time on school management than on either of their top priorities.[10] One principal said, "When I started as a principal, the assistant superintendent advised me, 'Harold, 75 percent of your time should be spent in evaluation, instruction, and curriculum.' I couldn't even do it then. Today, it's reversed. I don't spend 25 percent of my time with the people who are handling the instructional program!"[11]

Here is how one principal described his day:

> Generally I am working on four things at a time, but I know my priorities. I may have two students in my office to reinstate. I get a call, telling me there is a fight on the third floor. I ease the students out of my office and lock the door. As I move upstairs, a teacher confronts me, holding a student by the collar, upset about

his behavior. I must ignore her to get up to the fight. By the time I reach the third floor, that teacher informs me the situation is under control. All this effort, and what have I accomplished? The two students I started with are still not reinstated, and other teachers had to deal with their unauthorized presence in the hall. Another teacher is upset because I couldn't respond to her discipline problem. I didn't even settle the fight on the third floor.[12]

It is this state of perpetual motion, this need to deal on the run with a wide variety of people in brief, episodic fashion, that most characterizes the principalship. Little wonder that principals are restless.

According to a recent study of 1,600 principals, fully one-quarter said they intended to quit in the near future. In another survey, only 4 percent of the principals were interested in moving to another principalship, but 33 percent would say "yes" to a superintendency or central office position.[13] Over one-third cited lack of support from superiors and difficulties stemming from legislative and judicial mandates as reasons they might give up their jobs.[14]

Professional training rarely prepares principals adequately for the job. Most principals complete a graduate-degree program in educational administration, with courses in school management, school law, plant and personnel, finance, history and philosophy of education, and labor negotiations.[15]

The University Council for Educational Administration, after extensive study, was critical of typical existing state certification requirements, university-division standards, and preparatory programs in educational administration, and called for improvements.[16] Goldhammer and Becker, in their report on the principalship, conclude that principals who were effective could not be distinguished from those who were not on the basis of their formal preparation. In addition, certification requirements in many states appear to be irrelevant to the principal's actual needs. Universities appear to be indifferent toward the needs in this field.[17]

Educational administrators themselves disparage the usefulness of their training. In a survey of five hundred school districts, administrators gave low ranking to the value of college and university preparation. Over half said they looked to their state education agencies for help in professional development.[18]

The principal at one school we visited had his own candid and sharply critical view of the situation.

> The university people I dealt with in my educational administration courses hadn't been in a classroom in years; they didn't know what kids were like, and, to my mind, they didn't care. What really got to me was the sense of being patronized . . . as though I was limited and unaware of what secondary education was all about. . . . What they had to offer was really just Mickey Mouse courses that didn't reflect any of the realities in my high school. But that's what you have to put up with to get your ticket.[19]

This portrait of poor training, conflict, and frustration painted by many principals reveals more than private irritation. It portrays, in fact, a crisis in leadership, which seriously undermines the effectiveness of the school.

If the principal is key to an effective school, how can his or her leadership be strengthened?

First, new preparation and selection programs are required. Principals cannot exercise leadership without classroom experience. Specifically, we recommend that the preparation pattern for principals follow that of teachers. Without a thorough grounding in the realities of the classroom, principals will continue to feel uncomfortable and inadequate in educational leadership roles. Moreover, they will continue to lack credibility in instructional matters with their teachers.

One principal put it this way: "My own most useful preparation was really as a teacher, an English department chairman, and a deputy administrator, all of which gave me some notion of the relationships among school people and the chance to develop contacts I could call on for advice when I needed it."[20]

Following undergraduate academic work, a prospective principal should complete all requirements for licensing as a teacher. In addition, he or she should complete at least two years as an *associate teacher* (see Chapter 10) before entry into an administrative credential program. The candidate's strengths and weaknesses in the following critical administrative skills should be assessed: decision making, organization and planning, written and oral communication.

Upon successful completion of the formal program, the graduate should serve a year as an "administrative intern," working closely with an experienced and successful principal, after which he or she would be eligible for employment as an assistant principal. We suggest that a requirement of at least two years as an assistant principal be set before one could assume a full principalship.

Principals, once appointed, may wish to teach occasionally. They cannot exert leadership unless they stay in touch with teachers and classroom teaching. During our school visits, teachers were critical of the way principals dealt with them. Weekly staff meetings frequently turn out to be replicas of poorly-managed classrooms, where the principal talks at, rather than with, the teachers. Too often, these sessions concentrate on administrative details and ignore matters of educational policy. Such treatment alienates teachers and reduces the principal's effectiveness.

Further, if the role of the principal is to be strengthened, more authority must be given to the local school. In the early days, the principal possessed almost total autonomy. He was, quite literally, the head teacher—the one selected from a small group of teachers to handle administrative routine.

Today, most principals are caught in a complicated bureaucratic web. Far too many of our school systems are top-heavy with administration; they are administered to within an inch of their lives. School leadership is crippled by layer upon layer of administration. And, while control is rooted in the need for accountability, the reality is that it makes change in many schools all but impossible.

In one suburban school we visited, a teacher voiced resentment. "In 1968," she said, "we had 104 people in our central office and 28,000 students in the school system. Now we have 140 staff people in the central office, plus their secretaries, but only 19,000 students. That's just too many, when our school has to cut back on staff."[21]

One field report from our study contains the following indictment:

> The visitor need spend only a brief time in the school before becoming aware of an enveloping bureaucracy. It is the iron fist in the paper glove: memoranda is its hallmark. Daily, the school and its administration face a massive volume of generally unimaginative, arguably unnecessary, and often barely literate directives issued from Central Board headquarters. In addition to that, there is a union contract which frequently seems to have the effect of severely limiting thoughtful planning and support options. . . .
>
> The paper flow is virtually uninterrupted, and the volume is impressive. There are actually five separate administrative layers above the building principals, each a source of directives. In the course of one school year, an estimated forty-five pounds of documents came into the school; a count of the concerns addressed in the memoranda during one month added up to thirty-seven different topics.[22]

A teacher at Sequoia High School told us: "The principals have lost their responsibility. The district office has usurped the power so there is no leadership here."[23] And another: "The central office is out of touch; no one cares about the students or the teachers. We are ignored."[24]

Principals cannot exercise leadership without more authority over those functions for which they are responsible. Today, purchases—from pencils to window shades to textbooks—are centralized, and systemwide parsimony is likely to yield such added constraints as uniform building temperatures, standardized band instruments, identical library collections, and the time classrooms and corridors are to be repainted.

In sum, principals have limited time, few resources, and little leeway for decision making. They have little or no control over their budgets—and rarely have a discretionary fund. Their ability to reward outstanding teachers, deal with unsatisfactory teaching, or develop new programs is shockingly restricted.

Rebuilding leadership means giving each school more control over its own budget. Specifically, we recommend that the school principal and staff should have authority to allocate funds within guidelines set by the district office. Further, school systems should provide each high school principal with a Discretionary School Improvement Fund to provide time and materials for program development, or provide for special seminars or staff retreats.

Principals also should have more leeway in rewarding good teachers. In most schools they either inherit their staffs or are not consulted when the district decides which teachers should be assigned to which school. Principals we visited expressed frustration about the constraints they have in dealing with teachers under their supervision. "I have no control anymore," says a principal. "We have had five weeks of school, and already fifteen new teachers have come in—and fifteen have left because of 'bumpings,' teachers with seniority removing other teachers. In addition, each year, mostly through inheritance from somewhere else, I get three to five inept teachers."[25]

We recommend that principals, acting in consultation with their staffs, be given responsibility for the final selection of teachers for their schools. In districts where court-ordered mandates are in effect, we urge that principals participate with central office personnel in the assignment of teachers to the district schools. In meeting these responsibilities, principals should follow central office policies and civil rights requirements.

In making these recommendations, we recognize that issues of financing and equity, as well as court mandates, have placed heavy burdens on school districts. The impact of federal legislation and the courts on the daily operation of schools has been immense. Many districts have felt overwhelmed by the seemingly endless specifications, regulations, and detail involved in administering federal and state programs. We acknowledge, therefore, the key role of the central office and, particularly, that of the superintendent. District leadership is crucial.

In our school visits, we encountered superintendents who exercised superb leadership by establishing and maintaining high-quality education in their districts. In a number of cases, these superintendents transformed failing school systems into model ones for the nation.

Nonetheless, we believe that principals and staffs of individual schools need far more autonomy and authority to carry out their responsibility. Heavy doses of bureaucracy are stifling creativity in too many schools, and preventing principals and their staffs from exercising their best professional judgment on decisions that properly should be made at the local level.

We agree with John Goodlad, who said, "There is no educating of young people in the school 'system'; it takes place in tens of thousands of individual schools. Reconstruction must take place then in each of these schools. . . . Any overhaul of the system must be directed to increasing its ability to provide services to each local school."[26]

Principals caught up in endless problems and procedures have little time to study. Like teachers, they need time to reflect upon their work and stay in touch with developments in education. Specifically, we suggest that a network of Academies for Principals be established to provide for the continuing education of school administrators. State education departments may wish to follow the examples of Maryland, North Carolina, and New Jersey in creating statewide principal centers. Some individual school districts may be able to support regional centers on their own.

Professionalism among principals was given a boost when Harvard's Graduate School of Education announced in 1980 the creation of a special center to upgrade the skills of principals and help already successful ones to do an even better job. The Harvard program stresses the principal's responsibility in planning the curriculum. It also underwrites principals' visits to outstanding schools, where they can study first hand what makes such schools work better than others. Case studies are also used as texts from which principals learn to handle both routine and unforeseen problems.

Peabody College at Vanderbilt University has an intensive summer program attended by principals from eight states. The goal is to train education leaders rather than building managers. One of the principals who took part in a Peabody session said: "The longer you are in the principalship the more you tend to narrow your vision. This [program] opens up new horizons."[27]

What underlies these changed attitudes? Willis D. Hawley, dean at Peabody, says:

> In the past, principals were trained as if they were middle management. Real leadership was expected to come from the "system"—the superintendent or school board. In reality, however, those levels are generally preoccupied with the politics and financing of education, along with some mandating of standards and requirements. They resembled, to use a comparison from another arena, the Pentagon; principals, by contrast, ought to function like ship captains.[28]

Finally, we urge that outstanding principals be given special recognition. For ten years, the Danforth Foundation has funded a program for the renewal of urban school principals. Each year, five principals from five separate cities are chosen for participation.

For a full school year, the principals are freed one day a week from their regular duties to make site visits to other cities and engage in university-related study (a key university professor or administrator meets with the principals once a month). The principals meet six times a year in convenient locations with colleagues from other cities as well as with nationally recognized education leaders.

During the decade of its operation, 250 principals in 46 cities have participated in this program. Only one participant has left a principalship for reasons other than retirement. The benefit for individual principals has been enduring, and a national network of school leaders has been established.

What we seek are high schools in which the school community —students, teachers, and principals—sees learning as the primary goal. In such a community, the principal becomes not just the top authority but the key educator, too.

As the principal at Jenner High School told us: "I have a dream for the school and for what goes on in the classroom. I'd like every teacher to focus on problem solving, to make the process of learning, *not* factual recall, the center of instruction. I'd like us to challenge our students to think."[29]

Rebuilding excellence in education means reaffirming the importance of the local school and freeing leadership to lead.

14

FLEXIBILITY: PATTERNS TO FIT PURPOSE

C hanges come and go," one principal told us, "but in the end life here stays pretty much the same."[1] The principal was describing his own small school in the Southeast, but he might have been describing the high school as an institution. Vast changes have swept over education in recent decades, and yet the structure of schools remains much the same.

Over the years, a host of innovations have been introduced: open classrooms, "modular" scheduling, off-campus learning, to name a few. Some new programs were successful. Others were marred by poor planning or by excess. The basic pattern of public schools may make bureaucratic sense—but does it make educational sense?

American education is marked by great diversity. It must be able to adjust to a variety of conditions and strive for education of high quality in a variety of ways. More flexibility in the use of time, in school size, and in serving special groups of students must be carefully considered.

The Matter of Time

Our present school year was organized to fit an agrarian society. Children were asked to attend between "crop time" and "seed time," those few months from fall to early spring. In California in

1867, the average length of the school year for "free schools" was 7.2 months. However, in the smaller rural districts with less than one hundred children "free schools" were maintained only three months each year; in the somewhat larger districts, schools were kept open five months. Schools in the largest urban districts had a ten-month school year.[2]

At the turn of the century, when the school year was standardized by the Carnegie unit, it was deemed "that the length of the school year is from thirty-six to forty weeks."[3] And in 1908, a typical day in an American high school was "from 8:30 to 1:30, or 9 to 2, or 9 to 2:30; roughly a five hours' session with six or seven periods of forty, forty-five or fifty minutes each and a recess or break of twenty minutes to half an hour, rarely longer, for food and rest."[4]

Today, the typical school year is 178 days long, and the average school day convenes for over 5 hours (5 hours, 35 minutes).[5] The state of Missouri has the shortest school year (174 days), and Ohio has the longest (182 days). New Jersey has the shortest *minimum* day (4 hours) and Texas the longest (7 hours).

When compared to other developed countries, the modern American school day and year are relatively short. In the Soviet Union, East Germany, the People's Republic of China, and Japan, for example, the school year averages 240 days with a 5½ - or 6-day week and a school day of 6 to 8 hours. School vacations in these countries are brief and spaced throughout the year, in contrast to the long summer recess in America.[7]

Public opinion in America has not been enthusiastic about the idea of schooling in the summer even though children are no longer needed to tend the crops. In 1982, 53 percent of those surveyed opposed the idea of a longer school year.[8] Still, at least two states, North Carolina and Florida, are now considering lengthening the school year to as long as 200 days.[9] And the National Commission on Excellence in Education proposed that the school year be lengthened to between 200 and 220 days.[10]

Our school visits convinced us that lengthening the school year is not a top priority for school reform. The urgent need is not more time but better use of time. The great problem today appears to be the incessant interruption of the bell, the constant movement of students from room to room, the feeling that the class is over just as learning has begun. There is not sufficient time to set up and complete science laboratory experiments, no time to write essays and critique them, and no time to engage in extended foreign language conversation. The rigidity of the 50-minute class schedule, for example, often limits good instruction.

Lowell High School in Massachusetts has patterns to fit purpose. The daily schedule is arranged in 15- to 20-minute periods, beginning at 7:40 A.M. and running until 3:20 in the afternoon. Teachers at Lowell can design courses for varying lengths of time. Students can shape their own class schedule, with longer chunks of time for science labs, field work, and electives.

Colman McCarthy, Washington *Post* columnist, describes his own experience as a guest teacher at Washington, D.C.'s School Without Walls, where students attend only two classes every day.[11] Morning and afternoon classes run for 2½ hours, with a 10-minute break during class and an hour in between for lunch.

McCarthy makes the point that "learning needs intimacy" and that studying a subject one-half day each week permits greater depth and more serious contemplation than five short, fragmented sessions can provide. Aside from saving time not traveling to and from class, students have an opportunity not only to write essays but also to have them evaluated during class time, something that is almost impossible in a standard class.

We repeat. The urgent need is not lengthening the school day or school year, but using more effectively the time schools already have—more time to complete a science laboratory experiment, more time to write essays and critique them, more time to engage in extended foreign language conversation. Therefore, we recommend that the class schedule be more flexibly arranged to permit larger blocks of time, especially in courses such as laboratory science, foreign language, and creative writing.

The Matter of Size

In *The American High School Today*, James B. Conant devoted an entire section to the issue of school size. He supported consolidation, making big schools out of small ones. Conant concluded that no high school should have a graduating class of fewer than one hundred pupils.[12] The need for consolidation was based on persuasive evidence: small schools, Conant argued, were seldom able to offer students a rich curriculum, especially upper-level courses in foreign language, science, and mathematics.

School consolidation was already well under way when Conant issued his report. As early as the mid-nineteenth century, Horace Mann, a vigorous spokesman for public education, advocated merging rural schools.[13] The trend continued as the population shifted from farm to town. In 1932, the first year for which statistics on the subject were collected, the U.S. Office of Education reported 127,-531 school districts in America.[14] By 1950, this figure had dropped to 83,718.[15] Conant's pronouncement gave momentum to the consolidation movement. Between 1960 and 1970, the number of school districts shrank from 40,520 to 17,995,[16] and the number of small high schools also shrank.

There are now approximately 16,000 local school districts in the United States, with a median district enrollment of 827 pupils (though 4,270 districts have fewer than 300 pupils).[17] As reported earlier, however, about one-half of all high schools even now have fewer than 600 students.

Most students attend large urban or suburban high schools, often with troubling effects. A teacher at a high school in the Northeast with 3,000 students said, "This is a very big, impersonal place. It is very hard to get to know people. I know only four or five people and then only in passing. I worked before with a faculty where everyone knew everyone and supported each other. . . . Here, nothing works as a whole, nothing works at all. The school is too big."[18]

Soon after Conant's widely-heeded report was issued, Barker and Gump published *Big School, Small School,* challenging the assumption of large-school superiority. This book reported the findings of a study of 218 high schools in eastern Kansas, enrolling from 18 to 2,287 students. The authors concluded that students attending a small school have many more opportunities to participate in school life.

Barker and Gump also found that students in large schools were more polarized, with a group of active participants at one end and a large group of students who did not participate at the other. In small schools there were very few students who did not participate in anything. Also, large schools include a substantial group of "outsiders," students with poor academic records and no extracurricular involvement, a group almost unknown in small schools.[19]

In reviewing studies of school size, Stephen F. Hamilton, Associate Professor of Human Development and Family Studies at Cornell University, describes the issue vividly:

> A tiny school will field several athletic teams and offer the basic math, English, social studies, and science courses required for accreditation. A large school will have both varsity and junior varsity teams in several sports and offer elective courses in physics and trigonometry. But the increase in the number of different academic and athletic opportunities available in the large school does not keep pace with the increase in enrollment. Therefore, the number of opportunities per student declines steadily.[20]

Other researchers have described the social advantages of small schools. Edwin P. Willems, in 1967, found that the positive effects of the small school are greater for the "marginal" students.[21] And in 1980 James Garbarino reported that small schools are more orderly and coherent than large ones, and tend to have lower crime rates.[22] In sum, research during the past several decades suggests that small schools appear to provide greater opportunity for student participation and greater emotional support than large ones.

But Conant's expressed concern persists. Can a small school provide the education opportunities to match the social and emotional advantages that may accompany smallness? We believe the preferred arrangement is to have bigness *and* smallness—a broad education program with supportive social arrangements. Therefore, we recommend that small high schools expand their education offerings in ways discussed in Chapter 8, by using off-campus sites or mobile classrooms or part-time professionals to provide a rich experience for all students. We further recommend that large high schools organize themselves into smaller units—"schools-within-a-school"—to establish a more cohesive, more supportive social setting for all students.

It is difficult to say when a school is too big, the point where schools-within-a-school should be introduced. We do suggest, however, that schools enrolling 1,500 to 2,000 students are good candidates for reorganization into smaller units of several hundred each. An important caveat: those responsible for assigning students to smaller groups must avoid unintentional segregation by race or by socioeconomic status.

Rosemont High School, a suburban school with 2,000 students, has a school-within-the-school. A community of one hundred students and five teachers is organized within the larger setting. This arrangement started about thirteen years ago. It has survived its critics and is well-established. Students become a part of the school-within-the-school for a variety of reasons. One young woman talked about feeling lost and faceless during her freshman year in the "downstairs school" (the term used to refer to the total school). Feeling that in the smaller unit she had gained the self-confidence to thrive in a more competitive setting, she applied to a string of elite colleges.

At Rosemont there is only one such unit within the school. The idea could, we feel, be expanded, not only within Rosemont but also to other large high schools across the nation. There is, in short, a need for the American high school to be as flexible about size as about time.

Special Students, Special Structures

The new patterns proposed to this point have focused on flexible variations in the use of time and variations in school size. New patterns are equally important for special groups of students—the gifted and the disadvantaged—those who are not successfully served by conventional arrangements.

The Gifted Student

Today, gifted and talented students are often overlooked. Teachers and administrators just assume they'll "make it," "blossom on their own." Nothing could be further from the truth. What gifted students want is flexibility: to be allowed to go at their own pace, to satisfy course requirements as quickly as possible, and to move to new areas of learning. One bright young man put it this way:

> Believe it or not, we don't necessarily want to reduce the number of required courses (at least some of us do not). But must we be held to the same timetable as others, so many hours or months or years of a certain subject, if we are able to grasp the fundamentals and move on to a more complex treatment? Or to a new subject altogether?[23]

How can gifted students be encouraged to "move on"? Independent study is one of the simplest and most effective ways. An exceptional student should have the opportunity to select a topic for special study—in science, in literature, in the arts—and work closely with a teacher or with a specialist outside the school who serves as mentor.

Credit by examination is another way to break the logjam, permitting a student to "test-out" of a course in which he or she is already well prepared and then move on to other, more advanced subjects. Gifted students also can take college-level courses at their high school or on the campus of a nearby university or college. These possibilities are spelled out more fully in Chapter 15.

Another pattern for able students is the International Baccalaureate, a rigorous program of study for secondary school students. There are about 225 schools in nearly 50 countries that participate in this program, and approximately 100 of these schools (some private, some public) are in the United States and Canada. Wherever it is offered, the International Baccalaureate consists of three courses that are studied for two years each and three that are studied for one year each.

One course, Theory of Knowledge, is mandatory for two years, braiding the strands of the other courses into a unified intellectual experience. Some American high schools, such as Francis Lewis High School in Flushing, New York, and Wausau High School in Wausau, Wisconsin, have adopted the International Baccalaureate as an appropriate way to stretch able students.

Some school districts have established a separate high school exclusively for gifted students. Jenner High, one of the schools we visited, is such an institution. It is a competitive academic school in a large northeastern city. About 7,000 students apply each year for admission. Only 900 get in. At Jenner, expectations are high, the pressure intense; students are offered an extraordinarily diverse range of courses, and work in a heady atmosphere of discovery. Some see it as having a profound impact on their lives.

One student at Jenner told us, "A lot of things were opened up for me that I wouldn't have known about at the local high school. Math, biology, English, and constitutional law were great. I'm certainly a much different person than I was three years ago." Another said, "In advanced-placement biology we really delve into the subject . . . because we're interested in it. The teacher doesn't teach to get the course material done; he'll teach something that we don't have to know because it's interesting. He'll bring up questions that will make you stop and think . . . it's exciting."[24]

Not all large school districts can support an academic school like Jenner. For most districts regional or even statewide specialty schools may be an answer. In North Carolina, two residential schools for the gifted have been established to serve students from all across the state. The idea was born in 1965 when Governor Terry Sanford created the North Carolina School for the Arts. Talented students in music, drama, and the visual arts are selected to study in this state-supported residence school.

In 1980, the two-year North Carolina School of Science and Mathematics opened with 150 juniors hand-picked from around the state. There are currently 400 juniors and seniors enrolled; that number will eventually increase to about 700.

The state of North Carolina provided 75 percent of the funds needed to turn a twenty-seven-building former hospital compound, donated by Durham County, into a campus. The state also pays 90 percent of the school's operating costs. Parents are asked to contribute to a Parents Association fund, but their children pay no tuition or room and board. In exchange, students must spend five hours each week performing housekeeping or maintenance tasks.

While the school's focus is on science and mathematics, a full range of subjects is required. The academic core is enriched by evening tutorials, off-campus field trips, and a Special Projects Week. All science courses have laboratory periods of at least ninety minutes each week, with additional laboratory time available for independent study. In 1982, the North Carolina School of Science and Mathematics boasted fifty-one National Merit finalists, an almost unheard-of number for such a small school.

We conclude that every high school should have special arrangements for gifted students—credit by examination, independent study, or special study with universities. Since it is impossible for all high schools to provide the top teachers and the sophisticated equipment needed to offer advanced study, we also propose that in large urban areas, magnet schools in the arts or science be developed for gifted and talented students.

In addition, a network of Residential Academies in Science and Mathematics should be established throughout the nation. Some might be within a densely populated district. Others might serve entire states. And, in less densely populated areas, a residential school might serve several states. Some of these academies may be located on college campuses. Such schools should receive federal support since, clearly, the vital interests of the nation are at stake.

One final point. While the emphasis here is on science and mathematics, there also is a need to serve exceptional students in other fields, especially foreign languages and the arts.

The High-Risk Student

New patterns are also needed for students at the other end of the education spectrum. Year after year, about one out of every four students who enroll in school drops out before graduation. However, the rate varies greatly from one state to another (Table 20). Usually, students stay in school in the early years, but begin to leave in junior high. Dropping-out peaks during the junior year, when 10 percent of the age group leave school. During the senior year another 6 percent will drop out.[25]

While there has been a slight downward trend in the proportion of school dropouts among nonwhites (aged sixteen to twenty-four),[26] the dropout rates continue to be higher for blacks and Hispanics than for whites. This gap persists precisely at a time when minority groups represent an increasing proportion of the youth population (Chart 9). In 1980, for example, 30 percent of all white Americans were nineteen years of age or under. For blacks, the corresponding figure was 40 percent; for Hispanics, 43 percent. If minority students continue to leave school at the current rate, the number of school dropouts will significantly increase.

Table 20 Public High School Graduates and Nongraduates as a Percent of Ninth-Grade Enrollment, by State: School Year 1980–81

State	1980–81 graduates	Ninth-grade enrollments 4 years earlier	Graduates as a percent of ninth-grade enrollment	Nongraduates as a percent of ninth-grade enrollment
50 States and D.C.	2,724,564	3,779,486	72.1	27.9
Alabama	44,894	66,899	67.1	32.9
Alaska	5,343	7,779	68.7	31.3
Arizona	28,416	41,153	69.0	31.0
Arkansas	29,577	39,563	74.8	25.2
California	242,172	356,094	68.0	32.0
Colorado	35,869	46,902	76.5	23.5
Connecticut	38,369	53,970	71.1	28.9
Delaware	7,349	10,111	72.7	27.3
District of Columbia	4,848	8,886	54.6	45.4
Florida	88,755	139,272	63.7	36.3
Georgia	62,963	97,936	64.3	35.7
Hawaii	11,472	14,415	79.6	20.4
Idaho	12,679	16,509	76.8	23.2
Illinois	136,795	186,984	73.2	26.8
Indiana	73,381	97,440	75.3	24.7
Iowa	42,635	50,297	84.8	15.2
Kansas	29,397	36,510	80.5	19.5
Kentucky	41,714	62,003	67.3	32.7
Louisiana	46,199	72,900	63.4	36.6
Maine	15,554	21,795	71.4	28.6
Maryland	54,050	72,046	75.0	25.0
Massachusetts	74,831	97,423	76.8	23.2
Michigan	124,372	171,649	72.5	27.5
Minnesota	63,247	73,509	86.0	14.0
Mississippi	28,083	45,452	61.8	38.2
Missouri	60,359	81,548	74.0	26.0
Montana	11,634	14,384	80.9	19.1
Nebraska	21,411	26,325	81.3	18.7
Nevada	9,069	11,808	76.8	23.2
New Hampshire	11,552	14,989	77.1	22.9
New Jersey	93,168	121,501	76.7	23.3
New Mexico	17,934	24,947	71.9	28.1
New York	198,465	301,129	65.9	34.1
North Carolina	69,601	103,751	67.1	32.9
North Dakota	9,924	11,687	84.9	15.1
Ohio	143,503	182,955	78.4	21.6
Oklahoma	38,875	50,542	76.9	23.1
Oregon	28,629	40,744	70.3	29.7

Table 20 Public High School Graduates and Nongraduates as a Percent of Ninth-Grade Enrollment, by State: School Year 1980–81 (continued)

State	1980–81 graduates	Ninth-grade enrollments 4 years earlier	Graduates as a percent of ninth-grade enrollment	Nongraduates as a percent of ninth-grade enrollment
Pennsylvania	144,645	183,933	78.6	21.4
Rhode Island	10,719	14,715	72.8	27.2
South Carolina	38,338	55,731	68.8	31.2
South Dakota	10,385	12,549	82.8	17.2
Tennessee	50,758	76,133	66.7	33.3
Texas	171,665	249,397	68.8	31.2
Utah	19,886	24,800	80.2	19.8
Vermont	6,424	8,510	75.5	24.5
Virginia	67,126	91,623	73.3	26.7
Washington	50,040	66,460	75.3	24.7
West Virginia	23,580	31,849	74.0	26.0
Wisconsin	67,743	82,264	82.3	17.7
Wyoming	6,161	7,706	80.0	20.0

Source: U.S. Department of Education, National Center for Education Statistics, *Bulletin* (Washington: U.S. Government Printing Office, May 1983), p. 5.

What happens to the nearly one million young people who leave school each year? As they scan the help-wanted columns or enter unemployment lines, dropouts quickly confront a harsh reality: jobs are very hard to come by, especially for uneducated people. Even if they find a job, it will be menial work with the lowest pay; and they will be the first to go when the economy turns sour.

Many dropouts endure these harsh realities until their early twenties, when they may move into more stable employment. For some, marriage will be the key to settling down. And possibly as many as half will eventually return to some form of further education—a community college or adult education program—or they may complete the high school equivalency program, the General Education Diploma.[27]

For those least fortunate, perhaps one-fourth to one-third of all dropouts, prospects will be grim.[28] Often moving in a shadow world of drugs or crime, they suffer chronic unemployment, and end up

Chart 9　Age Distribution as Percent of Racial Ethnic Population: 1980

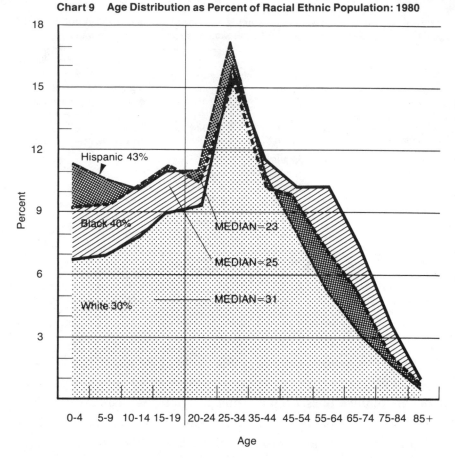

SOURCE: U.S. Department of Commerce, Bureau of the Census, "Population Profile of the United States: 1981," *Population Characteristics,* Series P-20, No. 374, p. 20.

**Table 21   Racial and Ethnic Distribution of Public Elementary/Secondary
School Enrollment, by State: Fall 1980**

State	Total	White Non-Hispanic	Minority	Black Non-Hispanic	Hispanic	American Indian/ Alaskan Native	Asian or Pacific Islander
			Percentage Distribution				
50 States and D.C.	100.0	73.3	26.7	16.1	8.0	0.8	1.9
Alabama	100.0	66.4	33.6	33.1	.1	.2	.2
Alaska	100.0	71.6	28.4	3.9	1.6	20.6	2.3
Arizona	100.0	66.3	33.7	4.2	24.2	4.1	1.1
Arkansas	100.0	76.5	23.5	22.5	.3	.4	.3
California	100.0	57.1	42.9	10.1	25.3	.8	6.6
Colorado	100.0	77.9	22.1	4.6	15.3	.5	1.7
Connecticut	100.0	83.0	17.0	10.2	5.8	.1	.9
Delaware	100.0	71.2	28.8	25.9	1.8	.1	.9
District of Columbia	100.0	3.6	96.4	93.4	2.0	0	1.0
Florida	100.0	67.8	32.2	23.4	7.9	.1	.0
Georgia	100.0	65.7	34.3	33.5	.3	0	.5
Hawaii	100.0	24.8	75.2	1.4	2.0	.2	71.4
Idaho	100.0	91.8	8.2	.5	4.6	2.1	1.0
Illinois	100.0	71.4	28.6	20.9	6.1	.1	1.5
Indiana	100.0	88.0	12.0	9.9	1.5	.1	.5
Iowa	100.0	95.9	4.1	2.2	.8	.2	.9
Kansas	100.0	87.3	12.7	7.8	3.0	.6	1.2
Kentucky	100.0	90.9	9.1	8.7	.1	0	.3
Louisiana	100.0	56.6	43.4	41.5	.8	.4	.8
Maine	100.0	99.1	.9	.3	.1	.2	.3
Maryland	100.0	66.5	33.5	30.6	.9	.2	1.8
Massachusetts	100.0	89.3	10.7	6.2	3.3	.1	1.1
Michigan	100.0	78.7	21.3	17.9	1.8	.8	.8
Minnesota	100.0	94.1	5.9	2.1	.7	1.6	1.5
Mississippi	100.0	48.4	51.6	51.0	.1	.1	.4
Missouri	100.0	85.2	14.8	13.6	.5	.1	.5
Montana	100.0	87.9	12.1	.3	1.2	9.8	.8
Nebraska	100.0	89.5	10.5	5.6	1.9	2.2	.8
Nevada	100.0	81.1	18.9	9.5	5.2	2.0	2.2
New Hampshire	100.0	98.7	1.3	.5	.4	0	.4
New Jersey	100.0	71.6	28.4	18.5	8.0	.1	1.7
New Mexico	100.0	43.0	57.0	2.2	46.5	7.8	.6
New York	100.0	68.0	32.0	17.9	12.0	.2	2.0
North Carolina	100.0	68.1	31.9	29.6	.2	1.6	.4
North Dakota	100.0	96.5	3.5	.5	.5	1.8	.7
Ohio	100.0	85.3	14.7	13.1	1.0	.1	.6
Oklahoma	100.0	79.2	20.8	9.3	1.6	9.1	.8

State	Total	White Non-Hispanic	Minority	Black Non-Hispanic	Hispanic	American Indian/ Alaskan Native	Asian or Pacific Islander
			Percentage Distribution				
Oregon	100.0	91.5	8.5	2.1	2.6	1.7	2.2
Pennsylvania	100.0	85.1	14.9	12.4	1.5	.2	.7
Rhode Island	100.0	91.8	8.2	4.7	2.1	.3	1.1
South Carolina	100.0	56.5	43.5	42.8	.2	.1	.4
South Dakota	100.0	92.1	7.9	.2	.2	7.2	.3
Tennessee	100.0	75.5	24.5	24.0	.1	0	.4
Texas	100.0	54.1	45.9	14.4	30.4	.2	1.1
Utah	100.0	92.7	7.3	.5	3.5	1.8	1.5
Vermont	100.0	99.0	1.0	.3	.1	.1	.5
Virginia	100.0	72.5	27.5	25.5	.5	.1	1.4
Washington	100.0	85.9	14.1	3.4	4.0	3.0	3.7
West Virginia	100.0	95.7	4.3	3.9	.1	0	.3
Wisconsin	100.0	90.7	9.3	6.2	1.5	.9	.7
Wyoming	100.0	92.5	7.5	.7	5.3	1.0	.4

Source: U.S. Department of Education, Office for Civil Rights, 1980 Elementary and Secondary Civil Rights
         Survey, *National Summaries,* 1982, and *State Summaries,* 1982, projected data.

on welfare, supplemented by part-time jobs or even petty theft. Rarely if ever do they return to formal education.

Why do young people drop out? The main reason students want to leave school is that they are discouraged and doing poorly. "Not interested in school" was mentioned most frequently by young white men as the reason for dropping out; whereas young nonwhite men were especially likely to mention economic reasons.[29] Marriage and pregnancy are the main reasons for dropping out given by white women, and are cited even more frequently by nonwhite women.[30]

Dropouts have, among other things, low grade averages, a lack of college plans, and a low evaluation of their own academic ability.[31] Deficiency in basic skills—in language and mathematics—is certainly a problem, too.

Dropouts tend to come from poor families. They have more

siblings, more broken homes, higher levels of parental punitiveness, and lower self-esteem. Their parents also have less schooling. Simply put, many students who leave school come from stressful homes.[32] As one student who threatened to drop out put it, "I don't feel close to any member of my family."[33]

What can be done? First, with all of its good intentions, the school has little influence over home and family environment. The high school cannot act in isolation. It cannot solve the dropout problem all alone. But schools can relieve some of the negative aspects of a poor environment. Patterns of school failure can be identified early.

It is in elementary school that dropout prevention must begin, with special emphasis on language, with continuous assessment of student progress, and with skilled counseling. Federally-supported remedial programs, most of which have been concentrated in the early grades, have demonstrated that improvements can be made in the academic achievement of even the most disadvantaged child. We recommend, therefore, that the federally-funded Elementary and Secondary Education Act (Title I) be fully funded to support all students who are eligible to participate in this effective program.

Again, we urge that the language proficiency of all students be tested before they enter high school, a proposal made in Chapter 6. Students who are deficient in reading and writing should receive special remedial help in a summer program and in the first year of high school. Improving language ability will, we believe, help give high-risk students the skill and confidence they need to stay in school.

Further, alternative schools might be organized to give intensive, continuous help to some high-risk students. We visited one such school, Neill Academy, a small institution located in an urban midwest school district. Some students at Neill were described as "fugitives" from their neighborhood schools. Others were bored and rebellious. Some had personal and emotional problems. All were ready to drop out. When these students were asked why they chose

Neill, the answers were generously sprinkled with words like "attachment," "belonging," "safety," and "a real home."

The Alternative School in Richmond, Indiana, was set up to help potential dropouts. Here students are placed in small groups so they don't get "lost" as they so often did in the past. The school is highly structured; rules are explicit; students know what to expect. At the same time, the faculty work to build up trust. Students have improved their attendance rate, reading and math scores, and behavior and attitude.[34]

Cooperative High School in New Haven, Connecticut, is another program for students who, for one reason or another, do not do well in a large school. Cooperative High was begun three years ago with a racially balanced enrollment of 90 students at all levels of ability. The enrollment now is about 300. The curriculum emphasis is on academic courses.[35]

Cities-in-Schools is an experimental program designed to link social services to education. Now operating in Atlanta, Houston, New York, and several other cities, it is financed by both public funds and private contributions. Cities-in-Schools students meet with counselors on a daily basis. The counselors monitor school work and school attendance, and are often from agencies outside the school. Attendance rates among chronically truant youths have increased.

Although we observed a variety of special programs for disadvantaged students, there was no single formula for success. However, at the heart of every effort that appeared to be succeeding, we noticed that there was a close relationship between a student and a counselor or teacher—there was a mentor with high standards and clear goals, one who had gained the student's confidence and trust. We recommend that programs be developed for high-risk students that provide special tutoring and a supportive relationship between a teacher and each student.

Serving disadvantaged students is the urgent unfinished agenda for American education. Unless we find ways to overcome the problem of failure in the schools, generations of students will continue to be doomed to frustrating, unproductive lives. This nation cannot afford to pay the price of wasted youth.

Keeping high-risk students in school is a top priority. But what about students who already have dropped out?

Students who leave high school are usually forgotten by the institution. Once the file has been closed, it is very difficult for it to be reopened. Dropouts become outcasts, socially adrift, with little or no guidance and support.

In North Carolina, community colleges are actively involved in dealing with school dropouts. This program—the National Model Dropout Information and Service Project—is operating through nine community colleges that, together, serve more than twenty school districts. A network has been established by the North Carolina community colleges to obtain the names of all students within a short time after they drop out of high school. The youngsters are contacted by phone or letter or in person. They are presented many options—from independent study to high school classes for adults to special help to prepare for a high school diploma by equivalency examination.[36]

The City University of New York has also taken an interest in dropouts. A program at six of its community colleges helps people prepare for the high school equivalency test. The program is run in conjunction with the New York City Board of Education, which pays for the coordinators, teachers, and paraprofessionals. In turn, the university actually does the hiring, training, and supervision of the staff. One of the keys to success in the New York City program is the fact that it operates on college campuses, where students feel a sense of greater self-esteem, and also have access to various college-level services, including counseling. Students also feel comfortable remaining on campus for further education after obtaining the diploma.[37]

We recommend that every high school district, working with a community college, have a reentry school arrangement to permit dropouts to return to school part time or full time or to engage in independent study to complete their education.

Schools are complex places, and if they are to function smoothly, they must be coordinated. The pieces must fit. Everything must work together. To introduce change in one place can throw a dozen other parts off balance. For that reason, disorder has always been one of the school administrator's deepest fears.

But the American high school is more than "a system"; it is a human environment, a place where young people come together for learning. Therefore, order and freedom must be carefully balanced, as must rigidity and flexibility.

There are over 16,000 high schools in the United States, with over 13 million students. And while the logistical problems are immense, so is the range of student needs. Meeting those needs remains the highest purpose of schooling. It is why, we believe, patterns must fit purpose.

PART VI

CONNECTIONS BEYOND
THE SCHOOL

15

THE COLLEGE CONNECTION

Hﾠigh schools do not carry on their work in isolation. They are connected to elementary and junior high schools and to higher education, to industry and businesses, to state and federal governments that provide support, and, above all, to the communities that surround them. In the end, the quality of the American high school will be shaped in large measure by the quality of these connections.

It happened in the late 1970s during one of those rituals when the presidents of Ohio's state-supported universities are summoned before a legislative committee. Several of them were there—Harold L. Enarson, the now retired president of Ohio State University; the late Hollis A. Moore, president of Bowling Green State University; and others. "All of us were lined up like so many blackbirds on a fence, each carrying one of those big books filled with numbers," recalled Enarson. "Then the steady drumfire began. 'Why,' they wanted to know, 'were the universities asking the State of Ohio to pay twice for the same thing? Why all this money for remediation after the high schools had already been paid to teach the same material?' "*[1]

And so it has gone all across the country as problems of the high schools remind everyone of the connection between what happens

*Parts of this chapter are adapted from a report prepared for this project entitled *School and College: Partnerships in Education* by Gene Maeroff, with a foreword by Ernest L. Boyer.

to students before they get to college and after they arrive on campus. Perhaps it took the shock treatment of remediation—having to offer college courses built around high-school-level content—to cause higher education to notice schools. Perhaps it was a loss of public confidence in education. Or the downturn in enrollments may have been what finally jolted higher education into a state of receptiveness.

In any event, college and high school educators are showing interest in each other. Conferences, conversations, and collaborative projects are cropping up from coast to coast. Such linkages between the nation's colleges and schools must be strengthened in order to establish academic standards, permit students to move more flexibly from one level to another, enrich the work of classroom teachers, and strengthen education programs at the local school.

Setting Academic Standards

"The high schools in this country are always at the mercy of the colleges," said A. Bartlett Giamatti, the president of Yale University. "The colleges change their requirements and their admissions criteria, and the high schools, by which I mean public and private parochial schools, are constantly trying to catch up with what the colleges are thinking. When the colleges don't seem to know what they think over a period of time, it's no wonder that this oscillation takes place all the way through the system."[2]

The particular courses a student takes are not important for getting into most colleges, although they may be critical to success once a student is there. Half the colleges set no specific course requirements, and only about one-fourth consider the courses taken in making a decision for or against admission. When specific courses are identified, the most frequently required are English (the usual requirement being four years), mathematics (two years is the average requirement), and the physical sciences (one year).

By the early 1980s, efforts were under way to tighten standards and let high school students know what would be expected of them. Admission requirements were being changed or reviewed for the public systems of higher education in twenty-seven states, according to a survey in 1982 by the National Association of Secondary School Principals.[3]

In Ohio, the clouds of legislative intervention hovered over Ohio State and the other state-sponsored campuses. This threat forced Ohio educators to reexamine the relationship between secondary schools and higher education. What had long been taken for granted became a subject for scrutiny. The State Board of Education and the Ohio Board of Regents formed an advisory commission to study school-college transition and to offer recommendations.[4]

The Ohio commission quickly concluded that there was a need to strengthen the English and mathematics courses in high schools across the state. It recommended that the college preparatory curriculum in every high school in Ohio include four years of English and at least three years of mathematics. Moreover, it recommended that every private and state-sponsored four-year college and university in Ohio require students to take these courses in order to gain unconditional admission.

What was so stunning about all this was that, for the first time, the State of Ohio was telling students they no longer would be unconditionally admitted to public college. The flexible policy of admissions was not abrogated, but suddenly students had an obligation to show that they had tried to prepare themselves adequately.

In Florida, a Postsecondary Education Planning Commission called for a detailed definition of the college curriculum, particularly in the first two years. This is viewed as a prerequisite to defining what the schools should be offering in preparing students for college study. The Florida Commission called for a phase-out of all remedial education at the college level by 1988. Such responsibility is to be totally assumed by the high schools.[5]

On the West Coast, the academic senates of the California Community Colleges, the California State University, and the University of California recommend that every student planning to pursue a bachelor's degree take at least four years of English and at least three years of mathematics in high school. Moreover, at least one course in each of these subjects should be taken in the senior year, which had disintegrated into an academic wasteland for many students in California high schools. The voluminous statement prepared by the academic senates includes lengthy descriptions of the kinds of skills that students should acquire in each subject and samples of the sort of work they should be able to handle.

In Utah, a full-page advertisement appearing in the Salt Lake *Tribune* said it all. Addressed to high school students and their parents as an open letter from the University of Utah, the advertisement listed a recommended course of study in high school that purportedly would increase chances for success at the institution.[6]

It was recommended that, beginning in 1987, students have four years of English, two years of mathematics, three years of science, four years of history and social studies, three years of foreign language, and two years of fine arts.

As if the message needed amplification, Utah announced that there would be no more remedial courses offered as part of the regular program on campus after the middle 1980s. Students will have to take remedial courses at off-campus extension sites, paying extra and receiving no credit.

Copies of the advertisement are pinned on the walls of advisors' offices in high schools from Logan to Cedar City, a not too subtle reminder that expectations are rising.

These moves to clarify standards for admission are in the right direction, but colleges should not act alone. We recommend that all states establish a School-College Coordination Panel to permit educators at both levels to define an integrated school-college curriculum that provides both continuity and coherence and assures smooth transfer from high school to higher education.

Accelerating Students

About the time high school students complete their sophomore years, they become very much like the rope in a game of tug of war in which schools and colleges are adversaries. Colleges pull bright high school juniors and seniors to the campus with special programs at the postsecondary level. Schools, on the other hand, occasionally try to hold students back and are reluctant to lose them.

Secondary schools and colleges have a special obligation to break the bureaucratic barriers and develop flexible arrangements for students as they move from one level to another. Such arrangements include advanced placement, credit by examination, early college admission, and "university in the school" programs, to name just a few.

In May of 1982, 141,626 students from 5,525 high schools took 188,933 advanced-placement examinations. Results were sent to 1,976 colleges and universities.[7] These examinations, prepared by the Educational Testing Service and given under the auspices of the College Board, make it possible for high school students to receive college credit. The scores, on a scale of 1 for the lowest and 5 for the highest, are submitted to the institutions of higher education that the students plan to attend, and it is up to each college to decide how much consideration to give the work.

During the year of our visit to Brette High School, 326 students took 489 advanced-placement examinations. A remarkable 90 percent of the examinees earned scores that ranged from 3.4 to 5, to qualify for college credit or advanced study—a success rate unmatched by any other secondary school of comparable size.

Some institutions, including the University of California at Berkeley, have had long-standing programs to bring high school students onto their campuses. At Berkeley, the Accelerated High School Student Program is aimed at seniors in the Bay Area who have demonstrated their potential for doing college-level work.

Their high school principals must nominate them for the program, and parents have to give their consent.

Students spend at least four periods a day at the high schools where they remain officially enrolled. They are restricted to no more than two courses per quarter at Berkeley and may earn up to a maximum of ten academic credits from the university as accelerated students.

High school students in Berkeley's accelerated program also sit in regular undergraduate courses. They are expected to do the same work as the others and are graded on the same basis. If they eventually enroll at Berkeley, the credits they earn count toward their degree requirements, and if they enroll elsewhere they can apply to have the credits transferred. The list of courses at Berkeley in which high school students have participated reads like an undergraduate transcript, cutting across subjects from anthropology to geology to Italian to physics and sociology.

Such programs have one serious drawback. High school funding is based on average daily attendance, and schools lose money when their students leave the campus. This difficulty is overcome by programs like Syracuse University's Project Advance, which permits students to earn college credits without leaving their high school classrooms. Youngsters who successfully complete a Project Advance course are guaranteed college credits from Syracuse. If the student decides eventually to attend the university, the credits are waiting there to be claimed. If he attends some other institution, a transcript will be sent.

Seventy-five high schools in four states—New York, New Jersey, Massachusetts, and Michigan—are participating in the Syracuse program. In six different subjects, ranging from biology to sociology, the program uses the same material and the same tests given to university freshmen in their introductory courses. The teachers are experienced and exceptionally well-qualified. Research comparing the performance of students who take the courses in high schools with those who take them at the university shows very similar achievement.[8]

The high school itself decides which students to admit to Project Advance. Syracuse requires only that the student has completed the normal curriculum through the eleventh grade. This means, for example, that the student has already taken a high school course in biology or chemistry and that the Project Advance course comes on top of, and not as a substitute for, the high school course. Thus, almost all of the participants are high school seniors, usually getting both high school and college credit for the courses.

Project Advance helps high school teachers feel more self-confident by giving them regular exposure to colleagues in higher education. Every Project Advance class is visited at least once a semester by a representative from Syracuse. Also, once a semester, university faculty members meet as a group with high school teachers from the same disciplinary area. This all comes on top of intensive summer workshops of seven to ten days in which campus professors discuss common problems with high school counterparts who are teaching the same courses.

Operating on a more limited scale, Kenyon College in Ohio has its School/College Articulation Program, through which six private schools are able to offer courses that lead to college credits. Kenyon, like Syracuse, awards its credits to students who successfully complete the courses in their high schools and a Kenyon transcript is sent to whichever college the student decides to attend.

Among the most extraordinary efforts to reach out to youngsters on the precollegiate level has been that of Johns Hopkins University in behalf of the gifted. It is a cooperative venture not so much between a university and the high schools as between a university and the students themselves. Julian C. Stanley, a psychology professor at Hopkins, laid the foundation for the program in 1971 when he sought a way to identify young mathematical geniuses. He wanted to create a program for allowing gifted students to work closer to their capacities than the traditional secondary school curriculum permitted.[9]

Courses on the university campus itself are thrown open to the students, and more than a few have raced through the secondary curriculum, or, in rare instances, skipped it altogether, and entered the university at the age of fifteen or sixteen or younger. "I didn't feel at all out of place in skipping four grades and going to college," said a student who went on from Hopkins to become a doctoral candidate in computer science at Cornell by the time he was twenty years old.[10]

There are also summer institutes for gifted junior and senior high school students. The sites in 1982 were the campuses of two colleges in Pennsylvania—Dickinson College and Franklin and Marshall College. Courses were given in such areas as Latin, computer science, biology, psychology, composition, German, astronomy, and chemistry. Students, on the average, completed two high school mathematics courses in three weeks of instruction during the summer program, according to officials. Furthermore, a quarter of the participants completed all four and a half years of their high school precalculus mathematics education in a three-week period.[11]

A few, largely experimental, institutions have been organized to merge school and college into "middle" or "transition" schools.

The idea is not new. In the 1920s, Pasadena City College brought the eleventh, twelfth, thirteenth, and fourteenth grades under the same roof. One modern version is Simon's Rock of Bard College in Great Barrington, Massachusetts. Located in the Berkshire Hills of Massachusetts, Simon's Rock is designed for restless young people for whom traditional high schools offer inadequate challenge. Students enter Simon's Rock directly after completion of the tenth grade, on the basis not only of academic performance, but also of maturity and evidence of ability to do college-level work. After two years at Simon's Rock, students are awarded associate of arts degrees. After two more years, they can receive bachelor's degrees.[12]

Matteo Ricci College in Seattle unites two private institutions, Seattle Preparatory School and Seattle University. They pool their resources to provide a joint program for students who complete the eighth grade and elect to spend six years on studies aimed at both the high school diploma and a college degree.[13]

The high school portion of the program is concentrated on the campus of Seattle Preparatory School and is referred to as Matteo Ricci I. The college program, Matteo Ricci II, is offered at Seattle University, and draws upon the university's faculty. Mathematics and foreign languages are taught conventionally, but such subjects as literature, history, and religion are handled in an interdisciplinary mode. Time shortening is not achieved by concentrating on gifted students or by accelerating traditional instruction. It is made possible by tightening the entire six-year course to eliminate overlap and duplication.

Middle College of La Guardia Community College in Long Island City, New York, serves students who might not, on their own, regard college as an option. It is operated jointly by the New York City Board of Education and La Guardia Community College, a part of the City University of New York. Both the high school and college portions of the program are physically located on the community college campus, and its students are encouraged to use many of the college's facilities. Some of the high school teachers spend time in the classrooms of the school. In some instances, high school students actually attend college classes and earn college credit for their work. A special feature of the program requires that every student in the Middle College spend a portion of the year in volunteer work in the community. Credit is awarded for such service.[14]

Students enter Middle College in their junior year and work toward a high school diploma and an Associate of Liberal Arts Degree. Gene Maeroff in his report on school-college connections observes:

After a shaky start in the middle 1970s, the high school has a lower drop-out rate than the citywide average and its average rate of daily attendance exceeds that of the city. Eighty-five percent of its graduates go on to college.[15]

In a recent survey, The Carnegie Foundation for the Advancement of Teaching identified about 260 programs that enrolled students in college-level programs before they finished high school.[16] We estimated that more than 28,000 students were served by such arrangements. The obvious question may be why, if the programs are so good, there are not more of them.

Part of the answer, of course, is that not all students in high school are college preparatory students. Moreover, not all college preparatory students are ready for acceleration. Another reason is that school-college collaboration is not easy. To succeed, it requires extraordinary agreement among administrators and faculty members on goals and the means by which they are to be reached.

Despite the difficulties and limitations of school-college cooperation, its potential is well worth securing for more of the nation's young people. We therefore urge that experiments in school-college cooperation be extended. Specifically, we recommend that every high school offer a "university in the school" program and other flexible arrangements—credit by examination, early admission, and advanced placement—to permit able students to accelerate their academic progress.

Enriching Classrooms and Teachers

All the talk about higher standards for new teachers, even if translated into action, will have a limited immediate effect on what happens in classrooms. The biggest difference in improving schools will be made by bolstering the skills and morale of those already on the job. They form the largest portion of the group that will be teaching in the schools during the 1980s.

Colleges and universities must plan to work with those they

trained in previous years in order to bring about profound improvements in secondary education. One organization puts schools in contact with humanists for just such purposes. The National Humanities Faculty, founded in 1968, is a group of some seven hundred people who teach at colleges and universities throughout the country. They have agreed to make themselves available to meet with schoolteachers to help them strengthen their grasp of the humanities.[17] The project belongs to the school, not to the National Humanities Faculty, which serves basically as a consulting firm.

Projects in which the National Humanities Faculty is involved are as varied as the humanities themselves. There has been a program to teach grammar and writing at a school in the mountains of West Virginia by using the region's folklore, music, and history. Another program, in a typical small industrial town in Indiana, involved teaching literature and history by having students interview their parents and grandparents about the impact of the Depression and then supplement the interview with appropriate readings.

Benjamin DeMott, Andrew W. Mellon professor of the humanities at Amherst College, is among the better-known members of the National Humanities Faculty. DeMott has discovered that professors who agree to help their precollegiate colleagues should not approach the task innocently.

"Once you are there," DeMott observes, "you may say you are just a visitor, but you are into it up to your ears and you are seen as an ally of the teacher who arranged to bring you to the school. You have to figure out how to enlarge the team and start building bridges immediately. Once they trust you, you are treated with warmth and you get a sense of common enterprise. When you do something like this, you get to know more about where your students come from."[18]

The Yale–New Haven Teachers Institute, begun in 1978, bridges the usual barriers between town and gown. About eighty teachers a year from the city's secondary schools study with senior professors on the campus of the Ivy League university.

A poll of the New Haven teachers who have been fellows at Yale through the institute revealed that, for almost half of them, the chance to participate in the program has been an important factor in helping them decide to remain as public schoolteachers in New Haven.[19]

The range of offerings in the spring of 1982 was typical of the institute. Seven separate seminars were running—Society and Literature in Latin America, Autobiography, The Constitution in American History and American Life, Society and the Detective Novel, An Unstable World: The West in Decline?, The Changing American Family, and Human Fetal Development.

The experience of Linda Powell, a New Haven teacher, illustrates how this works. A recent seminar in which she participated was devoted to study of British colonialism, and Powell used it to write a three-week curriculum unit on modern China. "I was able to talk about China in connection with what it did to stand up to colonialism," she said. "This program is a way to study what you know you are going to need to teach; you don't have to worry about a prescribed set of readings you may never use."[20]

A program that began at the University of Michigan in 1978 helps the schools in a different way. It is an outreach program designed to help high school teachers throughout Michigan—in all subjects—to train their students to be better writers. In this case, unlike Yale, the university eventually enrolls many of the students affected by the program.[21]

Five years ago, the faculty of the College of Literature, Science, and the Arts at Michigan approved new writing requirements that affect students from the time they enter the university until they graduate. After an evaluation of an hour-long essay that each incoming freshman writes, the student is placed in a small tutorial class or an introductory composition class or a group exempted from lower-division writing requirements. About 80 percent of the freshmen at the University of Michigan end up in the introductory composition class.

Something like this happens in many institutions of higher education. What is notably different at Michigan, however, is that all students—from those who were the least able writers to those who were the most able—must fulfill a thirty-six-page writing requirement in one of the courses they take in their major field of study during the junior or senior year.

Michigan's program has proved so popular that its professors are now carrying the gospel of good writing into high schools in other states. Yale's program has been so helpful to the teachers of New Haven that it is being permanently endowed.

Such successes should come as no surprise to those who watched the growth of the Bay Area Writing Project. What began as a small program at the University of California at Berkeley in 1974, expanded to cover the length and breadth of the country as the National Writing Project. At more than eighty sites in thirty-three states, schoolteachers were brought to college campuses to learn how to be better writers, so that, in turn, they could teach their fellow teachers and their students to be better writers.[22]

The point of all this is that there is a thirst among the nation's secondary teachers for all kinds of help that will improve and ease their work. If the quality of the teaching in America's public schools is going to rise, then the nation's institutions of higher education cannot afford to sit back as indifferent spectators while the schools struggle with problems that they cannot solve alone. We recommend that school-college partnerships for the continuing-education of teachers be collaboratively developed.

During our own school visits we found disappointingly few examples where colleges and universities were helping teachers. Garfield High is a case in point. It is in the shadow of a distinguished university. Some of the most quoted and respected research on teachers emanates from the pens of its famous professors, but there is no contact between them and Garfield educators. University faculty told us they were "interested" in Garfield High but they have other interests—a book or article, a research project to run.

Unless colleges and universities deepen their commitment to teachers and change their system of recognition and rewards, they cannot help the schools.

Special Models: One-to-One Connections

Some colleges are working comprehensively with single schools. If schools had parents, Queens College in New York City would be both mother and father to the Louis Armstrong Middle School. The college has been involved in the school since its opening three years ago. Faculty members and student teachers from the college have been integrated into the day-to-day life of the school, which runs from fifth through eighth grade.[23]

The focus of this attention is a building in the East Elmhurst area of northern Queens, a potpourri of ethnicity twenty minutes by subway from Times Square. It is smack between the roar of the jets at La Guardia Airport and the roar of the fans at Shea Stadium. The nearby Corona neighborhood, a black enclave, was the home of the musician whose memory the school honors. Carefully drawing its students from a waiting list of one thousand, the school has created a model of integration reflecting the makeup of the Borough of Queens.

No teacher in the school can fail to feel the effects of the collaboration with the college. The impact can be seen in the way it impinges on just one teacher, Mary Ellen Levin, whose subject is English. Like other teachers in the school, Levin has been able to take courses free at the college. Recently, after completing one such course in computer language, she was allowed to keep her terminal and take it back to school to use with her students. When Levin needed a library consultant, the college sent one. The college also provided a storytelling expert to meet with her students once a week. Most semesters, Levin is assisted by a student teacher from Queens College. She also is able to guide some of her students and their parents into the family counseling program that the college makes available for the school community.

Students and professors from Queens College are fixtures in the Armstrong School. The student teachers are primarily responsible for the Early Bird Program permitting youngsters to arrive at school at 8 A.M., forty-five minutes before the regular schedule begins, for sports and crafts activities. The college has been heavily involved in the museum that was established in the school. The guidance provided by the college has enabled the school to develop an elaborate outreach program to parents and other members of the community, an effort that includes counseling, adult education, and a host of activities that link the school to the people of Queens.

The model of cooperation developed between Queens College and the Armstrong School is not perfect, nor would it suit every pair of institutions. But it is the sort of relationship that ought to be found more frequently. Not all colleges have the opportunity to give birth to a school in the way Queens College did. However, we recommend that all institutions of higher education establish a comprehensive partnership with one or more secondary schools.

What makes a school-college project work?

First, to achieve effective school-college cooperation, educators at both levels must agree that they do, indeed, have common interests. This point is embarrassingly obvious—it is like Knute Rockne telling his players that first they need a football. Yet the harsh truth is that many educators are convinced that they can go it all alone. It is reported that Henry David Thoreau scorned the idea of stringing telegraph lines between Maine and Texas because he wondered what in the world New Englanders and Texans could possibly have to say to one another![24] Today, many school and college people are like Texans and New Englanders before the telegraph. They have no messages to send, or so they think. And yet education is a seamless web; communication between the sectors is urgently required.

Second, in order to achieve effective collaboration, the traditional academic "pecking order" must be overcome. Colleges and universities have had, for many years, a "plantation mentality" about schools. Higher education set the ground rules and schools were expected passively to go along.

Consider, for example, the way college admission requirements are established and abandoned. Faculty committees deliberate in splendid isolation. They make decisions that have enormous impact on the school curriculum. Yet, when these dramatic moves are made —when foreign languages are introduced or eliminated or reintroduced—high school teachers, principals and superintendents rarely are consulted.

Consider also the way continuing-education programs are unilaterally developed. All too often, schools of education decide what courses should be taught and when they should be taught. Frequently the real needs of teachers are not adequately considered.

Fortunately, this traditional pecking order is beginning to break down, as illustrated in the examples we have presented. But these are the exceptions, not the rule. Time and time again, programs are launched with very little consultation with the schools. The point is this: If the quality of American education is to improve, top-down planning will not do. Teachers and administrators in the public schools must be full partners in the process.

Third, if school-college collaboration is to succeed, cooperative projects must be sharply focused.

Recently, a school-college project was announced in a midwestern city. With great enthusiasm everyone agreed to work together. Greetings were exchanged, toasts were raised, but it soon became clear that everyone was vague about the problem they hoped to solve.

To put it simply, school-college "togetherness" must be something more than an academic love-in. Serious cooperation will occur only if school and college people agree to focus on a few specific goals and work to keep the programs sharply focused. Everything cannot be done at once.

Fourth, if school-college cooperation is to be successful, those who participate must get recognition. Collaboration will win or lose to the degree that participants understand that the projects are important and that there will be professional rewards.

Syracuse University's Project Advance has been successful because it is a true partnership and because the project is sharply focused. But the program also is a success because teachers are rewarded. High schools pay a stipend for teachers to participate in the Syracuse summer training program, which is viewed as professional development. Instructional materials are furnished by the university.

Syracuse gives Project Advance teachers the title of "Adjunct Instructor," which makes them eligible for scholarship grants at the university, or, in some cases, at other institutions close to home. Participating teachers also may receive 50 percent of the cost of graduate credits (for a master's or Ph.D.). And those participating are recognized, within their schools and communities, as outstanding teachers.

The fifth principle is equally important: For school-college cooperation to work, it must focus on action, not machinery.

Time and time again, when people think about collaboration they focus first on budgets and bureaucracy, on the costs involved, on hiring one or two directors, on renting space, on paper clips and a new letterhead.

This is self-defeating. And, quite frankly, this kind of talk frequently is a smoke screen for an unwillingness to act. While resources are important, they should not become the preoccupation of school and college planners. The most successful programs are those for which people see a need and find time to act with little red tape or extra funding.

The projects described in this chapter illustrate the five essential ingredients of collaboration. Schools and colleges are working together to establish standards, accelerate students' progress, create new kinds of institutions, educate teachers, and enrich the schools. The goal is to serve the student, not the system.

16

CLASSROOMS
AND CORPORATIONS

It is early afternoon at a large high school in a midwestern city. Classes are still in session. There is lively discussion in a remedial mathematics class. The day before, the class had been visited by three executives from the Mid-Continental Bottling Company. They had divided the class into three "companies" (Sunkist, Dr. Pepper, and Hawaiian Punch) and given each company mock grocery-chain accounts. On this day, the Sunkist group was discussing ways of conducting product-demand surveys. In another corner of the room, Hawaiian Punch group members were looking at various types of packaging that could be used for their product. A student from the third group stood at the chalkboard figuring out unit-pricing formulas with the help of her peers. As the teacher remarked, this day was a first for many. "They've never before found basic math so relevant or understandable."[1]

Traditionally, corporate America has stood aloof from public schools. While complaining about the quality of education, it has failed to get involved.

Several years ago, Willard Wirtz, former Secretary of Labor and a pioneer in industry-education collaboration, observed that, while business leaders have a stake in education, "in no sense do they become full partners in the joint enterprise. . . . Virtually every community in the country has an untapped reservoir of personnel and information. . . . What is lacking is the requisite collaborative process."[2]

Today, however, collaboration is in full swing.

James B. Hunt, Jr., governor of North Carolina, chairman of the Task Force on Economic Growth, and of the Education Commission of the States, has vigorously urged corporate America to rally around the public schools. The term "Adopt-a-School," first introduced over fifteen years ago, is now almost commonplace. A host of school-business partnerships are springing up from coast to coast. At last count, forty-two states had appointed task forces to build bridges between industry and the schools. Currently there are over one hundred business-education councils in major cities, involving many hundreds of high schools across the United States.[3]

In 1980, Tenneco Oil in Houston, Texas, hosted a kickoff reception for a new citywide program called Volunteers in Public Schools. Chief executive officers from one hundred major companies in the Houston area met with the president of the Chamber of Commerce and the superintendent of schools. Each corporate participant was asked to name a contact person to serve as program coordinator. The partnership between the schools and businesses of Houston was born. Today there are about eighty partnership programs in the city.

Several years ago, the St. Louis public schools developed a School Partnership Program. The project brings the resources of the St. Louis community to the aid of its public schools in a way that forms connections not only with businesses, but also with professional organizations, government and cultural agencies, and colleges.

Chicago has a citywide Adopt-a-School program. The superintendent of public schools asks each high school to supply an educational "wish list." A network of industries, in turn, have committed themselves to work with schools at least once a week, for a minimum of one year. Businesses generally target a school in their immediate area. Meetings are arranged between principals and industry representatives. A plan of action is agreed to with the Adopt-a-School coordinator. Currently, about 20 percent of Chicago's high schools have been "adopted."

Pittsburgh's Partnerships in Education began four years ago, led by the Allegheny Conference. The conference is a regional private partnership to promote the city's renaissance. It works with the greater Pittsburgh Chamber of Commerce and the Pittsburgh Board of Public Education. The conference sponsors the Allegheny Conference Education Fund, which has raised nearly $1 million from local corporations and foundations. School projects include enrichment programs for teachers, scholars in residence in the schools, and work connections with industry, to name a few.

David Bergholz, assistant executive director of the Allegheny Conference, says, "Public education is now on the private sector's agenda."[4] The Ford Foundation has singled out Pittsburgh's program as a model, and is providing grants to encourage similar programs in more than forty cities.

A school-industry partnership program was born in Boston during the 1974 school desegregation crisis. The first partnership, between one school and a telephone company, has expanded to include all of Boston's high schools and twenty-one corporations.

In 1977, in Los Angeles, a group of Atlantic Richfield employees wanted to do something for children in nearby schools. They "adopted" two inner-city elementary schools and agreed to tutor children several hours every week. The program became Atlantic Richfield's Joint Educational Project. Other businesses, large and small, followed in Atlantic Richfield's footsteps. In Los Angeles, the Adopt-a-School program is now citywide.

The private sector has a significant role to play in the support of education. Schools need the help of business, business needs the schools. The quality of work is linked to the quality of education.

What, specifically, can business do to enrich public education? Five separate strategies are proposed.

Helping "Needy" Students

First, businesses can work with students who are educationally disadvantaged.

B. Dalton Booksellers, the nation's largest chain of bookstores, has been supporting literacy projects since 1977. Dalton employees serve as tutors and donate time to local library boards in ten states and forty communities.[5]

In Chicago, a natural gas firm, People's Energy, sends tutors to the schools. Twenty employees tutor reading and math at Tilden High School for one and one-half hours twice weekly. In Houston the program that Tenneco first launched now sends twenty-five employees to primarily Hispanic inner-city schools, again providing tutorial help to students with language difficulty.

A Chicago candy manufacturer developed a creative project for one hundred nearby high school students in need of remedial help. The students were organized into small competitive teams that were challenged to produce a new candy and market it to fellow students. The teams were responsible for every aspect of the process, from market research to design, production, advertising, and evaluation.

Hughes Tool in Houston sends Hispanic and Vietnamese workers to tutor high school students of the same ethnic groups. These tutors serve as role models, and place special emphasis on communication skills. In Los Angeles, Atlantic Richfield employees are given released time to tutor Hispanic students in English usage. Atlantic Richfield volunteers also counsel students suffering from academic and personal problems.

The First Federal Bank of Chicago has developed a Foreign Language Resource Center to tutor three hundred students for whom English is a second language. In addition, the students are taken to Chicago's cultural centers, which would otherwise be inaccessible to many of them.

Other businesses have been active in helping students stay in school. Benito Juarez High School in Chicago had an average absenteeism rate of nearly 20 percent during the 1980–81 school year. Illinois Bell organized a "call squad" of bilingual employees. With the help of the Board of Education's computer, the squad identified all absentees and called their homes before nine o'clock each morning to determine if their absences were legitimate, and to alert their parents if they were not. At the end of the 1981–82 school year, absenteeism had fallen to 13 percent.

In Atlanta, Rich's department store created an academy for one hundred dropouts and potential dropouts. The program—a part of the national Cities-in-Schools program—offers classes in the basic skills, and personal and job counseling. The school is located in an unused portion of their central-city store.

The Greater Baltimore Committee has a dropout prevention program called "Operation Rescue." Each week, employees from a number of companies go to high schools to talk with students who are on the verge of leaving. The same employee goes to a particular school every week. Relationships develop between the volunteers and the students, and, along with them, a sense of trust.

Other programs attack the dropout problem by working directly with families. Some companies sponsor special events to bring parents into the high schools. At the James Monroe High School Adult Skills Center in the Bronx, New York, parents study office techniques, computer programming, and English as a second language.

Enrichment for the Gifted

Businesses also can help gifted students, especially in science and mathematics, and the new technologies.

Shell Development, for example, sends high-level technical and computing staff to Houston's Jones High School Vanguard Program for the Gifted. When questioned about the program, a student remarked that the volunteers "stretch us beyond what the teacher can do."[6] Similar reactions have been reported at Houston's Engineering High School, which is visited weekly by a team of engineers. A graduate, when asked who had had the greatest influence on his career choice, cited the IBM volunteer with whom he had worked in class for one year. The Oak Forest Bank, also of Houston, gives awards to students who demonstrate outstanding leadership qualities. A few programs provide summer scholarships for promising students. Bell Laboratories and other businesses provide sponsoring scholarships for college-bound students in fields of study related to the industry.

Advanced math students from Southwest High School in St. Louis travel to Monsanto, where engineers provide instruction in Fortran computer programming. Under the same program, biology students visit environmental labs and chemistry classes tour research and development laboratories at Monsanto.

In the student reactions to the Southwest-Monsanto partnership, one can sense the power and potential of these collaborative efforts. When asked, "What do you think is the most important thing you gained from this program?" students responded in these terms:

> I met and learned from three successful black engineers. They were all young and attended different schools. They set an example for me that I can pattern myself after.[7]

> I thought it was great that all the employees depend on each other and work as a team.[8]

> Now I *really* know what an engineer does—they solve problems, know how chemicals are used in industry and how what we're learning is applied to everyday life.[9]

> I learned how chemistry, physics, biology and mathematics are interwoven on a practical level.[10]

Helping Teachers

Perhaps the most promising role for corporations is the renewal of the teacher. McDonnell-Douglas Corporation has opened its Employee Voluntary Improvement Program to the staff at nearby Central High School—at no charge. Under this program, high school administrators take management seminars and teachers take courses in computer science, algebra, and trigonometry. Moreover, the head of the business department at Central went through the McDonnell-Douglas Secretarial School and as a result made major changes in the curriculum to better prepare students for vocations.

Helping teachers can take a variety of forms. A particularly creative project involved the Robert Bosch Corporation of Charleston, South Carolina. For eight weeks during the summer of 1977, Bosch employed high school guidance counselors to build fuel injection pumps at a local plant. For many of the participants, it was their first taste of life in the blue-collar world.

Science teachers, especially those who deal with gifted students, are frequently singled out to participate in special workshops. Houston teachers of science get together with scientists from industry to discuss new developments in their fields. Teacher "clinics" have been conducted in other subject areas too. In Pittsburgh, Westinghouse sponsors seminars and workshops to improve the communication skills of teachers.

In Boston, the Bank of New England set aside $300,000 to be used to recognize and reward outstanding teachers over a five-year period. The bank issues nine Teacher Excellence Awards of $6,500 each year.

Pittsburgh's Allegheny Conference on Community Development awards mini-grants to one hundred innovative teachers for proposed projects. A committee composed of representatives from the mayor's office, the superintendent of schools, the Urban League, and various corporations distributes grants to teachers totaling about $10,000. These grants can range from $50 to $1,000. They have been awarded for such creative projects as a course combining the teaching of art and geometry (now part of the school's electives curriculum) and an illustrated booklet describing how art objects can be created from industrial throw-aways.

The possibilities are almost endless. The idea of the endowed chair, typically a university practice, also might be used as a way to reward excellence among public school teachers. A minimum endowment of $25,000 would provide a small annual bonus for one teacher over the course of his or her career or it could be rotated from teacher to teacher or school to school.[11] For the teacher awarded an endowed chair, the boost in prestige and morale would be at least as valuable as the bonus, and would help keep outstanding teachers in the school. The endowed chair program could be administered by the school district, with the teacher chosen by a district-wide committee composed primarily of teachers, but also including school administrators and PTA members.

We urge that businesses in all communities support excellence in teaching by providing teacher grants, fellowships, and special recommendations.

Connections to Work

Businesses can help students take the step from school to work.

Before the name Adopt-a-School came along, General Electric donated a $5 million plant for use by the Cleveland Board of Education. That facility, located in the heart of the high unemployment district, became the Woodland Job Center. Students at Woodland work on various assembly lines, and are paid for their work. Shop work is supplemented by a thorough sixteen-session orientation program presented by General Electric foremen. Many graduates of the program move on to jobs in General Electric's main plant.

Over ten years ago, in Louisville, Kentucky, General Electric established a close relationship with the public schools. Corporate officials met with students to discuss employment requirements, working conditions, and job expectations. The result: school and job options were better linked.

In another midwestern city, industry experts come to school to lecture in work-related programs. In an advanced chemistry laboratory, for example, students prepare the basic chemical component of aspirin. Research chemists from Mallinkrodt Chemical discuss with the students the differences and similarities between their own laboratory work and the commercial production of pharmaceuticals.

In Los Angeles, Atlantic Richfield employees volunteer at Manual Arts High School to help students learn about the new microcomputers purchased by the school. The company also arranges field trips to the ARCO Word Processing Data Center, and employees help students fill out sample job applications. In addition, ARCO personnel join over one hundred other local industry representatives in career days that are held in the Los Angeles area.

The Volunteers in Public Schools program in Houston, Texas, maintains a speakers' bureau of over a thousand speakers. A lecture concerning almost any business or industry can be arranged at the request of a teacher. And Southwestern Bell has "adopted" an entire Houston high school senior class. Every member of the class who so desires fills out a job application, participates in a mock job interview, and is critiqued by the "interviewer." This experience is tremendously useful in helping students prepare for work.

The Boston Compact is a nonbinding agreement between the Boston school system, the Chamber of Commerce, and nearly two hundred businesses in the region. The compact stipulates that entry-level work requirements be identified by industry and that high school students be prepared to meet those requirements. In return, businesses in the compact have committed themselves to give these students top consideration for employment.

American business has a high stake in helping students make the transition from school to work. Introducing students to employment possibilities is, we conclude, a primary obligation of industry and business. We recommend that business provide apprenticeship experiences, as well as part-time and summer jobs, to high school students, to assist them as they consider options for the future.

School Management and Leadership

Business and industry also can be administrators, particularly in aiding the principals in their capacity as both manager and leader.

As early as 1966, the Olin Winchester Group loaned management trouble shooters to New Haven schools for six months of consultation. That same year, Warren King and Associates evaluated the management of schools in Ohio and Oregon. Eighty firms participated. Teams of executives visited two hundred schools and made recommendations, resulting in savings of over $100,000 each year.[12] And several years ago, the city of Baltimore saved $700,000 in its school-bus operations through changes proposed by business consultants.

A critically important—but often overlooked—possibility is the need to help administrators improve and better utilize school facilities and equipment. While the nation clamors for better teaching in science and mathematics, teachers often do not even have the basic equipment they need to do the job. Even outstanding teachers cannot succeed under these conditions.

During our school visits we were shocked by the lack of adequate supplies. Here is what we heard from one high school science teacher:

> When I entered through the door of this classroom for the first time, I was as depressed as I was when getting on the plane to Vietnam. The doors on the cupboards and workbenches were torn off. The equipment was broken, and when I went to the back storage room for the chemicals it was even more depressing. . . . I have little money for equipment. The pulleys are broken. There are few experiments where all the necessary equipment works.[13]

Keeping the school in good repair and making it attractive are not only good management but also can contribute enormously to the morale of teachers and students. A major oil company carpeted an entire high school with carpeting originally earmarked for its recycling center. Volunteers from this same company spent an entire day painting murals at another school.

Further, services that many industries take for granted, such as printing, can be major stumbling blocks for overburdened school systems. Such services can be provided to schools at minimal expense to business, and with maximal benefit to the school. Illinois Bell prints and mails newsletters, grades reports, and bilingual handbooks to parents of Chicago high school students. Providing business-related materials to be used in existing courses of study costs business almost nothing, but can do a great deal in the way of supplementing textbooks.

We propose that business and industry help schools improve their physical plants and science laboratories. Specifically, a school facility and equipment program should be sponsored by a business, providing for modest repairs and beautification. It would also be appropriate for industries to conduct inventories of the science laboratories to help upgrade the equipment.

We have focused on the management side of school administration. Corporations also can help school principals move from being manager to being leader. Outstanding principals could be given sabbaticals or small discretionary funds to work with teachers on creative programs. The principals' seminars, proposed in Chapter 13, could be funded by corporate grants. Specifically, businesses with corporate campuses should donate the use of these instructional facilities for a week or two each year to the schools to be used as Academies for Principals. The faculty at these academies could include outstanding scholars in the liberal arts, specialists in teaching and consultants in school management as well. We also recommend that corporations periodically provide scholarships to cover the cost of the continuing education of principals at the schools in their area.

What lessons can be learned from the partnership between business and the public school? There has as yet been little formal evaluation of the educational impact of such collaboration. We do sense, however, that individual students, teachers, and school administrators have been helped. And in our review of several dozen school-business partnerships, four key principles emerged:

First, business should enrich the school program, not control it. Business can benefit from aiding education, but this alone should not be the motivation. Larger social purpose should be sensed, and the watchword should be learning, not training. The corporate connection must promote high-quality education, not move students onto a narrow vocational track. All students, regardless of the special experiences provided by business, should complete a core of common learning, and all off-campus experience should fit within an approved elective cluster.

Second, goals should be realistic. Collaborative programs should have concrete objectives, ones that are attainable within a finite period of time. Specific strategies are bound to reap greater rewards than plans for global reform that are beyond the reach of a single organization. There are 80,000 public schools in the United States. Business leaders, quite understandably, ask, "Where do we begin?" The answer: Begin at home. "What can we do for *this* school?" is a more appropriate question than "How can we save public education in America?"

Third, businesses and schools should do what each can do best. A clear division of labor should be established. Schools should not try to become workplaces that specialize in "hands-on" experience; nor should businesses try to become experts in academic studies. Indeed, some career-related courses now offered in the schools might shift to a business site, where students would have access to up-to-date equipment and teachers. Schools, in turn, would have more time to teach the core of common learning.

Fourth, the spirit of cooperation should be rooted in mutual respect. There has been a tendency for business leaders to ascribe the problems of the schools to the incompetence of educators and for educators to caricature business persons as concerned only with profits. Neither side is above reproach, neither side beneath the other. School leaders, as well as business leaders, have unique contributions to make, and there must be a willingness to listen to and learn from one another. The incentive of excellence in the schools should be sufficient to bring both groups into the service of an institution that needs both.

Cooperation between industry and the schools yields a special profit. The pay-off cannot always be clearly measured in dollars and cents, but the chance to work with young people who may soon be employees, to help to cultivate in them a sense of responsibility and an excitement of discovery, to enrich the teachers, to give the principals support while at the same time enlarging the corporate vision by working for the betterment of society—these are among the returns that some executives are already including on their company's balance sheets. Rance Crain, editor-in-chief of Crain's *Chicago Business*, a financial weekly whose employees teach journalism at Carl Schurz High School, said that "in this case, self-interest is, in fact, for the good of all."[14]

17

EXCELLENCE:
THE PUBLIC COMMITMENT

I don't believe the public really cares about what goes on in this school. Only 20 percent of our parents ever come to open house. We send home progress reports, but few parents are concerned about their children's learning even when they are failing. The sad fact is that apathy is our biggest enemy."[1] With these words the principal of one school we visited highlighted one of the most formidable barriers to excellence in the schools—diminishing public commitment.

How we, as a nation, regard our schools has a powerful impact on what occurs in them. It helps determine the morale of the people who work there; it helps students calibrate their expectations; it contributes, one way or another, to the climate for reform. Whether a school succeeds or fails in its mission depends in no small measure on the degree of support received from the nation and from the community it serves. In this chapter, we examine America's commitment to public education as seen first from the home, then from the school board, and finally from the level of state and federal government. Only by deepening support can schools improve.

America believes in education. In 1982, every major group queried in a Gallup poll agreed that America's strength in the future will depend more on developing the finest educational system in the world than on developing the best industrial system or the strongest military force.[2] Similarly, four out of five people—young and old, rich and poor, well-educated and poorly educated—affirmed their faith in education as extremely important to one's future success.[3]

America believes in *education*. Increasingly, however, it has come to distrust its *schools*. Between 1970 and 1977, nonsectarian private school enrollments increased by about 60 percent, although the school-age population in the United States dropped by more than 3.9 million students.[4] While a variety of reasons have been given to account for this shift, the major one is invariably dissatisfaction with the public schools.[5]

Not until 1981 did the Gallup polls announce the grimly cheering news that the long decline in confidence in the public schools had at last bottomed out. But by then nearly twice as many Americans were giving the schools *D* or failing grades as in 1974.[6]

Small wonder that teachers and administrators feel like second-class citizens. One teacher we interviewed said that the criticism of schools at her summer job was so harsh that she declined to reveal her real profession. "I heard only that teachers did not know what they were doing, and that all of the schools are bad."[7] Another teacher complained, "You rarely get any kind of thank you from the parents or the community. In fact, there's no positive reinforcement for anything you do. Either they just don't care, or they think of us as goof-offs."[8]

The indifference of parents can be almost as destructive as criticism; it undermines staff morale, erodes standards, and slows students' progress. Over and over, teachers complained to us about lack of communication from parents. Remarked one, "Students won't do homework because there is parental apathy toward learning."[9] Said another, "If you send home fifty report cards, you might get one response from one parent."[10]

Most parents at one school we visited were employed in a city thirty-five miles away. As a consequence, many leave for work early and arrive home late. These circumstances discourage participation in school activities. A teacher noted, "We have students who can be absent from school for several days without their parents knowing because parents leave home before it is time for the children to attend school and arrive home after their children are scheduled to return. Only a basketball game will get parents out."[11]

In another school, a teacher expressed his frustration over parents who are casual about their children's school attendance. "They take their sons hunting, go to football games, let kids take time off."[12] The principal, too, was amazed by a mother who, at a parent-teacher conference, described the family's plans to take their son out of school for a few days to go to a pro football game. These absences would put the boy over the school's ten-day absence limit, and he would receive no credit in several classes. The mother's response to this information was that her son could graduate late.

On parent involvement in school affairs, one teacher remarked:

> I think there are three groups of parents. Half of them support you because you are a teacher. A smaller group, about ten percent, always supports their kids. The third group, forty percent, says to the school, "Handle it all and don't bother me."[13]

Here is another example:

> I think that as a teacher there is only so much I can do for students. I can stand on my head, cut my wrists, and bleed for them. Still, if they don't get the push at home to learn, there is nothing I can do. I think parents have messed up their priorities. One of my students was falling asleep in class a couple of weeks ago. She works until ten or eleven at night. She has no reason to work, but her parents let her. When does this girl do her homework? What is she learning? Her parents let her sacrifice school work so she can have a job and buy herself designer jeans![14]

Educators are far from blameless for the gap between home and school. We frequently heard parents complain that teachers were too often defensive or aloof. They turned away honest questions, hinting that they, not the parents, were the experts in education. If school-community ties are to be strengthened, each side must reach out to the other.

There are attempts to do just this at Garfield High School. Garfield is not strictly a neighborhood school. However, we found there a definite "community of parents" spread around the city. They were doing what they could to make sure that Garfield "worked" for their children. Parent-Teacher-Student Association meetings were held once a month. An Advisory Council, attended by the principal, some teachers, and about twenty parents met regularly to explore, in depth, such serious topics as school security, grading, parent-teacher conferences, and the support of extracurricular activities.

While attending a session of the council, we were impressed not only by the thoroughness of the discussions, but also by the mutual trust and concern of those involved. These were people—black and white, educated and uneducated, rich and poor—who knew each other well and were working hard to make Garfield the best school it could be for their children. White parents supported the school while at the same time they talked about the extra challenges they felt their children had to encounter as members of a minority. Black parents, on the other hand, seldom referred to race, other than to acknowledge that Garfield was the one school they felt they could send their children to and feel comfortable about the quality of instruction.

For schools to be effective, parents must be involved. To increase participation, we recommend that there be a Parent-Teacher-Student Advisory Council at every school. We further recommend that a parent volunteer program be established in all the nation's secondary schools.

Today, almost two-thirds of all public high schools in the United States use volunteers in some capacity. A third of these volunteers are parents. About a quarter are retired citizens, and another quarter are college students. The remainder are mostly business people.[15] These thousands of dedicated people across the nation demonstrate a strong grassroots support and concern for public education.

In addition to obvious volunteers—the mother who helps coach a team, the father who helps design scenery for a school play—high schools could invite parents to assist the librarian and to tutor individual students. Parents should also be asked to organize other volunteers—retirees to tutor, business executives to help reorganize the record-keeping and accounting system, newspaper reporters to lend a hand with student publications as well as supervise "interns" from the journalism class.

Parents are important; school boards and district office leaders are important, too. Among the fundamental responsibilities of the school board, we emphasize three:

- *Finances.* The school board should obtain adequate financial support and make it available in ways that are fiscally responsible yet minimally restrictive to individual schools.

- *Personnel.* The school board should ensure that the ablest and best-qualified people possible are employed to lead and teach in the system's schools. This must begin with the selection of a top-notch superintendent.

- *Coordination.* The school board should build a bridge between the school and those groups and agencies, including state and local governments, that seek to influence school programs, doing so with due regard for both the integrity of the individual school and the legitimate expectations of those beyond its walls.

Given the fact that school boards have a vital role to play, it was disturbing to find that tension between educators and school boards was a chronic and troublesome feature of the schools we visited. Teachers and principals said school boards were distant and unresponsive. Board members and district office people seemed to feel the local schools were out of touch.

Persistent misunderstanding among educators and school officials is a barrier to education. It need not exist. With closer contact, school board members, central school administrators, principals, and teachers would be able to work together far more productively.

Their goals need not remain so separate, their insights unshared. Therefore, we urge that more open and direct communication be established between the school and the district office. And we recommend that boards of education hold meetings, at least once a year, with principals and teachers from all schools in the district.

Serving on a school board was once a great honor, an assignment seriously accepted and responsibly carried out by concerned parents and the community's most respected leaders. Today, the status of school boards has declined. Too many parents and civic leaders refuse to get involved. In too many communities, school boards have become battlegrounds for special interest groups and platforms for politicians. We urge that parents and all concerned citizens become actively involved in school board elections, attend meetings, and participate constructively in discussions, and that they, themselves, consider serving as members of the board.

The high schools of the nation are only as strong as the communities of which they are a part. The renewal of the school must, quite literally, begin at home.

There is, at the same time, policy and financial responsibility for public education that state governments must assume. Over the last decade, state support for public schools has increased from 40 to 50 percent. This shift has occurred as a result of efforts to relieve local taxpayers or to achieve greater equity. In fact, more money now comes to schools from the state government than from any other source, although there is great variation in the pattern of school financing from one state to another (Table 22).

The constitutions of most states require that public schooling must be provided for all children; state law requires, in turn, that each child must go to school. But strung between these twin pillars is a web of additional laws, regulations, and procedures—covering attendance quotas, requirements for graduation, teacher certification, the nature of state aid, the selection of textbooks, and the structure of curriculum. Such elaborate state regulations often tend

Table 22 Percentage of Revenue Receipts for Public Elementary and Secondary Schools from Local, State, and Federal Governments, by State (Revised Estimates)

Region and State	Local 1971–72	Local 1982–83	State 1971–72	State 1982–83	Federal 1971–72	Federal 1982–83
United States	51.8	42.3	40.2	50.3	8.0	7.4
New England						
Connecticut	75.0	58.7	22.4	36.4	2.7	4.9
Maine	56.9	40.2	33.4	49.7	9.7	10.1
Massachusetts	71.4	55.8	23.2	39.4	5.4	4.8
New Hampshire	87.7	89.2	6.5	6.9	5.8	3.9
Rhode Island	55.7	58.3	35.3	37.0	9.0	4.7
Vermont	60.9	57.8	33.0	35.2	6.1	7.0
Mid-Atlantic						
Delaware	22.6	21.2	69.6	67.6	7.8	11.2
District of Columbia	86.7	84.5	NA	NA	13.3	15.5
Maryland	49.7	53.9	43.3	40.2	7.1	5.9
New Jersey	70.0	56.4	25.4	40.0	4.6	3.5
New York	51.9	54.1	42.3	41.9	5.8	4.0
Pennsylvania	46.5	47.4	47.0	45.2	6.5	7.5
Southeast						
Alabama	19.5	21.0	62.4	64.3	18.1	14.8
Arkansas	37.4	32.4	46.1	54.3	16.6	13.3
Florida	35.9	31.0	52.9	61.9	11.3	7.1
Georgia	34.5	34.2	51.8	55.6	13.7	10.2
Kentucky	29.8	18.7	53.5	70.5	16.6	10.7
Louisiana	29.9	34.7	56.0	55.9	14.1	9.4
Mississippi	24.2	23.7	48.2	53.3	27.6	23.0
North Carolina	21.5	22.4	62.6	61.5	15.9	16.1
South Carolina	27.0	29.3	55.0	57.1	18.0	13.6
Tennessee	41.5	39.8	44.4	47.2	14.0	13.0
Virginia	54.4	51.8	33.8	41.6	11.8	6.6
West Virginia	32.0	28.5	54.9	62.4	13.0	9.0
Great Lakes						
Illinois	55.4	53.4	37.8	38.0	6.8	8.5
Indiana	63.1	35.1	31.5	58.6	5.4	6.3
Michigan	51.7	55.8	44.5	36.1	3.8	8.1
Ohio	63.3	54.3	30.5	40.7	6.2	5.0
Wisconsin	65.4	57.2	30.4	37.4	4.3	5.4
Plains						
Iowa	65.0	50.6	31.3	42.1	3.7	7.3
Kansas	64.6	50.8	27.4	44.4	8.0	4.8
Minnesota	46.9	46.3	48.4	48.9	4.7	4.7
Missouri	58.1	52.3	33.7	39.6	8.2	8.1
Nebraska	75.9	65.0	17.8	27.9	6.3	7.1
North Dakota	58.7	41.1	29.4	51.5	11.9	7.3
South Dakota	72.3	63.7	15.1	27.6	12.5	8.7

Table 22 Percentage of Revenue Receipts for Public Elementary and Secondary Schools from Local, State, and Federal Governments, by State (Revised Estimates) *(continued)*

Region and State	Local 1971–72	Local 1982–83	State 1971–72	State 1982–83	Federal 1971–72	Federal 1982–83
Southwest						
Arizona	50.5	42.9	40.1	45.7	9.4	11.4
New Mexico	20.4	12.0	60.0	77.8	19.6	10.2
Oklahoma	44.7	29.5	44.5	60.2	10.8	10.3
Texas	41.7	39.5	47.0	50.6	11.3	10.0
Rocky Mountain						
Colorado	64.2	57.7	27.5	36.9	8.3	5.4
Idaho	47.6	30.4	39.4	62.6	13.0	6.9
Montana	67.7	44.2	23.9	47.4	8.5	8.5
Utah	38.6	38.5	52.1	56.3	9.3	5.2
Wyoming	55.6	61.3	33.8	34.7	10.6	4.0
Far West						
Alaska	10.4	16.0	74.1	78.3	15.5	5.7
California	56.5	8.9	36.7	85.8	6.8	5.3
Hawaii	2.9	0.3	88.7	89.8	8.4	9.9
Nevada	52.4	31.8	39.4	60.6	8.2	7.6
Oregon	75.6	54.4	19.9	36.8	4.5	8.8
Washington	42.6	19.4	49.0	75.2	8.4	5.4

Source: National Education Association, *Estimates of School Statistics 1972–73* (Washington: National Education Association, January 1973), p. 32; National Education Association, *Estimates of School Statistics 1982–83* (Washington: National Education Association, January 1983), p. 37.

to confuse the mission and diminish the authority of the local school.

The time has come for states to recognize that their overriding responsibility is to establish general standards and to provide support, but not to meddle. It is time for states to sift through the rules and regulations, sorting out what is needed and what should be discarded. To achieve this end, we recommend that the body of state education law be revised to eliminate confusing and inappropriate laws and regulations. Ways must be found to combat undue state intervention.

State education laws should be modest and general, answering a few very basic questions: What is a school? Who must attend it and until what age? What are the statewide requirements and stan-

Table 23 States Ranked by Sources of Revenue Receipts—Federal, State, and Local and Other: 1982–83

Federal		State		Local and Other	
Mississippi	23.0	Hawaii	89.8	New Hampshire	89.2
North Carolina	16.1	California	85.8	District of Columbia	84.5
District of Columbia	15.5	Alaska	78.3	Nebraska	65.0
Alabama	14.8	New Mexico	77.8	South Dakota	63.7
South Carolina	13.6	Washington	75.2	Wyoming	61.3
Arkansas	13.3	Kentucky	70.5	Connecticut	58.7
Tennessee	13.0	Delaware	67.6	Rhode Island	58.3
Arizona	11.4	Alabama	64.3	Vermont	57.8
Delaware	11.2	Idaho	62.6	Colorado	57.7
Kentucky	10.7	West Virginia	62.4	Wisconsin	57.2
Oklahoma	10.3	Florida	61.9	New Jersey	56.4
Georgia	10.2	North Carolina	61.5	Massachusetts	55.8
New Mexico	10.2	Nevada	60.6	Michigan	55.8
Maine	10.1	Oklahoma	60.2	Oregon	54.3
Texas	10.0	Indiana	58.6	Ohio	54.3
Hawaii	9.9	South Carolina	57.1	New York	54.1
Louisiana	9.4	Utah	56.3	Maryland	53.9
West Virginia	9.0	Louisiana	55.9	Illinois	53.4
Oregon	8.8	Georgia	55.6	Missouri	52.3
South Dakota	8.7	Arkansas	54.3	Virginia	51.8
Illinois	8.5	Mississippi	53.3	Kansas	50.8
Montana	8.5	North Dakota	51.5	Iowa	50.6
Michigan	8.1	Texas	50.6	Pennsylvania	47.4
Missouri	7.6	*50 States and D.C.*	50.3	Minnesota	46.3
Nevada	7.6	Maine	49.7	Montana	44.2
Pennsylvania	7.5	Minnesota	48.9	Arizona	42.9
50 States & D.C.	7.4	Montana	47.4	*50 States & D.C.*	42.3
Iowa	7.3	Tennessee	47.2	North Dakota	41.1
North Dakota	7.3	Arizona	45.7	Maine	40.2
Nebraska	7.1	Pennsylvania	45.2	Tennessee	39.8
Florida	7.1	Kansas	44.4	Texas	39.5
Vermont	7.0	Iowa	42.1	Utah	38.5
Idaho	6.9	New York	41.9	Indiana	35.1
Virginia	6.6	Virginia	41.6	Louisiana	34.7
Indiana	6.3	Ohio	40.7	Georgia	34.2
Maryland	5.9	Maryland	40.2	Arkansas	32.4
Alaska	5.7	New Jersey	40.0	Nevada	31.8
Colorado	5.4	Missouri	39.6	Florida	31.0
Wisconsin	5.4	Massachusetts	39.4	Idaho	30.4
Washington	5.4	Illinois	38.0	Oklahoma	29.5

Table 23 **States Ranked by Sources of Revenue Receipts—Federal, State, and Local and Other: 1982–83** *(continued)*

Federal		State		Local and Other	
California	5.3	Wisconsin	37.4	South Carolina	29.3
Utah	5.2	Rhode Island	37.0	West Virginia	28.5
Ohio	5.0	Colorado	36.9	Mississippi	23.7
Connecticut	4.9	Oregon	36.8	North Carolina	22.4
Kansas	4.8	Connecticut	36.4	Delaware	21.2
Massachusetts	4.8	Michigan	36.1	Alabama	21.0
Minnesota	4.7	Vermont	35.2	Washington	19.4
Rhode Island	4.7	Wyoming	34.7	Kentucky	18.7
New York	4.0	Nebraska	27.9	Alaska	16.0
Wyoming	4.0	South Dakota	27.6	New Mexico	12.0
New Hampshire	3.9	New Hampshire	6.9	California	8.9
New Jersey	3.5	District of Columbia	N/A	Hawaii	0.3

Source: Ranked from basic data in National Education Association, *Estimates of School Statistics, 1982–83.*

dards for entering high school? What is the state prepared to pay for, and on what terms? What are the minimum requirements for becoming a public high school teacher in the state?

None of these questions needs a long statutory answer, and we caution state education agencies (and their boards) against tedious and complex regulations in the interpretation of the statutes. For example, education requirements should be defined in terms of general skills and bodies of knowledge, not course labels, periods of time spent on a subject, or Carnegie units accumulated. The Education Commission of the States has developed model legislation that may be especially helpful in revising the education laws.[16]

In 1982, the Texas state legislature repealed outdated sections of the education code, calling also for a "well-balanced" curriculum in all districts. Typical of many states, Texas had a tangle of complicated, often irrelevant education laws. One section of the code, since repealed, required that kindness to animals be taught. Another required that "the daily program of every public school shall be set by the teacher, principal, or superintendent to include 10 minutes for the teaching of intelligent patriotism." Thomas E. Anderson, Jr.,

Deputy Commissioner for Education in the State of Texas, says, "As far as we can tell, this is the first time a state legislature has gone in and simply wiped everything off the books . . . and let the education community take it from there."[17]

The Institute for Educational Leadership, working with the Education Commission of the States, sponsors State Education Policy Seminars in thirty-eight states. One purpose is to bring together state political and educational leaders to explore and debate important policy issues. A second purpose is to improve the formulation of education policies by providing learning experiences for persons who make these policy decisions in public education.[18]

While state legislative involvement in the schools should be limited, the role of state education departments is becoming more important. In every state there is an agency responsible for public education, and the heads of these agencies—chief school officers—have important leadership and education responsibilities. In 1982, at Colorado Springs, the nation's chief school officials met with college and university presidents to talk about improving the quality of education in the nation. The two groups met again in 1983 in New Haven. Here the focus was on improved teaching in the schools. Since these national conferences, state and regional efforts have been made to enrich the schools. We believe chief education officers have a critical role to play in raising quality standards, in moving federal funds to local schools, and, increasingly, in stimulating school leadership and innovation.

In short, the state's role is to provide a framework for assuring equity and quality while avoiding overregulation.

In past decades, federal support of the nation's public schools has been critically important in the move toward quality and equality in education. It must remain important. Washington does not and should not run the schools. Still, public education presents a serious national challenge, and there should be a national response.

In June, 1983, four former United States Commissioners of Education described, in a letter to the *New York Times,* the significance of federal aid to education. "The evidence on the usefulness of the Federal presence in education," the commissioners said, "is overwhelming." A series of landmark actions were then cited:

- The Morrill Act of 1862 established our system of land grant universities, which have provided invaluable services to our people and our economy.

- The GI Bill after World War II and its successor legislation have opened opportunities to veterans and served the nation well.

- The National Defense Education Act of 1958 and accompanying activities of the National Science Foundation helped to modernize the curriculum and sustain the quality of teaching and learning in the schools.

- The 1965 program for augmenting the education of disadvantaged children has had positive effects that are now evident in test results among elementary school children, for whom most of the funds have been used.

- Clear testimony from school leaders underlines the value of federal funds for assisting desegregation.

- Thousands achieve advanced degrees and join the higher levels of our work force because of student aid programs launched in the '60s and '70s.

- Headstart has provided a useful life to millions of preschoolers.

The four former commissioners concluded, "Education initiatives like these have been launched and supported by both Republican and Democratic administrations, and most of them have bipartisan support in Congress and among the American people."[19]

As we see it, the federal role in elementary and secondary education should serve three broad purposes:

- First, the federal government has an obligation to provide information regarding the condition of American education, including the gathering, analysis, and dissemination of timely and accurate data about the nation's public schools.

- Second, the federal government has an obligation to help the nation's schools provide high-quality education for students with special needs: the disadvantaged and the handicapped.

- Third, consistent with such programs as the G.I. Bill and the National Defense Education Act, the federal government has an obligation to provide support to schools in response to emergency national needs. Such programs are designed to enlist the schools more effectively in the nation's service.

In this report, we have proposed recommendations to serve these three broad missions. We urge that the federal government help schools—through state grants—gather information about their graduates (Chapter 8). We propose that funding of Title I of the Elementary and Secondary Education Act be increased to support all eligible students (Chapter 14).

We call for a National Teacher Service and a federally funded network of Residential Academies in science and mathematics (Chapter 9). And we recommend that the federal government help create a National Film Library for schools to use, and that a network of Technology Resource Centers be established with federal support to teach teachers about technology and its uses (Chapter 11).

There remains one emergency that calls for a federal response. Many of our nation's schools have fallen into disrepair and are, in some cases, hazardous. The situation is as alarming as the decay of our highways, dams, and bridges. A 1983 survey of 100 school districts in 34 states showed:

- 71 percent of schools need roof repairs or replacements
- 27 percent need repair or replacement of heating and air-conditioning equipment
- 20 percent fail fire and safety standards
- 13 percent are not meeting building requirements for the handicapped
- 11 percent have not removed asbestos from buildings[20]

These are the cold statistics. At the human level they become personally frightening and depressing. One teacher lamented that his school

> had a fire on the first floor the previous year, but instead of repairing the damage, the Board chose to save money and simply walled off the damaged area. A bench in the carpentry shop was not secured to the floor, so one student had to hold it down while another worked. The school's television set was broken, the only pay phone was out of order . . . and several classroom radiators made a great deal of noise and did not function properly. School athletic facilities were in poor condition, the play yard was covered with potholes, and graffiti was abundant. There have been several instances of students being hit with plaster falling off the walls.[21]

In another school, observers found that paint was peeling from the walls, lights throughout the school were burned out, window shades were torn, some windows were cracked, walls were painted with different and often unmatching colors. In one classroom there was a large hole in the ceiling, which the teacher explained had not been repaired for five years. As a result the room was cold and uncomfortable.[22] Another teacher commented on the poor condition of facilities: "I begin to feel as if the school and children don't really matter to anyone."[23]

The total bill for repairing the nation's schoolhouses will be, it is estimated, at least $25 billion in current dollars. Meanwhile, much-needed repairs are being delayed for lack of funds. Tax and spending limits enacted in twenty-nine states since 1977 have brought about sharp cuts in maintenance. Only 6.7 percent of annual school budgets is currently spent for maintenance and capital improvements. This compares with 8.6 percent in 1970, 9.6 in 1960, and 14.1 percent in 1920.[24] One major report estimates that "To meet all maintenance and capital needs that have been deferred over the years, schools throughout the nation would be required to spend about 220 percent more on building improvements each year than they do now."[25]

There is another equally serious problem. Laboratory equipment in many schools is in poor shape or nonexistent. In a recent study of urban schools, it was found that "lack of supplies, poor condition of equipment, few repairs of facilities and inadequate maintenance in a majority of the schools observed made the teacher's primary task extremely difficult. Teachers lacked rudimentary materials like books and paper; special equipment often did not work."[26]

"The saddest place in this school is the chemistry and physics laboratory," said a teacher in one of our field visits.

> It has old black-topped science workbenches, the kind we all remember from thirty years ago, with gas jets sticking out, heavy drawers, and an electrical outlet on the side. A hood sits over a large workbench in the front center of the room (for demonstrations). Except for this, there are no signs of equipment that you would expect in a working laboratory. Chemistry and physics at this school are largely equipment-free. In fact, there is no single experiment that I can have the kids do, because for each experiment the necessary equipment is broken. So we rely on textbooks and worksheets instead. But I can tell you that's a pretty poor way of teaching science.[27]

Quality education does not require a luxurious setting, but surely it should provide adequate facilities. The schoolhouse itself should not place students in harm's way. More than that, it should be a place that is decent and safe.

The federal government has a leading role to play in rebuilding the nation's schools. A new federal program, the School Building and Equipment Fund, should be established to provide short-term, low-interest loans to schools for plant rehabilitation and for the purchase of laboratory equipment.

In 1963, Congress passed the Higher Education Facilities Act to make available to the nation's colleges low-interest loans to accommodate the post–World War II enrollment boom.[28] Today's emergency calls less for new buildings and more for the repair of existing facilities and the equipment of science labs. We cannot prepare a generation of first-rate scientists in second-rate facilities. Bold federal action is needed now to help meet an emergency in the schools, just as Washington responded so effectively to help colleges twenty years ago.

This report on the American high school has focused on education, not money. But the two, of course, are interlocked.

Support for education has been steadily losing ground. Between 1965 and 1980, the average proportion of public expenditures spent for welfare doubled; health expenditures increased by nearly a third, while expenditures for education decreased by over 20 percent.[29] This erosion of support has crippled many schools. The trend, as some states now acknowledge, urgently needs to be reversed. We cannot have bargain-basement education.

To talk of more money for public education is still sharply criticized by many. However, the issue is not the lack of money but misplaced priorities. In 1981, American men and women spent over $12.8 billion on beauty aids—hair preparations, cosmetics, and the like.[30] We spent more than $3.9 billion in 1981 to feed our dogs and cats.[31] And in fiscal year 1982 the nation's defense budget was $214.1 billion.[32] By comparison, Americans in 1981 spent $116.3 billion to educate more than 40 million children[33] in 80,000 public elementary and secondary schools. That was only 4 percent of our gross national product.

Schools in America should not be given a blank check, but neither should they be considered less important than health, welfare, or national defense. Our response is simple and straightforward. If the high school is to fulfill the nation's expectations, the cost of public education must be met.

We propose that coalitions of citizens—Citizens for Public Schools—be formed in every community to give leadership in the advocacy of more support for public education. These community action groups should include both parents and leaders of business and professions. The aim would be to match specific school needs with local resources and to broaden school support.

The success or failure of the American high school will determine the quality of our democracy, the strength of our economy, the security of our defense, and the promise of our ideals. The time has come for America to stand behind its belief in public education.

This report has identified twelve key strategies for achieving high quality in education: clear goals, the mastery of language, a core of common learning, preparation for work and further education, school and community service, better teachers, improved instruction, effective use of technology, flexible school patterns, strong leadership, connections with colleges and with corporations, and a renewed public commitment to the nation's schools. Obviously, money alone cannot make these strategies succeed, but neither can they succeed without cost. Quality has its price.

If we value our country and our heritage, we must invest in our children. We owe them a legacy of hope. James Agee once wrote: "In every child who is born . . . the potentiality of the human race is born again."[34]

There should never be a child—let alone a generation of children —who passes through our schools unawakened and unprepared for what will come. Educating a new generation of Americans to their full potential is still our most compelling obligation.

Every morning at 8 A.M. the doors of America's high schools are opened. Walk inside and look into the future of the nation.

This report asks for one thing above all else, the improvement of America's high schools. Problems have been identified with the confidence that solutions can be found. Suggestions have been made with the hope that they contribute constructively to the debate about the public schools. Our goal is to involve teachers, parents, students, school officials, and concerned citizens in the renewal of American education. For this reason we now bring together the major themes and key recommendations of our report. Placed side by side they become, we believe, an agenda for action.

18

HIGH SCHOOL: AN AGENDA
FOR ACTION

The world has changed, irrevocably so, and quality education in the 1980s and beyond means preparing all students for the transformed world the coming generation will inherit. To achieve this goal, a comprehensive school-improvement program must be pursued urgently. Without excellence in education, the promise of America cannot be fulfilled. We have identified twelve priorities that, taken together, provide an agenda for action.

I. Clarifying Goals

A high school, to be effective, must have a clear and vital mission. Educators must have a shared vision of what, together, they are trying to accomplish. That vision should go beyond keeping students in school and out of trouble, and be more significant than adding up the Carnegie course units the student has completed. Specifically, we recommend:

- Every high school should establish clearly stated goals—purposes that are widely shared by teachers, students, administrators and parents.

- School goals should focus on the mastery of language, on a core of common learning, on preparation for work and further education, and on community and civic service.

II. The Centrality of Language

The next priority is language. Formal schooling has a special obligation to help all students become skilled in the written and oral use of English. Those who do not become proficient in the primary language of the culture are enormously disadvantaged in school and out of school as well. The following recommendations are proposed:

- Elementary school should build on the remarkable language skills a child already has acquired. In the early grades, students should learn to read and comprehend the main ideas in a written work, write standard English sentences and present their ideas orally.

- The English proficiency of all students should be formally assessed before they go to high school. A pre-high school summer term and an intensive freshman year remediation program should be provided for students who are deficient in the use of English.

- Clear writing leads to clear thinking; clear thinking is the basis of clear writing. Therefore, all high school students should complete a basic English course with emphasis on writing. Enrollment in such classes should be limited to twenty students, and no more than two such classes should be included in the teacher's regular load.

- The high school curriculum should also include a study of the spoken word. Speaking and listening are something more than the mere exchange of information. Communication at its best should lead to genuine understanding.

III. The Curriculum Has a Core

A core of common learning is essential. The basic curriculum should be a study of those consequential ideas, experiences, and traditions common to all of us by virtue of our membership in the human family at a particular moment in history. The content of the core curriculum must extend beyond the specialties, and focus on more transcendent issues, moving from courses to coherence. The following are recommended:

- The number of required courses in the core curriculum should be expanded from one-half to two-thirds of the total units required for high school graduation.
- In addition to strengthening the traditional courses in literature, history, mathematics and science, emphasis should also be given to foreign language, the arts, civics, non-Western studies, technology, the meaning of work, and the importance of health.

Highlights of the core curriculum are as follows:

Literature: All students, through a study of literature, should discover our common literary heritage and learn about the power and beauty of the written word.

United States History: United States history is required for graduation from all the high schools included in our study, and it is the one social studies course uniformly required by most states. We favor a one-year United States history course that would build on the chronology of the emergence of America, including a study of the lives of a few influential leaders—artists, reformers, explorers who helped shape the nation.

Western Civilization: Beyond American history lies the long sweep of Western Civilization. We recommend that all students learn about the roots of our national heritage and traditions through a study of other cultures that have shaped our own.

Non-Western Civilization: All students should discover the connectedness of the human experience and the richness of other cultures through an in-depth study of the non-Western world. Specifically, we suggest a one-semester required course in which students study, in considerable detail, a single non-Western nation.

Science and the Natural World: The study of science introduces students to the processes of discovery—what we call the scientific method—and reveals how such procedures can be applied to many disciplines and to their own lives. We suggest a two-year science sequence that would include basic courses in the biological and physical sciences.

Technology: All students should study technology: the history of man's use of tools, how science and technology have been joined, and the ethical and social issues technology has raised.

Mathematics: In high school, all students should expand their capacity to think quantitatively and to make intelligent decisions regarding situations involving measurable quantities. Specifically, we believe that all high schools should require a two-year mathematics sequence for graduation and that additional courses be provided for students who are qualify to take them.

Foreign Language: All students should become familiar with the language of another culture. Such studies should ideally begin in elementary school and at least two years of foreign language study should be required of all high school students. By the year 2000, the United States could be home to the world's fifth largest population of persons of Hispanic origin. It does seem reasonable for all schools in the United States to offer Spanish.

The Arts: The arts are an essential part of the human experience. They are not a frill. We recommend that all students study the arts to discover how human beings use nonverbal symbols and communicate not only with words but through music, dance, and the visual arts.

Civics: A course in American government—traditionally called civics—should be required of all students, with focus on the traditions of democratic thought, the shaping of our own governmental structures, and political and social issues we confront today.

Health: No knowledge is more crucial than knowledge about health. Without it, no other life goal can be successfully achieved. Therefore, all students should learn about the human body, how it changes over the life cycle, what nourishes it and diminishes it, and how a healthy body contributes to emotional well-being.

Work: The one-semester study of work we propose would ask how attitudes toward work have changed through the years. How do they differ from one culture to another? What determines the status and rewards of different forms of work? Such a curriculum might also include an in-depth investigation of one specific occupation.

- All students, during their senior year, should complete a Senior Independent Project, a written report that focuses on a significant social issue and draws upon the various fields of study in the academic core.

IV. Transition: To Work and Learning

The high school should help all students move with confidence from school to work and further education. Today, we track students into programs for those who "think" and those who "work," when, in fact, life for all of us is a blend of both. Looking to the year 2000, we conclude that, for most students, twelve years of schooling will be insufficient. Today's graduates will change jobs several times. New skills will be required, new citizenship obligations will be confronted. Of necessity, education will be lifelong. We recommend:

- The school program should offer a single track for all students, one that includes a strong grounding in the basic tools of education and a study of the core curriculum. While the first two years would be devoted almost exclusively to the common core, a portion of this work would continue into the third or fourth year.

- The last two years of high school should be considered a "transition school," a program in which about half the time is devoted to "elective clusters."

- The "elective cluster" should be carefully designed. Such a program would include advanced study in selected academic subjects, the exploration of a career option, or a combination of both.

- In order to offer a full range of elective clusters, the high school must become a connected institution. Upper-level specialty schools (in the arts or science or health or computers, for example) may be appropriate in some districts. High schools should also establish connections with learning places beyond the schools—such as libraries, museums, art galleries, colleges and industrial laboratories.

There is also an urgent need to help students figure out what they should do after graduation. Therefore, we recommend:

- Guidance services should be significantly expanded. No counselor should have a case load of more than one hundred students. Moreover, school districts should provide a referral service to community agencies for those students needing frequent and sustained professional assistance.

- A new Student Achievement and Advisement Test (SAAT) should be developed, one that could eventually replace the SAT. The academic achievement portion of the test would be linked to the core curriculum, evaluating what the student has learned. The advisement section would assess personal characteristics and interests to help students make decisions more intelligently about their futures. The purpose is not to screen students out of options but to help them move on with confidence to colleges and to jobs.

The needs of the student for guidance are matched by the need of the school to be better informed about its graduates. To achieve this, the following is proposed:

- The United States Department of Education—working through the states—should expand its national survey of schools to include a sampling of graduates from all high schools at four-year intervals to learn about their post-high school placement and experience. Such information should be made available to participating schools.

V. Service: The New Carnegie Unit

Beyond the formal academic program the high school should help all students meet their social and civic obligations. During high school young people should be given opportunities to reach beyond themselves and feel more responsibly engaged. They should be encouraged to participate in the communities of which they are a part. We recommend:

- All high school students should complete a service requirement—a new Carnegie unit—that would involve them in volunteer work in the community or at school. Students could fulfill this requirement evenings, weekends and during the summer.

- Students themselves should be given the responsibility to help organize and monitor the new service program and to work with school officials to assure that credit is appropriately assigned.

VI. Teachers: Renewing the Profession

The working conditions of teachers must improve. Many people think teachers have soft, undemanding jobs. The reality is different. Teachers are expected to work miracles day after day and then often get only silence from the students, pressure from the principal, and criticism from the irate parent. To improve the working conditions of the teachers, we propose the following:

- High school teachers should have a daily teaching load of four regular class sessions. In addition, they should be responsible one period each day for small seminars and for helping students with independent projects.

- Teachers should have a minimum of sixty minutes each school day for class preparation and record keeping. The current catch-as-catch-can "arrangement" is simply not good enough.

- Teachers should be exempt from routine monitoring of halls, lunchrooms, and recreation areas. School clerical staff and parent and student volunteers should assume such noninstructional duties.

- A Teacher Excellence Fund should be established in every school—a competitive grant program to enable teachers to design and carry out a special professional project.

- Good teachers should be given adequate recognition and rewards—from a student's "thank you," to cash awards, to active support from parents. Outstanding teachers also should be honored annually in every school district, and, statewide, by the governor and the legislature, newspapers and other businesses in each community.

- Teachers should be supported in the maintenance of discipline based on a clearly stated code of conduct.

Teachers' salaries should be increased. When teachers' salaries are compared to those of other professionals, the contrast is depressing. For many teachers, moonlighting has become essential. Salaries for teachers must be commensurate with those of other professions, and with the tasks teachers must perform.

- As a national goal, the average salary for teachers should be increased by at least 25 percent beyond the rate of inflation over the next three years, with immediate entry-level increases.

Outstanding students should be recruited into teaching. We cannot have gifted teachers if gifted students do not enter the classrooms of the nation. When salaries and working conditions improve, prospects for recruiting talented young people will improve as well. We propose:

- Every high school should establish a cadet teacher program in which high school teachers identify gifted students and encourage them to become teachers. Such students should be given opportunities to present information to classmates, tutor other students who need special help, and meet with outstanding school and college teachers. Also some districts may wish to establish a magnet school for prospective teachers.

- Colleges and universities should establish full tuition scholarships for the top 5 percent of their gifted students who plan to teach in public education. These scholarships would begin when students are admitted to the teacher preparation program at the junior year.

- The federal government should establish a National Teacher Service, especially for those who plan to teach in science and mathematics. This tuition scholarship program would be for students in the top one-third of their high school graduating classes. Students admitted to the National Teacher Service would be expected to complete successfully an academic program and teach at least three years in the public schools.

The schooling of teachers must improve. There are serious problems with the education of our teachers. Many teacher training programs are inadequate. The accreditation of schools of education is ineffective. The careful selection of teacher candidates is almost nonexistent, and college arts and science departments fail to recognize the critical role they play in teacher preparation. The following is proposed:

- Prospective teachers should complete a core of common learning, one that parallels in broad outline the high school core curriculum proposed in this report.

- Every teacher candidate should be carefully selected. Formal admission to teacher training should occur at the junior year, the time when students begin a three-year teacher preparation sequence. Only students with a cumulative grade point average of 3.0 (B) or better and who have strong supportive recommendations from two professors who taught them in a required academic course should be admitted.

- Once admitted to the program, the teacher candidate should devote the junior and senior years to the completion of a major, plus appropriate electives. Every secondary school teacher should complete a sharply focused major in one academic discipline, not in education. During the junior and senior years, time also should be scheduled for prospective teachers systematically to visit schools.

- After grounding in the core curriculum and a solid academic major, prospective teachers should have a fifth-year education core built around the following subjects: Schooling in America, Learning Theory and Research, The Teaching of Writing, and Technology and Its Uses.

- The fifth year also should include classroom observation and teaching experience. This is the best way, we believe, to learn about students and to develop effective methods of instruction.

- In addition, the fifth year of teacher preparation should include a series of six one-day common learning seminars in which students meet with outstanding arts and science scholar-teachers who would relate the knowledge of their fields to a contemporary political or social theme. Such seminars would help provide the interdisciplinary perspective every high school teacher must acquire.

The continuing education of the teacher must be strengthened. We cannot expect a teacher trained twenty years ago to prepare students to live forty years into the future with no policy of systematic continued education for the teacher. Even the most dedicated teacher will fall behind, and students will learn how to live, not in the future, but in the past. School boards must accept lifelong learning as an essential condition for every teacher.

- A two-week Teacher Professional Development Term should be added to the school year, with appropriate compensation. This term for teachers would be a time for study, a period to improve instruction and to expand knowledge. The planning of such a term should be largely controlled by teachers at the school or district level.

- Every school district should establish a Teacher Travel Fund to make it possible for teachers, based on competitive application, to travel occasionally to professional meetings to keep current in their fields.

- Every five years, teachers should be eligible to receive a special contract—with extra pay to match—to support a Summer Study Term. To qualify and compete for this extended contract, each teacher would prepare a study plan. Such a plan would be subject to review and approval both by peers and by the school and district administrations.

A career path for teachers should be developed. Two of the most troublesome aspects of the teaching profession today are the lack of a career ladder and the leveling off of salaries. The irony is that to "get ahead" in teaching, you must leave it. Good teachers must be recognized and move forward within the profession, not outside it. Our proposals for restructuring the teaching career are these:

- The credentialing of teachers should be separated from college preparation. To qualify for a credential, each candidate should submit letters of recommendation from members of the faculty in his or her academic major, from faculty in his or her education sequence, and from a teacher who has supervised his or her school internship.

- Before being credentialed, the candidate would also pass a written examination administered by a Board of Examiners to be established in every state. The majority membership on such a board should be composed of senior classroom teachers.

- After credentialing, a career path based on performance should be available to the teacher, moving from associate teacher to senior teacher.

- With each professional advancement, salary increases should be provided. Such increases would be in addition to cost-of-living and merit pay earned within the ranks.

- The evaluation of teacher performance should be largely controlled by other teachers who themselves have been judged to be outstanding in the classroom.

Skilled professionals should be recruited to teach part-time in the nation's classrooms. More flexible arrangements will be needed to permit highly qualified nonacademic professionals to teach. Such "teachers" could serve in those fields where shortages exist—such as math and science—and provide enrichment in other fields as well. We recommend that:

- School districts should establish a lectureship program to permit qualified nonacademic professionals to teach on a part-time basis. Such teachers would devote most of their time to their regular jobs —in business or government or law or medicine—while also contributing significantly to education.

- School districts should look to recently retired personnel—college professors, business leaders, and others—who, after brief orientation, could teach part-time in high-demand subjects.

- School districts should enter into partnerships with business and industry to create joint appointments. In this way, two-member teacher teams could be created with one member of the team teaching in school for a year or two while the other works at a nonschool job. Then the cycle could be reversed.

- In-and-out teaching terms should be established—permitting a professional to teach for one to three years, step out, and then return for another one-to-three-year term.

- A Part-Time Practitioner Credential should be created in every state to put in place the recommendations we propose.

VII. Instruction: A Time for Learning

Much about good pedagogy is familiar. There remain, however, some old-fashioned yet enduring qualities in human relationships that still work: contagious enthusiasm, human sensitivity, optimism about the potential of the students. Improving instruction requires a variety of changes. We make the following recommendations:

- Teachers should use a variety of teaching styles—lecturing to transmit information, coaching to teach a skill and Socratic questioning to enlarge understanding. But there should be particular emphasis on the active participation of the student.

- For classroom instruction to be effective, expectations should be high, standards clear, evaluation fair, and students should be held accountable for their work.

- Textbooks seldom communicate to students the richness and excitement of original works. The classroom use of primary source materials should be expanded.

- States should ease their control over the selection of textbooks and transfer more authority to the district and local school. Teachers should have a far greater voice in selecting materials appropriate to their own subject areas.

VIII. Technology: Extending the Teacher's Reach

Technology, particularly computers, can enrich instruction. But educators are confused about precisely what the new machines will do. The strategy seems to be buy now, plan later. The absence of computer policy is itself a policy with major risks. A number of important steps should be taken to link computers to school objectives.

- No school should buy computers, or any other expensive piece of hardware, until key questions have been asked—and answered. Why is this purchase being made? Is available software as good as the equipment? What educational objectives will be served? Which students will use the new equipment, when, and why?

- In purchasing computers, schools should base their decisions not only on the quality of the equipment, but also on the quality of the instructional material available. School districts also should take into account the commitment of the computer company to work alone —or in collaboration with other companies—to develop instructional materials for schools.

- Every computer firm selling hardware to the schools should establish a Special Instructional Materials Fund. Such a fund would be used to develop, in consultation with classroom teachers, high-quality, school-related software.

- For technology to be used effectively, teachers must learn about the new equipment. Computer companies should provide technology seminars for teachers to keep them up-to-date on the uses of computers as a teaching tool.

- A National Commission on Computer Instruction should be named by the Secretary of Education to evaluate the software now offered for school use and propose an ongoing evaluation procedure that would be available to the schools. Outstanding teachers should comprise an important segment of such a panel.

- Federal funds should be used to establish ten Technology Resource Centers on university campuses—one in each major region of the nation. These centers would assemble, for demonstration, the latest technology. Also, federally funded regional networks should be developed to make computerized library services available to all schools.

- Schools should relate computer resources to their educational objectives. Specifically, all students should learn *about* computers; learn *with* computers; and, as an ultimate goal, learn *from* computers. The first priority, however, should not be hands-on experience, but rather educating students about the social importance of technology, of which the computer is a part.

Prospects for a technology revolution in education go far beyond computers. Through the use of television, films, video cassettes, the classroom can be enormously enriched. In this connection, we recommend:

- School districts with access to a cable channel should use the facility for school instruction and a district-wide plan for such use should be developed.

- All commercial television networks should set aside prime-time hours every week to air programs for education and thereby indirectly enrich the school curriculum.

- A National Film Library should be established with federal support. This resource center would secure outstanding film and television programs, both commercial and public offerings, index and edit them, and make them available for school use.

IX. Flexibility: Patterns to Fit Purpose

Our next priority is flexibility. There are many different high schools in the United States, with many different students. Greater flexibility in school size and the use of time will help schools achieve, more effectively, their educational objectives. The urgent need is not more time but better use of time. The following is proposed:

- The class schedule should be more flexibly arranged to permit larger blocks of instructional time, especially in courses such as a laboratory science, a foreign language, and creative writing.

- Small high schools should expand their education offerings by using off-campus sites or mobile classrooms or part-time professionals to provide a richer education for all students.

- Large high schools, particularly those with over 2,000 students, should organize themselves into smaller units—"schools-within-schools"—to establish a more cohesive, more supportive social setting for all students.

Gifted and talented students represent a unique challenge if they are to realize their potential. Therefore, we suggest:

- Every high school should develop special arrangements for gifted students—credit by examination, independent study, and accelerated programs.

- A network of Residential Academies in Science and Mathematics should be established across the nation. Some academies might be within a densely populated district. Others might serve an entire state. A residential school may serve several states. Academies might be located on college campuses. Such schools should receive federal support since clearly the vital interests of the nation are at stake.

Special arrangements are also needed for students at the other end of the education spectrum. Year after year, about one out of every four students who enroll in school drops out before graduation. This nation cannot afford to pay the price of wasted youth. We recommend:

- Federally supported remedial programs—most of which have been concentrated in the early grades—have demonstrated that improvements can be made in the academic achievement of even the most disadvantaged child. Therefore, the federally funded Elementary and Secondary Education Act (Title I) should be fully funded to support all students who are eligible to participate in this effective program.

- Every high school district, working with a community college, should have a reentry school arrangement to permit dropouts to return to school part time or full time or to engage in independent study to complete their education.

X. The Principal as Leader

What we seek are high schools in which the school community —students, teachers, and principals—sees learning as the primary goal. In such a community, the principal becomes not just the top authority but the key educator, too. Rebuilding excellence in education means reaffirming the importance of the local school and freeing leadership to lead. We make the following recommendations:

- The principal should be well prepared. The basic preparation should follow that of teachers.

- A principal should complete all requirements for licensing as a teacher and serve a year as an "administrative intern." At least two years as an assistant principal should be served before one could assume a full principalship.

- Principals and staff at the local school should have more control over their own budgets, operating within guidelines set by the district office. Further, every principal should have a School Improvement Fund, discretionary money to provide time and materials for program development and for special seminars and staff retreats.

- Principals should also have more control over the selection and rewarding of teachers. Acting in consultation with their staffs, they should be given responsibility for the final choice of teachers for their schools.

- In order to give principals time to reflect upon their work and stay in touch with developments in education, a network of Academies for Principals should be established.

XI. Strengthening Connections

High schools do not carry on their work in isolation. They are connected to elementary and junior high schools and to higher education. In the end, the quality of the American high school will be shaped in large measure by the quality of these connections. School-college relationships can be improved in a variety of ways:

- All states should establish a School-College Coordination Panel to define the recommended minimum academic requirements to smooth the transfer from school to public higher education.

- Every high school in the nation should offer a "university in the school" program and a variety of other arrangements—credit by examination, early admission and advanced placement—to permit able students to accelerate their academic programs.

- Each college or university should form a comprehensive partnership with one or more secondary schools.

Schools need the help of industry and business, and business needs the schools. The quality of work is linked to the quality of education. The following school-business partnerships are proposed:

- Businesses should provide help for disadvantaged students through volunteer tutorial and family counseling service, and support special school and part time apprenticeship experience for high risk students.

- Businesses should provide enrichment programs for gifted students, especially those in science and mathematics, and for those in the new technologies.

- Businesses should provide cash awards for outstanding teachers. In addition, they should consider establishing Endowed Chair Programs in the schools, and summer institute arrangements.

- Corporate grants should provide sabbaticals to outstanding principals and a discretionary fund for principals to work with teachers on creative programs. Further, large corporations should donate the use of their training facilities for a week or two each year to house an Academy for Principals.

- To help schools improve their physical plant and science laboratories, business should sponsor a facilities and equipment program. In addition, appropriate industries should conduct inventories of science laboratories and help upgrade school equipment.

XII. Excellence: The Public Commitment

Finally, school improvement is dependent on public commitment. How we as a nation regard our schools has a powerful impact on what occurs in them. Support for schools can take many forms, and it must come from many sources. Citizens, local school boards, state agencies and legislatures, and the federal government must work together to help bring excellence to our public schools. A number of steps are imperative:

- Parent-Teacher-Student Advisory Councils should be established at all schools. Further, a Parent Volunteer Program should be organized to tutor students, provide teacher aides, and other administrative, counseling, and clerical support.

- Parents should become actively involved in school board elections, attend meetings, and be willing to serve as members of the board.

- Boards of education should hold special meetings with representatives of the schools in their districts—principals and teachers—at least once a year.

- A network of community coalitions—Citizens for Public Schools—should be formed across the nation to give leadership in the advocacy of support for public education.

- The states should recognize that their overriding responsibility to the schools is to establish general standards and to provide fiscal support, but not to meddle. The state education law should be revised to eliminate confusing and inappropriate laws and regulations.

To achieve excellence in education the federal government also must be a partner in the process. In this report, we propose that funding of Title I of the Elementary and Secondary Education Act be increased to support all eligible students. We call for a National Teacher Service and a federally-funded network of Residential Academies in Science and Mathematics. We recommend that the federal government help create a National Film Library for schools and that a network of Technology Resource Centers be established with federal support to teach teachers about technology and its uses.

There is yet another urgent school need that calls for a national response. Many of our public schools have fallen into disrepair.

Laboratory equipment is in poor shape. The situation is as alarming as the decay of our highways, dams and bridges. Federal action is needed now to help meet an emergency in the schools. We propose:

- A new School Building and Equipment Fund should be established, a federal program that would provide short term, low interest loans to schools for plant rehabilitation and for the purchase of laboratory equipment.

No one reform can transform the schools. The single solution, the simple answer, may excite a momentary interest but the impact will not last.

In this report we have tried to think inclusively, and to search out interconnected solutions to the schools' interconnected problems. The result is something that is at once a yardstick to measure the need for reform and an agenda for action to bring about that reform.

Not every recommendation we present is appropriate for every school. Each institution will have its own agenda for renewal. What is important is that all high schools take steps to achieve excellence and that this effort be sustained.

We conclude this report on the American high school with the conviction that the promise of public education can be fulfilled and that, as a nation, we will meet the challenge.

APPENDIX A
THE FIFTEEN HIGH SCHOOLS
IN THE STUDY

1. *Archer High School* is a small rural school (approximately 400 students) in the Southeast with a predominantly black student body. The students' families are in the low to middle socioeconomic range. Community support for the school appears to be essentially nonexistent. Although the mayor and most of the city council members are black, the wealth and power in the town are largely in the hands of white citizens. People in positions of influence who have school-age children send them to a private school in another community. The financial support businesses formerly provided for school activities has been greatly reduced and in many instances it has been discontinued.

2. *Brette High School* is a West Coast urban academic high school with an enrollment of nearly 3,000 students on a campus designed for 1,800. Brette's student population now includes more children of working-class and poor families than it once did; about one-third of the students are eligible for the federal lunch subsidy. Brette is a minority school with a large population of Asians (45.5 percent). Blacks (7 percent of the student body) and Hispanics (6.5 percent) are underrepresented at Brette in comparison with their numbers in the whole district's student population. The school sends 99 percent of its students on to college—the majority to campuses of the University of California.

3. *Calvert High School* is located in the suburbs in the mid-Atlantic area of the United States. With an enrollment of 1,377, Calvert is one of the smaller high schools in a large county school system. Most of its students are white and come from middle-class families. A small number of students come from lower-upper class and poverty level. Seventeen percent of the student body is minority—5 percent black, 9 percent Asian, and 3 percent Hispanic. Because it serves a population in two different districts, there is no single governmental entity with which the school can identify. About 80 percent of the graduating students at Calvert go on to college, with 60 percent enrolling in four-year colleges and the other 20 percent in trade or technical schools. The student population is declining and there is a very real prospect that enrollment will continue to fall until the school is forced to close.

4. *Carver High School* is a magnet school—an urban vocational-technical school in the Southwest catering to non-college-bound youth. The student body are primarily black (71 percent) and Hispanic (23 percent). Vandalism is nearly unknown at Carver. Students are well disciplined and extremely serious about their chosen fields. Few students aspire to go to college. Instead, they want to go to work once they graduate. Many already have jobs after school and on weekends.

5. *DeSoto High School* is a magnet school in the Midwest concentrating on basic skills relevant to a variety of careers, with a specialty program in finance and small business. Opportunities for career exploration and work experience are offered along with academic work for students intending to go on to technical schools or to college. For many students, the school is a second choice when they cannot get into other, more attractive magnet schools in the district. The student body is relatively small, with an enrollment of approximately 1,100. Its small size has, at times, led to the possibility of closing—a threat that still concerns DeSoto's constituents.

6. *Garfield High School* is a big-city school in the Midwest with an enrollment of over 2,000 students. The school has a relatively new building located in a neighborhood that is integrated in both color and social class. Its students, predominantly minority, come from families in the low- to lower-middle-class socioeconomic range. It is reputed to be one of the best academic institutions in the city, a reputation supported by Student Aptitude Test (SAT) scores and advanced placement of its students in college, by daily attendance rates of over 96 percent, as well as by the favorable attitudes of students and parents and teachers.

7. *Jenner High School,* one of two academic high schools in the study, is located in an eastern metropolitan area. Its multiethnic, multiracial enrollment of approximately 3,000 students is drawn from the entire school district; only one-twentieth of those who apply are admitted. The school recruits and caters to students with specific academic aptitudes in mathematics and science; it does not attempt to serve all who are talented, such as those gifted artistically, athletically, or mechanically. One of Jenner's goals is to prepare students well for higher education. Over 90 percent of its graduates go on to a college or university.

8. *Neill House* is an alternative school encompassing grades K through 12. Located in an urban midwestern school district, it has a very small enrollment (181 students: 114 in grades K-8 and 67 in grades 9-12). The current student body is 37 percent minority, including 7 percent black and 30 percent Native American students. Graduation from Neill House is determined by completion of a comprehensive set of competency-based graduation requirements—a system unique to this school within the district. For the most part, the curriculum meets rough district guidelines, though teachers assume a high level of autonomy in determining the specific content of their classes. Many secondary students travel to more conventional high schools to take specific courses that are not available at Neill.

9. *Prairie View High School,* located in the rural Midwest, serves only 213 stu-

dents. The school's geographic isolation and small size are important aspects of what it means to be a rural school on the prairie. The school superintendent and his secretary are housed in the high school building. The teachers—nearly all from rural communities in the state—are a homogeneous group, with broad teaching responsibilities. There are no reading or special-education specialists; two teachers have five different subjects to teach during the six-hour day; six teachers have four; and eight teachers have three subjects to teach. The student body is not homogeneous: about half the students are Native American.

10. *Ridgefield High School* is a rural midwestern high school with a student body of about 1,000. Most students are from blue-collar families—low to lower-middle socioeconomic levels. Many parents commute to jobs in a nearby metropolitan area. What once was a stable rural community with strong local support for schools has, in the last 25 years, become a bedroom community with little attachment to its schools. Its rural ambience notwithstanding, Ridgefield has problems similar to those in more populous areas—in particular, problems with drugs.

11. *Rosemont High School* is a suburban school in the Northeast with an enrollment of 2,100 students. The diversity of the student body is considered one of its strengths. Thirty percent of the student body is minority, the largest proportion being Asian (including Chinese, Japanese, Korean, Indian, and Iranian in significant numbers). Twelve percent of the student body is black, half of whom come from a nearby metropolitan area. With the exception of the latter students, who have a working-class background, most of the Rosemont students are the children of upper-class professionals. The student body is divided into four houses (500 students are randomly assigned to each house). In addition, there is a school-within-a-school (SWS) of 100 students and 5 teachers offering an alternative for those who need or prefer a smaller school environment.

12. *Sage Vocational District High School* is a regional vocational education center in the West—a cooperative effort among five school districts and a community college to provide vocational training for secondary and postsecondary students and adults in the community. The center serves more than 1,500 students in more than 20 vocational programs taught in 12 different training locations. The vocational programs are designed to be an integral part of the students' high school educational program. Students elect to attend Sage and for that reason are committed to the school and its work.

13. *Sands High School*, located in the suburban Southeast, has an enrollment of 2,600 to 2,800 students. Sands is a school that has remained persistently middle class as its student population has been transformed from traditional American to Cuban-American youth. Almost half of the heads of families are in either managerial or professional occupations. In 70 percent of the families, both parents work. They prefer their adolescent children to be engaged in part-time jobs. While considerable emphasis is placed on doing well in school, parents tend to perceive academic achievement as a means to the more important goal of economic achievement.

14. *Sequoia High School* is a predominantly white school enrolling over 1,500

students from middle- to upper-middle-class families. It is located in a suburban area in the Pacific Northwest. A number of changes have affected Sequoia within the last few years, the major ones being a significant drop in school population (10,000 within the district), severe financial retrenchments leading to staff reductions and cutbacks in class offerings, and crowded classes. Nonetheless, both students and faculty consider Sequoia one of the best high schools in the state and are, on the whole, happy with their school. About 50 percent of the students go on to college, most within the state.

15. *Valley High School* is an urban school in the Southwest enrolling approximately 2,400 students, most of whom (68 percent) are Hispanic. About 16 percent of the student body is Asian, including relatively recently arrived "boat people" from Southeast Asia; the remainder of the students are American Indian, black, and "Anglo." The school shows a large incidence of transiency and dropouts. Of the total number of students entering the tenth grade in 1979, only about 55 percent graduated. Most students come from blue-collar families; about one-third qualify for free school breakfast or lunch programs. Of the 1982 graduating class, 80 percent went on to postsecondary school—about 30 percent to four-year schools.

APPENDIX B
OBSERVERS FOR THE
CARNEGIE FOUNDATION
HIGH SCHOOL STUDIES

Ms. Marianne Amerel
Development Research Division
Educational Testing Service
Princeton, New Jersey

Dr. Robert Anderson
Chairman
Program of Instructional Leadership
College of Education
University of Alabama
University, Alabama

Dr. Maja Apelman
Mountain View Center for
  Environmental Education
University of Colorado
Boulder, Colorado

Dr. Eva Baker
Center for the Study of Evaluation
UCLA Graduate School of Education
Los Angeles, California

Dr. Amity Buxton
Director of Staff Development
Oakland Unified School District
Oakland, California

Dr. Marilyn Cohn
Assistant Professor of Education and
Director of Elementary Teacher
  Training
Washington University
St. Louis, Missouri

Ms. Ann Cook
Co-director
Community Resources Institute
New York, New York

Ms. Kathleen Devaney
Director
Teacher Centers Exchange
Far West Laboratory
San Francisco, California

Dr. Ann diStefano
Graduate Institute of
  Education
Washington University
St. Louis, Missouri

Dr. B. Dell Felder
College of Education
University of Houston
Houston, Texas

Dr. G. Thomas Fox, Jr.
Research Associate
School of Education
University of Wisconsin
Madison, Wisconsin

Dr. Robert Houston
Associate Dean
School of Education
University of Houston
Houston, Texas

Mr. Wayne B. Jennings
Principal
Central High School
St. Paul, Minnesota

Dr. Jack Kleinert
Professor of Education
University of Miami
Miami, Florida

Dr. Sara Lightfoot
Harvard Graduate School of
  Education
Gutman Library
Cambridge, Massachusetts

Mr. Herb Mack
Co-director
Community Resources Institute
New York, New York

Dr. Marlene McCracken
Associate Professor
School of Education
University of North Dakota
Grand Forks, North Dakota

Dr. Robert McCracken
Professor of Education
Western Washington University
Bellingham, Washington

Dr. Fred M. Newmann
Professor of Curriculum and
  Instruction
University of Wisconsin
Madison, Wisconsin

Ms. Ruth Anne Olson
Evaluation Specialist
Minneapolis Public School System
Minneapolis, Minnesota

Dr. Warren Strandberg
Professor
College of Education
Virginia Commonwealth University
Richmond, Virginia

Dr. Cecilia Traugh
Center for Teaching and Learning
University of North Dakota
Grand Forks, North Dakota

Ms. Inez Wilson
Director
Chicago Teaching Center
Northeastern Illinois State
  University
Chicago, Illinois

APPENDIX C

Table 24 Total Population and Percentage of Population of School Age, by State: 1972 and 1982

State	1972		1982	
	Total population (in thousands)	Percentage of total population of school age	Total population (in thousands)	Percentage of total population of school age
United States	209,284	24.7	231,534	19.7
New England				
Connecticut	3,070	24.9	3,153	18.8
Maine	1,035	24.5	1,133	20.5
Massachusetts	5,762	26.6	5,781	18.4
New Hampshire	782	23.9	951	20.1
Rhode Island	976	22.6	958	18.0
Vermont	463	25.1	516	20.2
Mid-Atlantic				
Delaware	574	25.6	602	19.4
District of Columbia	744	21.5	631	14.4
Maryland	4,081	25.4	4,265	19.6
New Jersey	7,337	24.3	7,438	19.2
New York	18,352	23.6	17,659	18.7
Pennsylvania	11,905	24.1	11,865	18.8
Great Lakes				
Illinois	11,258	25.2	11,448	19.8
Indiana	5,296	25.8	5,471	20.8
Michigan	9,025	26.8	9,109	21.2
Ohio	10,747	25.9	10,791	20.1
Wisconsin	4,498	26.3	4,765	17.0
Plains				
Iowa	2,861	25.5	2,905	19.3
Kansas	2,256	24.9	2,408	18.4
Minnesota	3,867	26.7	4,133	19.5
Missouri	4,753	24.5	4,951	19.3
Nebraska	1,518	25.0	1,586	19.3
North Dakota	631	27.1	670	19.1
South Dakota	677	26.9	691	19.8

Table 24   Total Population and Percentage of Population of School Age, by State: 1972 and 1982 (continued)

State	1972 Total population (in thousands)	1972 Percentage of total population of school age	1982 Total population (in thousands)	1982 Percentage of total population of school age
Southeast				
Alabama	3,540	25.9	3,943	21.4
Arkansas	2,018	24.2	2,291	21.3
Florida	7,520	21.1	10,416	17.6
Georgia	4,807	25.0	5,639	21.7
Kentucky	3,336	24.9	3,667	21.3
Louisiana	3,762	27.2	4,362	21.9
Mississippi	2,307	27.0	2,551	22.9
North Carolina	5,296	24.6	6,019	20.3
South Carolina	2,718	26.0	3,203	21.6
Tennessee	4,088	24.1	4,651	20.4
Virginia	4,828	24.4	5,491	19.5
West Virginia	1,797	24.2	1,948	21.0
Southwest				
Arizona	2,009	23.8	2,860	20.7
New Mexico	1,078	28.2	1,359	21.9
Oklahoma	2,657	23.3	3,177	19.6
Texas	11,759	25.1	15,280	21.0
Rocky Mountain				
Colorado	2,405	24.1	3,045	19.2
Idaho	763	25.4	965	22.5
Montana	719	26.4	801	19.7
Utah	1,135	27.0	1,554	24.1
Wyoming	347	25.9	502	21.9
Far West				
Alaska	326	26.7	438	19.4
California	20,585	23.9	24,724	18.5
Hawaii	828	24.3	994	19.4
Nevada	547	23.4	881	19.0
Oregon	2,195	23.5	2,649	19.6
Washington	3,447	25.1	4,245	19.5

Source: 1972 population figures from U.S. Department of Commerce, *Survey of Current Business, August 1982.* 1982 population figures from U.S. Department of Commerce News, Bureau of Economic Analysis Report 83-21. Percentage of total population of school age computed from basic data in NEA, *Estimates of School Statistics,* selected years and total population figures.

Table 25 Public Elementary/Secondary School Enrollment, Number of Teachers, Average Teacher Salary and Per-Pupil Expenditure, by State: 1982–83

State	Public elementary/ secondary school enrollment	Number of teachers	Average teacher salary	Per-pupil expenditure
United States	39,505,691	2,138,572	$20,531	$2,917
Alabama	724,037	39,400	$17,850	$1,546
Alaska	86,683	5,630	$33,953	$6,620
Arizona	546,000	28,856	$18,849	$2,603
Arkansas	437,021	23,505	$15,176	$2,093
California	3,958,775	170,397	$23,555	$2,490
Colorado	544,800	29,000	$21,500	$2,986
Connecticut	505,400	31,698	$20,300	$3,746
Delaware	92,645	5,344	$20,665	$4,008
District of Columbia	87,581	4,909	$26,048	$3,767
Florida	1,476,000	82,041	$18,538	$3,009
Georgia	1,045,900	57,016	$17,412	$2,369
Hawaii	161,874	8,124	$24,796	$3,213
Idaho	205,020	10,125	$17,549	$2,110
Illinois	1,875,199	104,249	$22,618	$3,201
Indiana	1,005,159	50,692	$20,067	$2,672
Iowa	496,300	31,013	$18,709	$3,147
Kansas	405,810	26,280	$18,299	$3,094
Kentucky	652,000	32,200	$18,400	$2,193
Louisiana	774,000	42,499	$19,265	$2,529
Maine	211,986	12,277	$15,772	$2,651
Maryland	699,136	37,746	$22,786	$3,486
Massachusetts	925,160	52,000	$19,000	$2,958
Michigan	1,761,906	77,206	$23,965	$3,648
Minnesota	718,662	40,643	$22,296	$3,157
Mississippi	461,000	24,842	$14,285	$2,076
Missouri	806,400	48,257	$17,726	$2,587
Montana	151,988	8,906	$19,463	$2,981
Nebraska	264,478	16,249	$17,412	$2,605
Nevada	151,100	7,442	$20,944	$2,311
New Hampshire	161,298	10,105	$15,353	$2,341
New Jersey	1,157,000	73,291	$21,642	$4,190
New Mexico	269,111	14,250	$20,600	$2,904
New York	2,693,100	163,100	$25,100	$4,302
North Carolina	1,104,220	56,459	$17,836	$2,680
North Dakota	116,569	7,499	$18,390	$3,055
Ohio	1,850,800	95,010	$20,360	$2,807
Oklahoma	580,832	33,900	$18,110	$2,792
Oregon	447,449	24,500	$22,334	$3,643

Table 25 Public Elementary/Secondary School Enrollment, Number of Teachers, Average Teacher Salary and Per-Pupil Expenditure, by State: 1982–83 *(continued)*

State	Public elementary/ secondary school enrollment	Number of teachers	Average teacher salary	Per-pupil expenditure
Pennsylvania	1,781,000	102,700	$21,000	$3,290
Rhode Island	137,538	8,758	$23,175	$3,792
South Carolina	604,600	32,080	$16,380	$2,016
South Dakota	123,625	7,974	$15,595	$2,386
Tennessee	827,857	39,233	$17,425	$2,124
Texas	2,982,000	166,800	$19,500	$2,299
Utah	369,338	14,889	$19,677	$2,128
Vermont	91,597	6,591	$15,338	$2,940
Virginia	975,717	56,892	$18,707	$2,740
Washington	738,571	34,497	$23,413	$2,887
West Virginia	375,126	22,001	$17,370	$2,480
Wisconsin	784,800	52,200	$20,940	$3,421
Wyoming	101,523	7,297	$24,000	$3,467

Source: Selected data from National Education Association, *Estimates of School Statistics 1982–83.*

Table 26 Enrollments in Public Secondary Schools and Percentage Change, by State: 1972–73 to 1982–83

State	Public secondary school enrollment 1972–73	1982–83	Percentage change from 1972–73 to 1982–83
United States	19,149,677	15,719,450	−17.9
Alabama	375,646	337,209	−10.2
Alaska	33,312	38,014	14.1
Arizona	148,972	164,000	10.1
Arkansas	217,850	201,248	−7.6
California	1,755,241	1,246,203	−29.0
Colorado	262,718	234,800	−10.6
Connecticut	195,001	168,100	−13.8
Delaware	62,367	44,894	−28.0
District of Columbia	56,049	38,809	−30.8
Florida	763,647	681,470	−10.8
Georgia	397,801	396,100	−0.4
Hawaii	81,300	74,949	−7.8
Idaho	92,816	86,777	−6.5
Illinois	882,986	586,981	−33.5
Indiana	562,805	474,596	−15.7
Iowa	288,811	233,000	−19.3
Kansas	213,751	160,310	−25.0

Table 26 Enrollments in Public Secondary Schools and Percentage Change, by State: 1972–73 to 1982–83 (continued)

State	Public secondary school enrollment 1972–73	1982–83	Percentage change from 1972–73 to 1982–83
Kentucky	264,402	219,333	−17.0
Louisiana	334,952	224,000	−33.1
Maine	70,055	65,138	−7.0
Maryland	412,923	356,560	−13.6
Massachusetts	527,000	311,186	−40.9
Michigan	1,024,539	844,569	−17.6
Minnesota	439,820	360,360	−18.1
Mississippi	224,124	207,400	−7.5
Missouri	292,124	251,608	−13.9
Montana	55,076	44,971	−18.3
Nebraska	149,134	114,667	−23.1
Nevada	58,917	69,460	17.9
New Hampshire	71,275	67,759	−4.9
New Jersey	525,384	428,090	−18.5
New Mexico	136,081	119,211	−12.4
New York	1,616,545	1,384,500	−14.4
North Carolina	358,840	333,357	−7.1
North Dakota	47,216	35,922	−23.9
Ohio	946,142	733,500	−22.5
Oklahoma	273,939	248,000	−9.5
Oregon	198,724	172,120	−13.4
Pennsylvania	1,136,326	900,900	−20.7
Rhode Island	72,756	68,337	−6.1
South Carolina	237,246	183,500	−22.6
South Dakota	52,037	37,907	−27.1
Tennessee	339,883	237,434	−30.1
Texas	1,287,232	1,076,000	−16.4
Utah	142,192	147,817	4.0
Vermont	41,002	43,336	5.7
Virginia	404,035	375,331	−7.1
Washington	377,710	357,157	−5.4
West Virginia	180,527	150,357	−16.7
Wisconsin	420,305	339,800	−19.2
Wyoming	40,141	42,403	5.6

Source: Feistritzer Associates, Washington, D.C.

NOTES

Foreword

1. John I. Goodlad and others, "A Study of Schooling: Series of Introductory Descriptions," *Phi Delta Kappan,* November 1979 to February 1980. John I. Goodlad, *A Place Called School* (New York: McGraw-Hill, forthcoming).
2. James Coleman, "High School and Beyond: A National Longitudinal Study for the 1980's." Survey conducted by the National Opinion Research Center, Chicago, for the National Center for Education Statistics.

Prologue: The Globe, the Nation, and Our Schools

1. Dwight D. Eisenhower, "Special Message to Congress on Education," *Public Papers of the Presidents of the United States* (Washington, D.C.: Office of the Federal Register, National Archives and Records Service, January 27, 1958), p. 127.
2. U.S. Congress, House, Committee on Science and Technology, *Astronauts and Cosmonauts: Biographical and Statistical Data* (Washington, D.C.: Government Printing Office, 1981), pp. 5, 202–3.
3. *NORAD Satellite Boxscores* (Colorado Springs, Colorado: North American Aerospace Defense Command), March 30, 1983, p. 5.
4. Personal communication from Alan Needell, National Air and Space Museum, Space Science Division, March 29, 1983, and Rockwell International, *Press Information: Space Shuttle Transport System: February 1981* (Canoga Park, California: Rocket Dyne Information, 1981), p. 2.
5. United Nations, Department of International Economics and Social Affairs, *Demographic Year Book: 1958,* 10th issue (New York: United Nations, 1958), p. 104.
6. United Nations, Department of International, Economic and Social Affairs, *Demographic Year Book: 1981,* 33rd issue (New York: United Nations, 1983), p. 163, and Carnegie Foundation calculation based on a 1.8 percent annual rate of growth for period 1975–1980.

7. Based on 23,535,000 live births estimated for 1983 by the Population Reference Bureau, Washington, D.C., March 1983. Unpublished data.

8. U.S. Department of State, Office of the Geographer, *Status of the World's Nations* (Washington, D.C.: Government Printing Office, 1980), pp. 1, 12–15.

9. U.S. Department of Commerce, Bureau of the Census, *Statistical Abstract of the United States: 1958*, 79th ed. (Washington, D.C.: U.S. Government Printing Office, 1958), p. 522.

10. U.S. Department of Commerce, Bureau of the Census, *Statistical Abstract of the United States: 1983*, 103rd ed. (Washington, D.C.: Government Printing Office, 1983), pp. 555, 753.

11. Ruth Leger Sivard, *World Military and Social Expenditures* (Leesburg, Virginia: World Priorities, 1982), p. 43.

12. John Naisbitt, *Megatrends: Ten New Directions Transforming Our Lives* (New York: Warner Books, 1982), p. 14.

13. Bureau of the Census, *Statistical Abstract of the United States: 1983*, p. 386.

14. Naisbitt, *Megatrends*, p. 56.

15. U.S. Department of Commerce, Bureau of the Census, "Projections of the Population of the United States: 1982 to 2005 (Advance Report)," *Current Population Reports*, Series P-25, No. 922 (Washington, D.C.: U.S. Government Printing Office, 1982), p. 11.

16. Bureau of the Census, *Statistical Abstract of the United States: 1983*, p. 27.

17. U.S. Department of Commerce, Bureau of the Census, "Population Profile of the United States: 1981," *Current Population Reports*, Series P-20, No. 374 (Washington, D.C.: U.S. Government Printing Office, 1982), p. 20.

18. U.S. Department of Commerce, Bureau of the Census, "Household and Family Characteristics: March 1981," *Current Population Reports*, Series P-20, No. 371 (Washington, D.C.: U.S. Government Printing Office, 1982), pp. 131–34.

19. U.S. Department of Commerce, Bureau of the Census, unpublished data.

1. *A Day at Ridgefield High*

1. U.S. Department of Education, National Center for Education Statistics, *Digest of Education Statistics: 1982* (Washington, D.C.: Government Printing Office, 1982), p. 63.

2. U.S. Department of Education, National Center for Education Statistics, *The Condition of Education: 1982* (Washington, D.C.: Government Printing Office, 1982), p. 44.

3. Carnegie Foundation High School Visits, 1982.

4. U.S. Department of Education, National Center for Education Statistics, *1980 Survey of High School and Beyond*, public schools only.

2. *Report Card: How Schools Are Doing*

1. Staff communication with Sarah Van Allen, Gallup Poll Organization, Education Division, June 1983.

2. U.S. Department of Commerce, Bureau of the Census, *Statistical Abstract of*

the United States: 1983, 103rd edition (Washington: U.S. Government Printing Office, 1982), p. 136.

3. U.S. Department of Education, National Center for Education Statistics (NCES), unpublished data.

4. NCES, *1980 Survey of High School and Beyond,* public schools only.

5. NCES, *The Condition of Education: 1982* (Washington, D.C.: Government Printing Office, 1982), p. 50; and Carnegie Foundation calculation for median public high school enrollment in 1978–79.

6. NCES, *Digest of Education Statistics: 1982* (Washington, D.C.: Government Printing Office, 1982), p. 63.

7. Ibid., p. 43.

8. "St. Louis Proposes Ambitious Plan for Area Desegregation," *Education Week,* vol. 1, no. 23, November 12, 1981, p. 2.

9. *American Demographics,* vol. 3, no. 11 (New York: Dow Jones & Company, December 1981), p. 26, and staff communication with Carolyn Weeman, Atlanta Public Schools, Division of Research and Evaluation, March 4, 1983.

10. Personal communication of Neal Showalter, Milwaukee Public Schools, Department of Education and Program Assessment, Milwaukee, Wisconsin, March 4, 1983.

11. NCES, *Condition of Education: 1982,* p. 72.

12. National Education Association, *Estimates of School Statistics: 1982–83,* (Washington, D.C.: January 1983), p. 37.

13. NCES, *Digest of Education Statistics: 1982,* p. 74.

14. Susan Abramowitz and Ellen Tenenbaum, *High School '77: A Survey of Public Secondary School Principals* (Washington, D.C.: U.S. Department of Health, Education, and Welfare, National Institute of Education, December 1978), p. 29.

15. Computed from National Education Association, *Estimates of School Statistics, 1982–83,* pp. 30–34.

16. NCES, *1980 Survey of High School and Beyond.*

17. NCES, *Digest of Education Statistics: 1982,* p. 65.

18. NCES, *1980 Survey of High School and Beyond.*

19. National Education Association, *Nationwide Teacher Opinion Poll: 1981* (West Haven, Connecticut, 1981), p. 26.

20. Ibid., p. 29.

21. NCES, *1980 Survey of High School and Beyond.*

22. George H. Gallup, "Gallup Poll of the Public's Attitude Toward the Public Schools," *Phi Delta Kappan,* September 1982, p. 39.

23. Lyle V. Jones, "Achievement Test Scores in Mathematics and Science," *Science,* vol. 213, July 24, 1981, p. 412.

24. W. Willard Wirtz, *Report of the Advisory Panel on the Scholastic Aptitude Test Score Decline* (New York: College Entrance Examination Board, 1977), pp. 22, 24, 48.

25. Ibid., p. 48.

26. Lawrence Biemiller, "Board Says Minority-Group Scores Helped Push Up

Average on SAT," *The Chronicle of Higher Education,* October 20, 1982, vol. xxv, no. 8, p. 10.

27. Unpublished data, The American College Testing Program, Iowa City, Iowa, February 15, 1983.

28. The American College Testing Program, *The High School Profile Report: 1975–76* (Iowa City, 1976), p. 3; The American College Testing Program, *The High School Profile Report, 1981–82* (Iowa City, 1982), p. 2.

29. Ibid.

30. National Assessment of Educational Progress (NAEP), *Writing Achievement: 1969–79,* vol. 1, 17-year-olds (Denver: Education Commission of the States, December 1980), pp. 14, 26.

31. Ibid., p. 44.

32. NAEP, *The Third National Mathematics Assessment; Results, Trends, and Issues* (Denver: Education Commission of the States, April 1983), p. xiii.

33. NAEP, *Three National Assessments in Science: Changes in Achievement: 1969–1977* (Denver: Education Commission of the States, June 1978), p. 10, and *Science Achievement in the Schools: a Summary of Results from the 1976–77 National Assessment of Science* (December 1978), pp. 6–16.

34. Ina Mullis, "Citizenship/Social Studies Achievement Trends Over Time," paper presented at the 1978 Annual Meeting of the American Educational Research Association, Toronto, Canada, March 1978, p. 9; and National Assessment of Educational Progress, *Education for Citizenship: A Bicentennial Survey,* (Denver: Education Commission of the States, November 1976), pp. 26–27.

35. National Assessment of Educational Progress, *The First Social Studies Assessment: An Overview* (June 1974), p. vii; National Council for the Social Studies, *National Assessment and Social Studies Education,* (Washington, D.C.: Government Printing Office, 1975), p. 111.

36. Phillip R. Rinhel, "Public Education in Transition," *The University of Michigan School of Education Innovation,* vol. 14, no. 2, September 1982.

37. "Achievement Scores Rise in California, Reversing Decline," *Education Week,* November 2, 1981, p. 2.

38. Torsten Husén, *The School in Question: A Comparative Study of the School and Its Future in Western Society* (Oxford: Oxford University Press, 1979), pp. 96, 88, 101.

39. Ibid., p. 98

40. Richard M. Wolf, *Achievement in America: National Report of the United States for the International Project* (New York: Teachers College Press, 1977), pp. 3, 44.

41. Husén, p. 97.

42. Torsten Husén, "Are Standards in U.S. Schools Really Lagging Behind Those in Other Countries?" *Phi Delta Kappan,* March 1983, p. 456.

43. Lerner, "American Education," no. 69.

44. Harold G. Shane, "An Interview with W. Willard Wirtz—The Academic Score Debate, Are Statistics the Enemy of Truth?," *Phi Delta Kappan,* October 1977, pp. 84, 85.

45. U.S. Department of Commerce, Bureau of the Census, *Statistical Abstract of the United States: 1983*, p. 82.
46. U.S. Department of Commerce, Bureau of the Census, "Household and Family Characteristics: March 1981," *Current Population Reports*, Series P-20, No. 371 (Washington, D.C.: Government Printing Office, 1982), p. 7.
47. U.S. Department of Labor, "Education Level of Labor Force Continues to Rise: Also Reports Proportion of Multi-Earner Families Hold Steady," News Release USDL-83-276, August 10, 1982, p. 4.
48. Unofficial estimates from U.S. Department of Commerce, Bureau of the Census.
49. Eva Hoffman and Margot Slade, "Teachers in the Hot Seat," *New York Times*, vol. 131, section 4, p. E19, February 7, 1982.
50. Ibid.

3. We Want It All

1. Carnegie Foundation High School Visits, 1982.
2. Lawrence A. Cremin, *The Genius of American Education* (New York: Vintage Books, 1965), p. 6.
3. David B. Tyack, *Turning Points in American Educational History* (Waltham, Massachusetts: Blaisdell Publishing Company, 1967), p. 353.
4. Adolphe E. Meyer, *An Educational History of the American People*, 2nd ed. (New York: McGraw-Hill, 1967), p. 207.
5. Ibid.
6. Fred and Grace Hechinger, *Growing Up in America* (New York: McGraw-Hill, 1975), p. 106.
7. Jim B. Pearson and Edgar Fuller (eds.), *Education in the States: Vol. 1, Historical Development and Outlook* (Washington, D.C.: National Education Association, 1969), pp. 596–97.
8. Henry Barnard, "Woodward High School in Cincinnati," *American Journal of Education*, December 1857, pp. 520–22, 525.
9. Tyack, *Turning Points in American Educational History*, p. 354.
10. Hechinger, *Growing Up in America*, pp. 114, 115.
11. Ibid.
12. David H. Cohen and Barbara Neufeld, "The Failure of High Schools and the Progress of Education," *Daedalus*, Summer 1981, vol. 110, no. 10, p. 72.
13. U.S. Department of Commerce, Bureau of the Census, *Historical Statistics of the United States: Colonial Times to 1970*, Part I (Washington, D.C.: Government Printing Office, 1975), p. 369.
14. Ibid., pp. 10, 369, and Carnegie Foundation Calculations.
15. A. Harry Passow, *Secondary Education Reform: Retrospect and Prospect*, Julius and Rosa Sachs Memorial Lecture, April 7–8, 1976 (New York: Teachers College, Columbia University, 1976), p. 10.
16. Sol Cohen (ed.), *Education in the United States: A Documentary History*, vol. 3 (New York: Random House, 1974), p. 1953. Reprint of Charles W. Eliot,

"The Fundamental Assumptions in the Report of the Committee of Ten," *Educational Review*, vol. XXX, pp. 325–43.

17. Hechinger, *Growing Up in America*, pp. 108, 109.

18. A. R. Dugmore, "New Citizens for the Republic," *The World's Work*, April, 1903, vol. 5, no. 6, pp. 3323–26.

19. Commission on the Reorganization of Secondary Education, *Cardinal Principles of Education*, Bulletin 1918, no. 35 (Washington, D.C.: Government Printing Office, 1918), p. 9.

20. William James, *Talks to Teachers on Psychology and to Students on Some of Life's Ideals* (New York: W. W. Norton, 1958); William James, *The Principles of Psychology*, 3 vols. (Cambridge: Harvard University Press, 1981); and John Dewey, *The Child and the Curriculum* (Chicago: University of Chicago Press, 1902).

21. John Dewey, *School and Society* (Chicago: University of Chicago Press, 1899), pp. 21–24.

22. Ibid., p. 19.

23. Tyack, *Turning Points in American Educational History*, p. 321.

24. Charles Prosser, as quoted in Richard Hofstadter, *Anti-Intellectualism in American Life* (New York: Random House, 1962), p. 346.

25. Hofstadter, *Anti-Intellectualism in American Life*, pp. 340, 346.

26. Edward A. Krug, *The Shaping of the American High School*, vol. 2, 1920–1946 (Madison, Wisconsin: University of Wisconsin Press, 1972), pp. 292–293.

27. William Chandler Bagley, *Education and Emergent Man: A Theory of Education with Particular Application to Public Education in the United States* (New York: T. Nelson and Sons, 1934), p. 151.

28. David Tyack and Elisabeth Hansot, "Hard Times, Then and Now: Public Schools in the 1930s and 1980," n.d., mimeographed, p. 2.

29. Personal correspondence with Ralph Tyler.

30. U.S. Department of Commerce, Bureau of the Census, *Historical Statistics of the United States: Colonial Times to 1970*, Part I (Washington, D.C.: Government Printing Office, 1975), pp. 10, 368, and Carnegie Foundation calculations.

31. Cohen and Neufeld, "The Failure of High Schools," p. 72.

32. Arthur Eugene Bestor, *Educational Wastelands: The Retreat from Learning in Our Public Schools* (Urbana: University of Illinois Press, 1953), pp. 29–33, 203.

33. Charles E. Silberman, *Crisis in the Classroom: The Remaking of American Education* (New York: Random House, 1970), p. 168.

34. James Bryant Conant, *The American High School Today: A First Report to Interested Citizens* (New York: McGraw-Hill, 1959), pp. 37, 38

35. U.S. Department of Health, Education and Welfare, Office of Education, National Panel on High School and Adolescent Education, *The Education of Adolescents: The Final Report and Recommendations* (Washington, D.C.: Government Printing Office, 1976) pp. 47, 48, 52.

36. Ibid., p. 5.

37. The National Commission on the Reform of Secondary Education, *The Reform of Secondary Education: A Report to the Public and the Profession* (New York: McGraw-Hill, 1973), p. 101.
38. Bestor, *Educational Wastelands*, p. 75.

4. *Four Essential Goals*

1. Ernie Knee, *Accreditation Standards and Procedures for Secondary Schools* (Boise: Idaho State Department of Education, Idaho State, 1981), p. 3.
2. "Standards for Accreditation of Teachers and Secondary Schools," *Mississippi State Department of Education Bulletin*, no. 171, July 1981, p. 2.
3. *Elementary-Secondary Guide for Oregon Schools, 1980: Standards for Public Schools* (Salem, Oregon: Department of Education, 1981), p. viii.
4. Maine Revised Statutes Annotated, Title 20-SS 1221, 1980.
5. California State Board of Education, Curriculum Development and Supplemental Materials Commission. History–Social Science Framework Committee. *History, Social Science Framework for California Public Schools, Kindergarten through Grade 12* (Sacramento: California State Department of Education, 1981), pp. 38–39.
6. Illinois Revised Statutes, 1981, ch. 122, para. 27–12ff.
7. National Association of Secondary School Principals, *State-Mandated Graduation Requirements*, 1980 (Reston, Virginia: National Association of Secondary School Principals, 1980), p. 5.
8. Rhode Island State Department of Education, *Rhode Island Laws Relating to Education*, Title 16 of the General Laws, 1975.
9. *Wisconsin State Statutes*, SS-18.01, 1977, pp. 519–520.
10. Carnegie Foundation High School Visits, 1982.
11. Ibid.
12. Ibid.
13. Ibid.
14. Ibid.
15. Ibid.
16. Ibid.
17. Ibid.
18. Ibid.
19. Ibid.
20. Ibid.
21. Ibid.
22. Ibid.

5. *Something for Everyone*

1. Carnegie Foundation High School Visits, 1982.
2. National Association of Secondary School Principals, *State Mandated Graduation Requirements, 1980* (Reston, Virginia, 1980), pp. 2, 3.
3. Clifford Adelman, and others, "Devaluation, Diffusion and the College Connection: A Study of High School Transcripts, 1964–1981," prepared for The

National Commission on Excellence in Education, March, 1983, mimeographed, p. 13.
4. S. Frederick Starr, "Foreign Languages in the American School," in U.S. Department of Health, Education, and Welfare/Office of Education, President's Commission on Foreign Language and International Studies: background papers and studies (Washington, D.C.: Government Printing Office, 1979), p. 10.
5. National Association of Secondary School Principals, *State Mandated Graduation Requirements, 1980* (Reston, Virginia; 1980), p. 15.
6. Ibid., p. 8.
7. Susan Walton, "Florida Panel Urges Statewide Graduation Standards," *Education Week*, December 22, 1982, p. 4.
8. "Maine Considers Requiring Science, Math for Diploma," *Education Week*, October 12, 1981, p. 2; Peggy Caldwell, "Ohio Board Approves New Minimum Standards," *Education Week*, December 22, 1982, p. 4; "Arizona Gov. Wants to Require Students to Take More Courses," *Education Week*, October 13, 1982, p. 3.
9. National Commission on Excellence in Education, *A Nation at Risk* (Washington, D.C.: Government Printing Office, 1983), p. 24.
10. Carnegie Foundation High School Visits, 1982.
11. William Humm and Robert L. Buser, "High School Curriculum in Illinois," *Educational Leadership*, May, 1980, pp. 670–672.
12. Carnegie Foundation High School Visits, 1982.
13. Ibid.
14. Ibid.
15. Ibid.
16. Carnegie Foundation Analysis of National Center for Education Statistics, *1980 Survey of High School and Beyond*, 1972 Longitudinal Survey.
17. Ibid.
18. Adelman and others, "Devaluation, Diffusion and the College Connection," p. 17.
19. Paul Campbell, John Gardner, and Patricia Seitz, *High School Vocational Graduates: Which Doors Are Open?* (Columbus, Ohio: National Center for Research in Vocational Education, 1982), pp. 3, 4.
20. National Institute of Education, *The Vocational Education Study: The Interim Report* (Washington, D.C.: September 1981), pp. vi–16.
21. Daniel P. and Lauren B. Resnick, "Standards, Curriculum, and Performance: A Historical and Comparative Perspective," A Report to the National Commission on Excellence in Education, August 31, 1982, mimeographed, pp. 13, 14.

6. Literacy: The Essential Tool

1. John Dewey, *The Public and Its Problems* (Chicago: The Swallow Press, 1954), pp. 151–152.
2. For a discussion of communication among nonhuman species, see Carol Grant

Gould, "Out of the Mouths of Beasts," *Science 83,* April, 1983, pp. 68–72.

3. See, for example, Herbert H. and Eve V. Clark, *Psychology and Language: An Introduction to Psycholinguistics* (New York: Harcourt Brace Jovanovich, 1977), pp. 554–557, and Roger Brown, *Psycholinguistics: Selected Papers* (New York: Free Press, 1970).
4. Morton Bloomfield, "The Study of Language," *Daedalus,* Summer 1973, vol. 102, no. 3, p. 5.
5. John Stewig, *Exploring Language with Children* (Columbus, Ohio: Charles A. Merrill, 1974), pp. 3–21.
6. See, for example, Roach Van Allen and Claryce Allen, *Language Experience Activities* (Boston: Houghton Mifflin Company, 1976).
7. Conversation with Herminia Uresti, April 4, 1983.
8. Ibid.
9. Conversation with Robert Stokes, April 7, 1983.
10. Jeanne S. Chall, as quoted in Daniel and Lauren B. Resnick, "The Nature of Literacy: An Historical Exploration," *Harvard Educational Review,* August 1977, vol. 47, no. 3, pp. 383–384.
11. Patricia Albjerg Graham, "Literacy: A Goal for Secondary Schools," *Daedalus,* Summer 1981, p. 132.
12. Donald H. Graves, *Balance the Basics: Let Them Write* (New York: Ford Foundation, 1978), p. 7.
13. Carnegie Foundation High School Visits, 1982.
14. Ibid.
15. Arthur H. Applebee, *A Study of Writing in the Secondary School: Final Report* (Urbana, Illinois: National Council of Teachers of English, September, 1980), pp. 140–141.
16. Henry Barnard, "Woodward High School in Cincinnati," *American Journal of Education,* December 1857, p. 521.
17. Wayne Booth, "Mere Rhetoric, Rhetoric, and the Search for Common Learning," in *Common Learning* (Washington D.C.: The Carnegie Foundation for the Advancement of Teaching, 1981), p. 34.
18. Ibid., p. 54.

7. The Curriculum Has a Core

1. E. D. Hirsch, Jr., "Cultural Literacy," *The American Scholar,* Spring 1983, vol. 52, no. 2, pp. 159–169.
2. Arthur N. Applebee as quoted in ibid., p. 159.
3. M. H. Abrams, *The Mirror and the Lamp: Romantic Theory and the Critical Tradition* (New York: Oxford University Press, 1953).
4. Carnegie Foundation High School Visits, 1982.
5. Murray Sidlin, "Someone's Priority," speech given at the Aspen Conference on the Talented and Gifted, sponsored by the U.S. Department of Health, Education, and Welfare in the Office of the Gifted and Talented, Aspen, Colorado, June 1978.
6. S. Frederick Starr, "Foreign Languages in the American School," in U.S.

Department of Health, Education, and Welfare/Office of Education, *President's Commission on Foreign Language and International Studies: Background Papers and Studies* (Washington, D.C.: U.S. Government Printing Office, November 1979), p. 11.

7. James A. Perkins, in U.S. President's Commission on Foreign Language and International Studies, *Strength Through Wisdom: A Critique of U.S. Capability* (Washington, D.C.: U.S. Government Printing Office, November 1979), p. i.

8. Eric H. Lenneberg, *Biological Foundations of Language* (New York: John Wiley, 1967), p. 176.

9. U.S. Department of Commerce, Bureau of the Census, "Geographical Mobility: March 1980 to March 1981," *Current Population Reports, Population Characteristics* (Washington, D.C.: Government Printing Office, 1983), Series P-20, no. 377, p. 33.

10. Unpublished data from Population Reference Bureau, Washington, D.C.

11. "China, Pop. 1,008,175,288, has 4th of World's People," *New York Times*, October 28, 1982, p. A-1.

12. Ralph Waldo Emerson, *Journals*, ed. by Edward Waldo Emerson and Waldo Emerson Forbes, vol. 2 (Boston: Houghton Mifflin, 1909), p. 448.

13. Thomas Jefferson, *Letters*, arranged by Willson Whitman (Eau Claire, Wisconsin: E. M. Hale, 1940), pp. 338, 339 (emphasis added).

14. Alexis de Tocqueville, *Democracy in America*, edited by Francis Bowen, 3rd ed. (Cambridge: Sever and Francis, 1863).

15. Walter Lippmann, *Public Opinion* (New York: Macmillan Company, 1922), p. 31.

16. Karl R. Popper, *The Logic of Scientific Discovery* (New York: Basic Books, 1959), p. 278.

17. Lewis Thomas, "On the Uncertainty of Science," *Harvard Magazine*, September-October 1980, vol. 83, no. 1, p. 21.

18. Carnegie Foundation analysis of National Center for Education Statistics, *High School and Beyond*, 1980.

19. Ibid.

20. Interview with Professor Robert McDowell, Washington University, St. Louis, Missouri.

21. Thomas Carlyle, *Sartor Resartus: The Life and Opinions of Herr Teufelsdrockh*, with an introduction by Ernest Rhys, Camelot Series (London: Walter Scott, 1888), p. 35.

22. N. Bruce Hannay and Robert McGinn, "The Anatomy of Modern Technology: Prolegomenon to an Improved Public Policy for the Social Management of Technology," *Daedalus*, Winter 1980, vol. 109, no. 1, p. 35. Emphasis added.

23. Oscar Handlin, "Science and Technology in Popular Culture," in Gerald Holton (ed.), *Science and Culture: A Study of Cohesive and Disjunctive Forces* (Boston: Houghton Mifflin, 1965), pp. 186, 194.

24. Jeremy Bernstein, "Science Education for the Non-Scientist," *The American Scholar*, Winter 1982–83, vol. 52, no. 1, p. 12.

25. Information from National Clearinghouse on Alcohol Abuse, Washington, D.C.

26. The national chairman of the National Institutes of Health, Washington, D.C., reports teenage pregnancies increased from 94.8 per thousand in 1976 to 103.5 per thousand in 1980.

8. *Transition: To Work and Learning*

1. U.S. Department of Labor, Bureau of Labor Statistics, *Employment and Earning Report* (Washington, D.C.: Government Printing Office, 1983), p. 149. Also, unpublished data from Bureau of Labor Statistics.
2. Unpublished data, National Center for Education Statistics.
3. Alexander W. Astin, Margo King Hemond, and Gerald T. Richardson, *The American Freshmen: National Norms for Fall 1982* (Los Angeles: University of California at Los Angeles, 1982), p. 9.
4. U.S. Department of Labor, *Student Force to Decline*, news release, April 12, 1983.
5. George J. Nolfi et al., *Experience of Recent High School Graduates* (Lexington, Massachusetts: Lexington Books, 1978), p. 53.
6. Joseph Froomkin and J.R. Endriff, *School and Work: An Analysis of Teenage Labor Force Status and School Enrollment*, Final Report (Washington, D.C.: Education Policy Research Center, Joseph Froomkin Inc., 1979), p. 28.
7. Paul Osterman, *Getting Started: The Youth Labor Market* (Cambridge: MIT Press, 1980), p. 31.
8. Staff communication with U.S. Department of Labor, April 1983.
9. Paul Campbell, John Gardner, Patricia Seitz, *High School Vocational Graduates: Which Doors Are Open?* (Columbus, Ohio: National Center for Research in Vocational Education, Ohio State University, 1982), pp. 3, 4.
10. Elinor M. Woods and Walt Haney, *Proposed Propositions and Framework for Study* (Cambridge, Massachusetts: Huron Institute, revised October 1979), p. 89.
11. Carnegie Foundation High School Visits, 1982.
12. Bette C. Overman, *Functions of Schooling: Perceptions and Preferences of Teachers, Parents, and Students* (Los Angeles: Graduate School of Education, University of California, 1980), Technical Report no. 10, pp. 23, 25, 39.
13. Carnegie Foundation High School Visits, 1982.
14. National Institute of Education, *The Vocational Education Study: The Final Report* (Washington, D.C.: September 1981), pp. vii–6, vii–9.
15. Carnegie Foundation High School Visits, 1982.
16. Osterman, *Getting Started*, p. 28.
17. Elinor M. Woods and Walt Haney, "Does Vocational Education Make a Difference? A Review of Previous Research and Reanalysis of National Longitudinal Data Sets," final report to the National Institute of Education (Cambridge, Massachusetts: Huron Institute, September 30, 1981), p. 4-1-19.
18. Charles S. Benson, "The Question of Quality," *Voc Ed*, vol. 57, no. 6, September 1982, p. 29.
19. Paul E. Petersen and Barry G. Rabe, *Urban Vocational Education and Managing the Transition from School to Work: A Review of a Series of Case Studies of*

Vocational Education Programs in Four Cities, ERIC Doc. No. ED 211 A 741 (Arlington, Virginia: ERIC Document Reproduction Service, 1981), p. 25.
20. Alan Woodruff, *The National Study of Vocational Education Systems and Facilities*, vol. 1. Technical Report Prepared for the Office of Planning, Budgeting and Evaluation, U.S. Department of Education, by Institutional Development Associates, Inc., Silver Spring, Maryland, and by Westat Incorporated, Rockville, Maryland, October 1978, p. 133.
21. Carnegie Foundation High School Visits, 1982.
22. Max L. Carey, "Occupational Employment, Growth Through 1990," *Monthly Labor Review*, U.S. Department of Labor (Washington, D.C.: Government Printing Office, August 1981), p. 48.
23. Henry M. Levin and Russell W. Rumberger, *The Educational Implications of High Technology*, Project Report No. 83-A4, Institute for Research on Educational Finance and Governance, Stanford University, February 1983, p. 5.
24. Ibid.
25. Carnegie Foundation High School Visits, 1982.
26. Ibid.
27. Ibid.
28. Ibid.
29. Ibid.
30. Ibid.
31. Ibid.
32. Jeannie Oakes, *A Question of Access: Tracking and Curriculum Differentiations in a National Sample of English and Mathematics Classes*, Technical Report No. 24, *A Study of Schooling Technical Report Series*, pp. 187, 189.
33. Carnegie Foundation High School Visits, 1982.
34. Center for Public Resources, *Basic Skills in the U.S. Work Force* (New York: Center for Public Resources, 1982), pp. 23, 5, 19, 20.
35. Carnegie Foundation High School Visits, 1982.
36. Ibid.
37. Ibid.
38. Lawrence A. Cremin, *Public Education* (New York: Basic Books, 1976), pp. 25–53.
39. National Center for Education Statistics, *1980 Survey of High School and Beyond*.
40. Carnegie Foundation High School Visits, 1982
41. Ibid.
42. Ibid.

9. Instruction: A Time to Learn

1. Kenneth A. Sirotnik, *What You See Is What You Get: A Summary of Observations in Over 1000 Elementary and Secondary Classrooms*. A Study of Schooling in the United States. Technical Report Series no. 29, ERIC Doc. no. ED 214 897 (Arlington, Virginia: ERIC Document Reproduction Service, 1981), p. 18.

2. Carnegie Foundation High School Visits, 1982.
3. Ibid.
4. Ibid.
5. Sherry Keith, *Politics of Textbook Selection* (Palo Alto: Institute for Research on Educational Finance and Governance, 1981), p. 19.
6. Carnegie Foundation High School Visits, 1982.
7. Ibid.
8. Ibid.
9. Ibid.
10. Ibid.
11. Mortimer J. Adler, *The Paideia Proposal: An Educational Manifesto* (New York: Macmillan, 1982), p. 32.
12. Ibid., p. 23.
13. Ibid., p. 50.
14. Sirotnik, *What You See Is What You Get*, pp. 8–9.
15. Lois V. Edinger, Paul L. Houts, and Dorothy V. Meyer (eds.), *Education in the 80's: Curriculum Challenges* (Washington, D.C.: National Education Association, 1981), p. 74.

10. *Teachers: Renewing the Profession*

1. Dan Clemente Lortie, *Schoolteacher: A Sociological Study* (Chicago: University of Chicago Press, 1975), p. 10 (emphasis added).
2. Staff conversation with Sarah Van Allen, Gallup Poll Organization, Education Division, June 1983.
3. National Education Association, *Nationwide Teacher Opinion Poll: 1980* (Washington: National Education Association, 1980), p. 14.
4. Carnegie Foundation High School Visit, 1982.
5. National Education Association, *Estimates of School Statistics 1982–83* (Washington: National Education Association, January 1983), p. 33.
6. Based on an average of 5 teaching classes and 1 preparation period per day of an average length of 54 minutes. National Education Association, *Status of the American Public School Teacher 1980–81* (Washington: National Education Association, 1982), pp. 143, 146, 148.
7. Carnegie Foundation High School Visits, 1982.
8. Ibid.
9. Ibid.
10. National Center for Education Statistics, *1980 Survey of High School and Beyond*, public schools only.
11. Carnegie Foundation High School Visits, 1982.
12. National Education Association, *Status of the American Public School Teacher 1980–81* (Washington: National Education Association, 1982), pp. 132–133.
13. Ann Lieberman and Lynne Miller, "The Social Realities of Teaching," *Teachers College Record*, vol. 80, September 1978, p. 60.
14. Ibid.
15. Carnegie Foundation High School Visits, 1982.

16. Edward B. Fiske, "Survey of Teachers Reveals Morale Problem," *New York Times,* September 19, 1982, pp. 1, 52.
17. National Education Association, *Status of the American Public School Teacher 1980–81* (Washington, D.C.: National Education Association, 1982), p. 74.
18. Robert Schaefer, *School as the Center of Inquiry* (New York: Harper & Row, 1967), p. 3.
19. Carnegie Foundation High School Visits, 1983.
20. Donna H. Kerr, "Teaching Competence and Teacher Education in the United States," *Teachers College Record,* Spring 1983, p. 531.
21. Carnegie Foundation High School Visits, 1982.
22. Lortie, *Schoolteacher,* p. 105.
23. Ibid., pp. 104–105.
24. Carnegie Foundation High School Visits, 1982.
25. Ibid.
26. National Education Association, *Nationwide Teacher Opinion Poll: 1980* (Westport, Connecticut: NEA Distribution Center, 1980), p. 14.
27. Carnegie Foundation High School Visits, 1982.
28. Ibid.
29. Ibid.
30. Ibid.
31. Ibid.
32. Staff conversation with Pam Holler, *The Washington Post,* June 1983.
33. Carnegie Foundation High School Visit, 1982.
34. National Education Association, *Status of the American School Teacher, 1980–81* (Washington, D.C.: 1982), p. 229.
35. David L. Henderson, Charles E. Darby, and Cleborne Maddux, "Moonlight, Salary, and Morale," *TSTA Advocate,* vol. 2, no. 7, November 1982, p. 9.
36. Ibid., p. 8.
37. Staff conversation with Dr. Clifford Swartz, Department of Physics, SUNY at Stony Brook, New York, April 1983.
38. James Koerner, *The Miseducation of American Teachers* (Boston: Houghton Mifflin, 1963), pp. 39–40.
39. Ibid., p. 41.
40. Ibid., p. 18.
41. Self-reported SAT scores, National Center for Education Statistics, *1972 National Longitudinal Survey,* Washington, D.C.; and College Board, *College Bound Seniors: 1982* (New York: College Board, 1982), Table 14.
42. "SAT Scores Rise for First Time in 19 Years," *Higher Education Daily,* September 22, 1982, vol. 10, no. 183, p. 1.
43. Thomas Barrows, John Clark, and Stephen Klein, "What Students Know About Their World," *Change,* vol. 12, no. 4, May–June 1980, p. 10.
44. Gerald Grant, "The Teacher's Predicament," *Teachers College Record,* Spring 1983, p. 593.
45. Gary Syles, "Teacher Preparation and the Teachers' Workforce," a background paper (Washington, D.C.: National Institute of Education, 1982), p. 5.

46. *Congress and the Nation, 1973–1977*, vol. IV (Washington, D.C.: Congressional Quarterly, Inc., 1977), pp. 362 and 382.
47. Carnegie Foundation High School Visits, 1982.
48. Reported in Marjorie Hunter, "Fight Brews on Aid to Teach Science," *New York Times*, April 19, 1983, p. C7.
49. Personal conversation with Joan Myers, Maryland Department of Education, Office of Teacher Certification, June 1983.
50. Robert G. Scanlon, *Report of the Council of Chief State School Officers' Ad Hoc Committee on Teacher Certification, Preparation, and Accreditation* (Washington: The Council, July 1982), p. 39.
51. Carnegie Foundation High School Visits, 1983.
52. Paul F. Kleine and Richard Wisniewski, "Bill 1706: A Forward Step for Oklahoma," *Phi Delta Kappan*, vol. 63, no. 2, p. 115.
53. Carnegie Foundation Telephone Interview with South Carolina School Officials, May 1983.
54. New Jersey Commission to Study Teacher Preparation Programs, *Final Report*, Submitted to the Governor, Senate and General Assembly, June 1981, p. 5.
55. Ibid., pp. 30–32.
56. Staff conversation with Arlene Kelliebrew, District of Columbia Public Schools, Department of Staff Development, June 1983.

11. *Technology: Extending the Teachers' Reach*

1. *Time*, vol. 121, no. 1, January 3, 1983, pp. 12–18, 21–24.
2. Patrick Suppes, "The Uses of Computers in Education," *Scientific American*, vol. 215, no. 3, September 1966, p. 207.
3. Alvin Eurich, *Reforming American Education: The Innovative Approach to Improving Our Schools and Colleges* (New York: Harper & Row, 1969), p. 220.
4. National Center for Education Statistics, "Instructional Use of Computers in Public Schools," *Early Release* (Washington, D.C.: National Center for Education Statistics, September 1982), p. 14.
5. Market Data Retrieval, *Update for the School Market for Microcomputers* (Westport, Connecticut: Market Data Retrieval, October 1982), pp. 9–10.
6. Carnegie Foundation High School Visits, 1982.
7. Ibid.
8. National Science Foundation, *The Five-Year Outlook on Science and Technology, 1981*, publication no. NSF 81-40 (Washington, D.C.: Government Printing Office, January 26, 1982), p. xxii.
9. Peter J. Dirr and Ronald J. Pedone, *Uses of Television for Instruction 1976–77: Final Report of the School TV Utilization Study* (Washington, D.C.: Corporation for Public Broadcasting, 1979), p. 8.
10. Bonnie Brownstein, as quoted in Fred M. Hechinger, "Computer Software Found Weak," *New York Times*, April 20, 1982, p. C4.
11. Karen Sheingold, *Issues Related to the Implementation of Computer Technology in Schools: A Cross Sectional Study*, a preliminary report presented to the Na-

tional Institute of Education Conference on Issues Related to the Implementation of Computer Technology in Schools, Washington, D.C., February 19, 1981 (New York: Bank Street College of Education, 1981), pp. 4, 10, 15.

12. Linda G. Roberts, "The Future of Electronic Learning: Implications for Curriculum and Instruction," paper presented at Conference on the Future of Electronic Learning, Teachers College of Columbia, April 2, 1982, p. 4.

13. Andrew Pollack, as quoted in Andrew Zucker, "Computers in Education: National Policy in the USA," *European Journal of Education*, vol. 17, no. 4, 1982, p. 397.

14. Peter J. Dirr and Ronald J. Pedone, 1979, p. 11.

15. Patrick Daly, "The Need for Cooperative Effort," a paper presented at the National Workshop on Television and Youth, Washington, D.C., March 12–13, 1980.

16. Carnegie Foundation High School Visits, 1983.

17. Carnegie Foundation High School Visits, 1982.

18. Robert T. Grieves, "Short Circuiting Reference Books," *Time*, vol. 121, no. 24, June 13, 1983, p. 76.

19. Ithiel de Sola Pool, "The Culture of Electronic Print," *Daedalus*, vol. 111, no. 4, Fall, 1982, p. 30.

20. Dick Moberg and Ira Laefsky, "Videodiscs and Optical Data Storage," *Byte*, vol. 7, no. 6, June 1982, p. 148.

21. Staff communication with Craig Ritter, Unified School District, Irvine, California, May 1983.

22. Ibid.

23. Harold Livingston, "How Schools Use the Cable . . . ," *Educational & Industrial Television*, April 1974, p. 20.

24. Ibid., p. 22.

25. Ibid., p. 20.

26. Ibid.

27. Ned White, *Inside Television* (San Francisco: Far West Laboratory for Educational Research and Development, 1980), p. 145.

12. *Service: The New Carnegie Unit*

1. Carnegie Foundation High School Visits, 1982.

2. George Gallup, Jr., as quoted in Dan Morgan, "Coming of Age in the '80s: Part 3," Washington *Post*, December 29, 1981, p. A6.

3. Morgan, "Coming of Age in the '80s: Parts 1 and 3," 1981, Washington *Post*, Dec. 27, p. A16, and Dec. 29, 1981, p. A6.

4. Carnegie Council on Policy Studies in Higher Education, *Giving Youth a Better Chance: Options for Education, Work, and Service* (San Francisco: Jossey-Bass Publishers, 1980), pp. 14–15.

5. National Panel on High Schools and Adolescent Education, *The Education of Adolescents: Summary Conclusions and Recommendations of the Report of the National Panel* as submitted to the U.S. Office of Education and the Department of Health, Education, and Welfare, 1974, p. 6.

6. Harold Howe II, "The High School: Education's Centerpiece for the 1980s," *College Board Review,* no. 120, Summer 1981, p. 27.
7. Carnegie Foundation High School Visits, 1982.
8. Ibid.
9. Ibid.
10. Ibid.
11. Ibid.
12. Ibid.
13. Ibid.
14. Ibid.
15. Ibid.
16. Ibid.
17. Ibid.
18. Ibid.
19. Ibid.
20. National Center for Education Statistics, *1980 Survey of High School and Beyond,* public schools only.
21. Ibid.
22. Ibid.
23. Carnegie Foundation High School Visits, 1982.
24. Robert L. Buser, *Special Report on Cocurricular Offerings and Participation* (Springfield, Illinois: Illinois State Board of Education, 1980), p. 6.
25. Carnegie Foundation High School Visits, 1982.
26. Ibid.
27. B. T. Collins, as quoted in Dan Morgan, "Coming of Age in the '80s: Part 3," 1981, p. A6.
28. Carnegie Foundation High School Visits, 1982.
29. Ibid.
30. Jerome Kagan, "The Moral Function of the School," *Daedalus,* vol. 110, no. 3, Summer 1981, pp. 163–164.
31. Staff communication with Alma Jones, Northern High School, Detroit, Michigan, June 1983.
32. Carnegie Foundation High School Visits, 1982.
33. Ibid.
34. Ibid.
35. Ibid.
36. Ibid.
37. Ibid.
38. Ibid.
39. Ibid.
40. Ibid.
41. Reginald D. Archambault (ed.), *John Dewey on Education: Selected Writings* (New York: Random House, 1964), p. 300.

13. *The Principal as Leader*

1. Carnegie Foundation High School Visits, 1983.
2. Michael Rutter, *Fifteen Thousand Hours: Secondary Schools and Their Effects on Children* (Boston: Harvard University Press, 1982); R. R. Edmunds and J. R. Frederiksen, *Search for Effective Schools: The Identification and Analysis of City Schools That Are Instructionally Effective for Poor Children* (Cambridge: Harvard University, Center for Urban Studies, 1978); William Wayson, *A Handbook for Developing Schools with Good Discipline*, a report of Phi Delta Kappan Commission on Discipline, *Phi Delta Kappan*, 1982.
3. Carnegie Foundation High School Visits, 1983.
4. Ibid.
5. National Association of Secondary School Principals, *The Senior High School Principalship* (Reston, Virginia: National Association of Secondary School Principals, 1978), vol. 1, pp. 1, 2, 6.
6. Ibid., pp. 4, 20.
7. Educational Research Service, *ERS Research Digest* (Arlington, Virginia: Educational Research Service, Inc., March 1983), p. 3.
8. Catherine D. Baltzell and Robert A. Dentler, "Local Variations in the Selection of School Principals," paper prepared for the 1982 Annual Meeting of the American Educational Research Association, New York, pp. 7–8.
9. W. J. Martin and D. J. Willower, as quoted in William D. Greenfield, Jr., *Research on Public School Principals: A Review and Recommendations*, submitted as the Final Report to the National Institute of Education, U.S. Department of Education, June 1, 1982, p. 26.
10. National Association of Secondary School Principals, *The Senior High School Principalship*, 1978, p. 20.
11. Harry Wolcott, as cited in *R & D Perspectives*, Winter 1982, p. 2.
12. Carnegie Foundation High School Visits, 1983.
13. National Association of Secondary School Principals, *Senior High School Principalship*, p. 7.
14. Nancy De Leonibus, *Principal Attrition Surveys* (Reston, Virginia: National Association of Secondary School Principals, 1979), p. 65, unpublished.
15. National Association of Secondary School Principals, *Senior High School Principalship*, pp. 3, 9, 10.
16. University Council for Educational Administration, *The Preparation and Certification of Educational Administration: A UCEA Report* (Columbus, Ohio: January, 1973), and staff communication with Charles L. Willis, executive director, June 1983.
17. Staff communication with Keith Goldhammer, former dean and professor emeritus, College of Education, University of Michigan, June, 1983.
18. Jeanette Goor and Elizabeth Farris, *Training Needs of Public School Administrators: A Survey of Local School Districts*, FRSS Report No. 5, prepared for the National Center for Education Statistics by Westat, Inc., Rockville, Maryland, Summer 1978, pp. 7, 12.

19. Carnegie Foundation High School Visits, 1983.
20. Carnegie Foundation High School Visits, 1983.
21. Ibid.
22. Ibid.
23. Ibid.
24. Ibid.
25. Ibid.
26. John Goodlad, "Schooling: Issues and Answers," St. Louis *Post-Dispatch*, special magazine section: "Ideals in Transition: Tomorrow's America," March 25, 1979, p. 72.
27. "Comments by 1982 Participants," Appendix to *The 1983 Principals Institute*, Peabody College for Teacher, Vanderbuilt University, draft brochure, October 18, 1982.
28. Fred M. Hechinger, "About Education: Preparing Principals to Take Charge," *New York Times*, September 21, 1982, p. 20.
29. Carnegie Foundation High School Visits, 1983.

14. *Flexibility: Patterns to Fit Purpose*

1. Carnegie Foundation High School Visits, 1982.
2. John Swett, *History of the Public School System in California*, reprinted in Sol Cohen (ed.), *Education in the United States: A Documented History*, vol. 2 (New York: Random House, 1974), p. 1047.
3. *The Fourth Annual Report of the President and the Treasurer of The Carnegie Foundation for the Advancement of Teaching* (New York: October, 1909), p. 132.
4. "An English Headmistress Describes a Typical Day in an American High School (1908)," in Sara A. Burstall, *Impressions of American Education in 1908*, in Sol Cohen (ed.), *Education in the United States*, vol. 4, p. 2108.
5. National Center for Education Statistics, *1980 Survey of High School and Beyond*, public schools only, and Carnegie Foundation staff survey of state departments of education, 1983.
6. Carnegie Foundation staff survey of state departments of education, 1983.
7. Paul De Hart Hurd, "State of Precollege Education in Mathematics and Science," paper prepared for the National Convocation on Precollege Education in Mathematics and Science, National Academy of Sciences and National Academy of Engineering, Washington, D.C., May 1982, p. 9.
8. George H. Gallup, "Gallup Poll of the Public's Attitude Toward the Public Schools," *Phi Delta Kappan*, September 1982, p. 48.
9. Staff communication with Christine Smith, Florida Association for Secondary School Principals, June 1983; and *Education Daily*, June 21, 1983, p. 5.
10. The National Commission on Excellence in Education, *A Nation at Risk: The Imperative for Education Reform* (Washington: U.S. Government Printing Office, 1983), p. 29.
11. Colman McCarthy, "An Alternative to Factory Schools," Washington *Post*, May 7, 1983, p. A-23.

12. James B. Conant, *The American High School Today: A First Report to Interested Citizens* (New York: McGraw-Hill, 1959), p. 37.
13. B. A. Hinsdale, *Horace Mann and the Common School Revival in the United States* (New York: Charles Scribner's Sons, 1900), p. 177.
14. U.S. Department of Commerce, Bureau of the Census, *Historical Statistics of the United States: Colonial Times to 1970, Part 1* (Washington, D.C.: U.S. Government Printing Office, 1975), p. 368.
15. Ibid.
16. Ibid.
17. National Center for Education Statistics, unpublished data for Fall 1980, June 1983, and Carnegie Foundation calculation for median school district enrollment.
18. Carnegie Foundation High School Visits, 1982.
19. Roger G. Barker and Paul V. Gump, *Big School, Small School: High School Size and Student Behavior* (Stanford, California: Stanford University Press, 1964), pp. 123–125.
20. Stephen F. Hamilton, "Synthesis of Research on the Social Side of School," *Educational Leadership,* February 1983, p. 70.
21. Edwin P. Willems, "Sense of Obligation to High School Activities as Related to School Size and Marginality of Student," *Child Development,* no. 38, 1967, p. 1255.
22. James Garbarino, "Some Thoughts on School Size and Its Effects on Adolescent Development," *Journal of Youth and Adolescence,* no. 9, 1980, pp. 19–21.
23. The National Student Symposium on Education of the Gifted and Talented, *On Being Gifted: Student Perspectives* (Washington, D.C.: Council for Exceptional Children, 1977), p. 67.
24. Carnegie Foundation High School Visits, 1982.
25. U.S. Department of Commerce, Bureau of the Census, *Statistical Abstract of the United States: 1982–83* (Washington, D.C.: U.S. Government Printing Office, 1982), p. 156, and Carnegie Foundation calculations for average eleventh- and twelfth-grade retention rates between 1974 and 1980.
26. U.S. Department of Commerce, Bureau of the Census, "School Enrollment: Social and Economic Characteristics of Students," October 1981 (Advance Report), *Current Population Reports, Part 1* (Washington, D.C.: Government Printing Office, February 1983), series P-20, No. 373, pp. 8, 9; and earlier series P-20 reports.
27. Jerald G. Bachman, Swazer Green, and Ilona D. Wirtman, *Youth in Transition, Dropping Out: Problem or Symptom?* (Ann Arbor, Michigan: Survey Research Center, Institute for Social Research, University of Michigan, 1971), p. 163.
28. Russell W. Rumberger, "Why Kids Drop Out of School," paper presented at the annual meeting of the American Educational Research Association, Los Angeles, April 13–17, 1981, p. 1.
29. Ibid., p. 3.
30. Ibid.
31. Bachman, Green, and Wirtanan, *Youth in Transition, Dropping Out,* pp. 54–58.

32. Ibid., pp. 27–34.
33. Carnegie Foundation High School Visits, 1982.
34. Ed Hinkley, "An Instructional Program for Dropouts," *NASSP Bulletin*, February 1979, pp. 59–64.
35. Staff communication with Julie Grillo, Administrative Offices, Cooperative High School, June 1983.
36. Gene I. Maeroff, *School and College: Partnerships in Education* (Princeton, New Jersey: The Carnegie Foundation for the Advancement of Teaching, 1983), p. 72.
37. Ibid.

15. *The College Connection*

1. Gene I. Maeroff, *School and College: Partnerships in Education* (Princeton, New Jersey: The Carnegie Foundation for the Advancement of Teaching, 1983), p. 1.
2. Paul Barry, "Interview: A Talk with A. Bartlett Giamatti," *College Board Review*, Spring 1982, p. 7.
3. National Association of Secondary School Principals, *College Admissions: New Requirements by the State Universities* (Reston, Virginia: 1982), p. 4.
4. Ohio Advisory Commission on Articulation Between Secondary Education and Ohio Colleges, *Final Report* (Columbus: Ohio Board of Regents and the State Board of Education, April 1981), p. 2.
5. Maeroff, *School and College: Partnerships in Education*, p. 12.
6. "An Open Letter to High School Students and Their Parents from the University of Utah," Salt Lake *Tribune*, February 7, 1982, p. 20a.
7. Maeroff, *School and College: Partnerships in Education*, p. 17.
8. Ibid., pp. 20–22.
9. Ibid., p. 23.
10. Ibid., p. 24.
11. Ibid., pp. 24–25.
12. Ibid., p. 44.
13. Ibid., pp. 46–48.
14. Ibid., pp. 50–53.
15. Ibid., p. 52.
16. Carnegie Council on Policy Studies in Higher Education, *Catalog Study, 1976*, unpublished report.
17. Gene I. Maeroff, *School and College: Partnerships in Education*, pp. 34–35.
18. Ibid., p. 36.
19. Ibid., pp. 36–37.
20. Ibid., p. 38.
21. Ibid., pp. 39–41.
22. Ibid., p. 42.
23. Ibid., pp. 67–68.
24. Brooks Atkinson (ed.), *Walden and Other Writings of Henry David Thoreau* (New York: Random House, 1950), p. 47.

16. Classrooms and Corporations

1. Staff communication with Wayne Walker, director of the St. Louis School Partnership Program, April 5, 1983.
2. Willard Wirtz and the National Manpower Institute, *The Boundless Resource: A Prospectus for an Education-Work Policy* (Washington, D.C.: The Manpower Institute, 1975), mimeographed, pp. 1, 7.
3. Mary E. Moran, "Improving Schools Through Private Sector Partnerships," *American Education*, January-February, 1983, vol. 19, p. 5.
4. Staff communication with David Bergholz, assistant executive director, Allegheny Conference on Community Development, March, 1983.
5. *Stakeholder Issues and Strategies*, Human Resource Network, Philadelphia, Pennsylvania, May 1983.
6. Staff communication with Jean Myers, Houston Volunteers in Public Schools, March, 1983.
7. Staff communication with Wayne Walker.
8. Ibid.
9. Ibid.
10. Ibid.
11. Traci Bliss, "Endowed Chairs in Public Schools," *Phi Delta Kappan*, December 1982, vol. 64, p. 272.
12. Samuel M. Burt and Leon M. Lessinger, *Voluntary Industry Involvement in Public Education* (Lexington, Massachusetts: Heath Lexington Books, 1970), p. 106.
13. Carnegie Foundation High School Visits, 1982.
14. Rance Crain, "Adopt-a-School Off and Running," *Crain's Chicago Business*, September 27, 1982, p. 10.

17. Excellence: The Public Commitment

1. Carnegie Foundation High School Visits, 1982.
2. George H. Gallup, "The 14th Annual Gallup Poll of the Public's Attitudes Toward the Public Schools," *Phi Delta Kappan*, September 1982, p. 46.
3. Ibid.
4. Jacob B. Michaelson, "Efficiency, Equity, and the Need for New Educational Policy," in James W. Guthrie (ed.), *School Finance Policies and Practices in the 1980s, a Decade of Conflict* (Cambridge, Massachusetts: Ballinger Publishing Co., 1980), p. 207.
5. Ibid.
6. George H. Gallup, "Taking Education's Pulse: The 13th Annual Gallup Poll of the Public's Attitudes Toward the Public Schools," *Principal*, September 1981, p. 23.
7. Carnegie Foundation High School Visits, 1982.
8. Ibid.
9. Ibid.
10. Ibid.

11. Ibid.
12. Ibid.
13. Ibid.
14. Ibid.
15. Sandra Grey, executive director, National School Volunteer Program, June 1983.
16. Education Commission of the States, *Model State Legislation Report no. 39* (Denver: The Commission, June 1973).
17. Alex Heard, "Texas Curriculum to Undergo Complete Revision for 1984," *Education Week,* vol. 1, no. 6, January 12, 1982, p. 6.
18. Education Commission of the States and the Institute for Educational Leadership, *State Education Policy Seminars,* 1983 brochure.
19. Ernest Boyer, Harold Howe II, Francis Keppel, and Sidney Marland, "Education Is in Dire Need of New Federal Efforts," *New York Times,* June 20, 1983, p. A-14.
20. American Association of School Administrators, Council of Great City Schools, and National School Boards Association, *The Maintenance Gap: Deferred Repair and Renovation in the Nation's Elementary and Secondary Schools,* a joint report by the associations and the council, January, 1983, p. 10.
21. Henrietta Schwartz et al., *School as a Workplace: The Realities of Stress,* report supported by a grant to the American Federation of Teachers and conducted at Roosevelt University, Chicago, unpublished, 1983, p. 12.
22. Ibid., vol. 2, p. 39.
23. Ibid., vol. 1, p. 12.
24. American Association of School Administrators, Council of Great City Schools, and National School Boards Association, *The Maintenance Gap,* pp. 7–8.
25. Ibid., p. 7
26. Henrietta Schwartz et al., *Schools as a Workplace,* 1983, p. 12.
27. Carnegie Foundation High School Visits, 1982.
28. Higher Education Facilities Act of 1963, Public Law 88-204; 77 STAT. 363
29. Guthrie, *School Finance Policies and Practices,* p. 66.
30. "Consumer Expenditure Study," *Product Marketing/Cosmetic and Fragrance Retailing,* August 1982, p. 38.
31. Staff communication with Robert Bregenzer, Nielson Company, Northbrook, Illinois, June 1983.
32. Staff communication with personnel of the U.S. Department of Defense, January 1983.
33. U.S. Department of Commerce, Bureau of the Census, *Statistical Abstract of the United States: 1983,* 103rd ed. (Washington: U.S. Government Printing Office, 1982), p. 136; National Education Association, *Estimates of School Statistics 1981–82* (Washington: National Education Association, January 1982), p. 7.
34. James Agee and Walker Evans, *Let Us Now Praise Famous Men* (Boston: Houghton Mifflin, 1960), p. 289.

INDEX

teachers *(cont.)*
  interdisciplinary approach of, 115
  isolation of, 158, 160, 171
  mentors of, 180, 182
  moonlighting of, 166–168
  negative public image of, 154, 155
  noninstructional chores of, 156–158, 159,
    307
  part-time, 183–185, 311–312
  powerlessness and frustrations of,
    142–144
  preparation time of, 155–156, 159, 307
  principals as, 224
  real vs. professional regard for, 154, 161,
    185
  recognition and rewards of, 155,
    161–165, 182–183, 226, 274–275,
    307–308
  recruitment of, 155, 161, 168, 171–174,
    308
  regular status of, 180–182
  reviews and evaluations of, 180, 311
  safety of, 160–161
  salaries of, 19, 155, 165–171, 179, 182,
    183–184, 308, 311
  selection of, 226
  senior, 182–183
  shortages of, 184, 311
  strengthening and renewal of, 7,
    154–185
  styles of, 148–153, 312
  subject distribution of, 74
  supportive environments for, 87, 160,
    163
  technology and, 187–188, 193–194,
    197–199, 200–201
  time problems of, 141–142, 144
  in troubled schools, 16–17
"teacher teams," 176
teacher training, 46, 61, 174–178
  complaints about, 174
  five-step program for, 175–177, 180,
    309–310
  four-course sequence in, 176
  selection procedures for, 175
Teacher Travel Fund, 171, 310
teaching clubs, 172
teaching machines, 187
teaching materials, shortages of, 158–159
Teaching of Writing, The, 176
technology:
  "breakthroughs" in, 187
  content of, 190–192
  educational role of, 7, 186–201, 312–314
  global interdependence and, 3–4
  potential of, 200–201

technology *(cont.)*
  school goals and, 194–201
  study of, 77, 109–111, 195–196, 304
  in teacher education, 176, 193, 198
  teachers and, 187–188, 193–194,
    197–199, 200–201
Technology Resource Centers, 194, 293,
  313, 318
television, 3, 24
  educational, 187–188, 190–191, 197–199,
    200
Tenneco Oil, 269, 271
testing, validity of, 133
test scores:
  decline in, 22–30, 37, 39
  of education majors, 171–172
Texas, 231, 290–291
  business–education link in, 269, 271,
    272–273, 274, 276
  moonlighting in, 166
  teachers of the year in, 164
textbooks:
  selection of, 143, 312
  standards for, 24
  weaknesses of, 143, 312
Thomas, Lewis, 106
Tilden High School, 271
time, use of, 141–153, 230–233
  improvements in, 232–233, 314
  interruptions and, 142
  paper work vs. teaching and, 141–142
Tocqueville, Alexis de, 105
tracking patterns:
  curriculum decisions and, 79–81
  single, 126–128, 305
  vocational education and, 123–126
transcripts, curriculum standards evaluated
  with, 81–83
transition schools, 128–130, 258–260, 305
Trinity University, 164
troubled schools, description of, 16–17
Tyack, David B., 46, 52
Tyler, Ralph W., 52
typewriters, talking, 188

unemployment, 16, 119, 241–244
University Council for Educational
  Administration, 222
urban schools, 16, 20
  development of, 43–46
  extracurricular activities in, 207
  supply shortages in, 158–159
  troubled, 16–17
  vocational education in, 122
Uresti, Herminia, 87